FOR ORGANS, PIANOS & ELECTRONIC KEYBOARDS

E-Z PLAY® TODAY

160

THE **GRAM** RECORD OF THE YEAR

1958 – 2011

MW00817500

GRAMMY, GRAMMY Awards and the gramophone logo are registered
trademarks of The Recording Academy® and are used under license.

Visit The Recording Academy Online at
www.grammy.com

ISBN 978-1-4584-1588-2

HAL•LEONARD®
CORPORATION

7777 W. BLUEMOUND RD. P.O. BOX 13819 MILWAUKEE, WI 53213

Visit Hal Leonard Online at
www.halleonard.com

» Adele at the 54th GRAMMY Awards

THE RECORDING ACADEMY®

When it comes to music on TV, the last few years alone have seen some very memorable moments: Paul McCartney, Bruce Springsteen, Dave Grohl, and Joe Walsh jamming on "The End" from the Beatles' classic *Abbey Road*; Adele making her triumphant first live singing appearance after throat surgery to perform "Rolling In The Deep"; Pink dripping wet and hovering 20 feet above the stage while singing a note-perfect version of "Glitter In The Air"; and Lady Gaga hatching from a massive egg to perform "Born This Way." All of these performances, and many more, took place on the famed GRAMMY Awards® stage.

The GRAMMY® Award is indisputedly the most coveted recognition of excellence in recorded music worldwide. Over more than half a century, the GRAMMY Awards have become both music's biggest honor and Music's Biggest Night®, with the annual telecast drawing tens of millions of viewers nationwide and millions more internationally.

And with evolving categories that always reflect important current artistic waves — such as dance/electronica music — as well as setting a record for social TV engagement in 2012, the GRAMMYs keep moving forward, serving as a real-time barometer of music's cultural impact.

The Recording Academy is the organization that produces the GRAMMY Awards. Consisting of the artists, musicians, songwriters, producers, engineers, and other professionals who make the music you enjoy every day on the radio, your streaming or download services, or in the concert hall, The Academy is a dynamic institution with an active agenda aimed at supporting and nurturing music and the people who make it.

Whether it's joining with recording artists to ensure their creative rights are protected, providing ongoing professional development services to the recording community or supporting the health and well-being of music creators and music education in our schools, The Recording Academy has become the recording industry's primary organization for professional and educational outreach, human services, arts advocacy, and cultural enrichment.

The Academy represents members from all corners of the professional music world — from the biggest recording stars to unsung music educators — all brought together under the banner of building a better creative environment for music and its makers.

» Paul McCartney at the 2012 MusiCares Person of the Year gala in his honor

Christopher Polk/WireImage.com

» Trombone Shorty and Mavis Staples at the GRAMMY Foundation's Music Preservation Project event in 2012

Michael Kovac/WireImage.com

MUSICARES FOUNDATION®

MusiCares® was established by The Recording Academy to provide a safety net of critical assistance for music people in times of need. MusiCares has developed into a premier support system for music people, providing resources to cover a wide range of financial, medical and personal emergencies through innovative programs and services, including regular eBay auctions of one-of-a-kind memorabilia that are open to the public. The charity has been supported by the contributions and participation of artists such as Neil Diamond, Aretha Franklin, Paul McCartney, Bruce Springsteen, Barbra Streisand, and Neil Young — just to name the organization's most recent annual Person of the Year fundraiser honorees — and so many others through the years.

THE GRAMMY FOUNDATION®

The GRAMMY Foundation's mission is to cultivate the understanding, appreciation and advancement of the contribution of recorded music to American culture. The Foundation accomplishes this mission through programs and activities designed to engage the music industry and cultural community as well as the general public. The Foundation works to bring national attention to important issues such as the value and impact of music and arts education and the urgency of preserving our rich cultural legacy, and it accomplishes this work by engaging music professionals — from big-name stars to working professionals and educators — to work directly with students.

>> Secretary of the Department of Health and Human Services Kathleen Sebelius and Recording Academy President/CEO Neil Portnow present the Recording Artists' Coalition Award to John Mayer at the GRAMMYs on the Hill Awards in Washington, D.C. in 2012

Paul Morigi/WireImage.com

>> The GRAMMY Museum in downtown Los Angeles

Courtesy of the GRAMMY Museum

FIGHTING FOR MUSICIANS' RIGHTS

Over the last 15 years, The Recording Academy has built a presence in the nation's capital, working to amplify the voice of music creators in national policy matters. Today, called the "supersized musicians lobby" by *Congressional Quarterly*, The Academy's Advocacy & Industry Relations office in Washington, D.C., is the leading representative of the collective world of recording professionals — artists, songwriters, producers, and engineers — through its GRAMMYs on the Hill® Initiative. The Academy has taken a leadership role in the fight to expand radio performance royalties to all music creators, worked on behalf of musicians on censorship concerns and regularly supported musicians on legislative issues that impact the vitality of music.

THE GRAMMY MUSEUM®

Since opening its doors in December 2008, the GRAMMY Museum has served as a dynamic educational and interactive institution dedicated to the power of music. The four-story, 30,000-square foot facility is part of L.A. Live, the premier sports and entertainment destination in downtown Los Angeles. The Museum serves the community with interactive, permanent and traveling exhibits and an array of public and education programs. We invite you to visit us when you're in the Los Angeles area.

As you can see, The Recording Academy is so much more than the annual GRAMMY telecast once a year, even if that one show is Music's Biggest Night®. To keep up with all The Academy's activities, visit GRAMMY.com regularly, and join the conversation on our social networks:

 Facebook.com/TheGRAMMYs

 Twitter.com/TheGRAMMYs

 YouTube.com/TheGRAMMYs

 TheGRAMMYs.tumblr.com

 Foursquare.com/TheGRAMMYs

 Instagram (user name: TheGRAMMYs)

 Google+ (gplus.to/TheGRAMMYs)

TABLE OF CONTENTS (ALPHABETICAL)

TABLE OF CONTENTS (CHRONOLOGICAL)

All I Wanna Do

Registration 8
Rhythm: Rock or Pop

Words and Music by Kevin Gilbert, David Baerwald,
Sheryl Crow, Wyn Cooper and Bill Bottrell

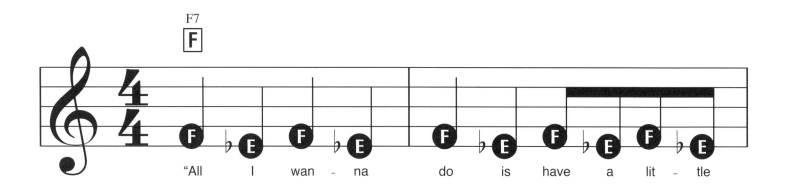

"All I wan - na do is have a lit - tle

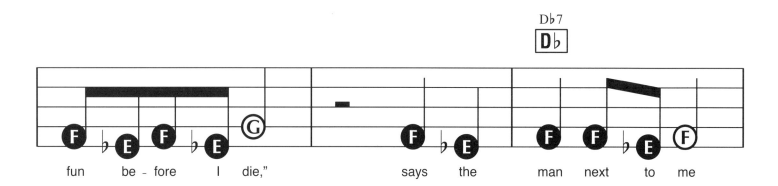

fun be - fore I die," says the man next to me

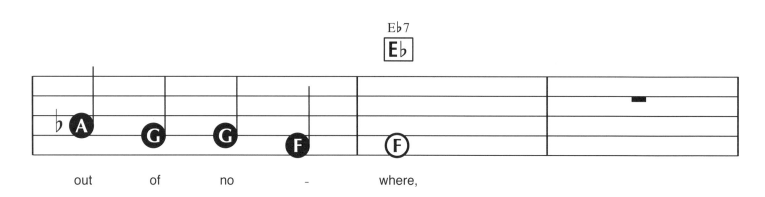

out of no - where,

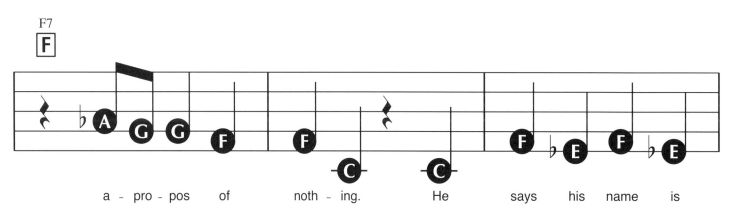

a - pro - pos of noth - ing. He says his name is

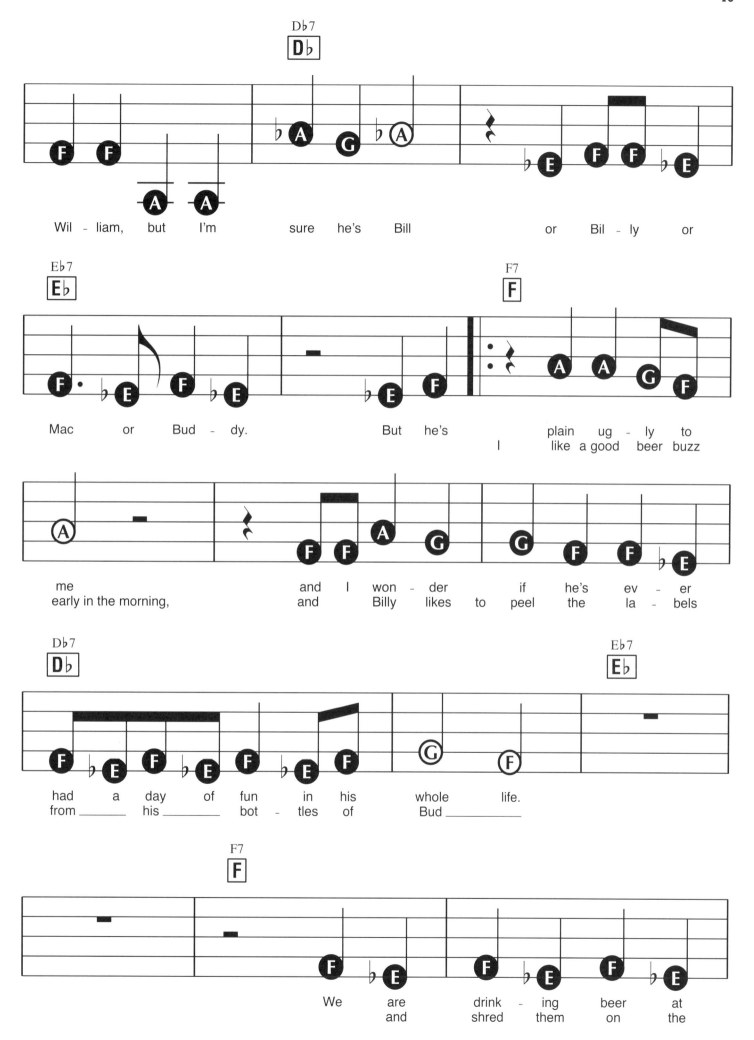

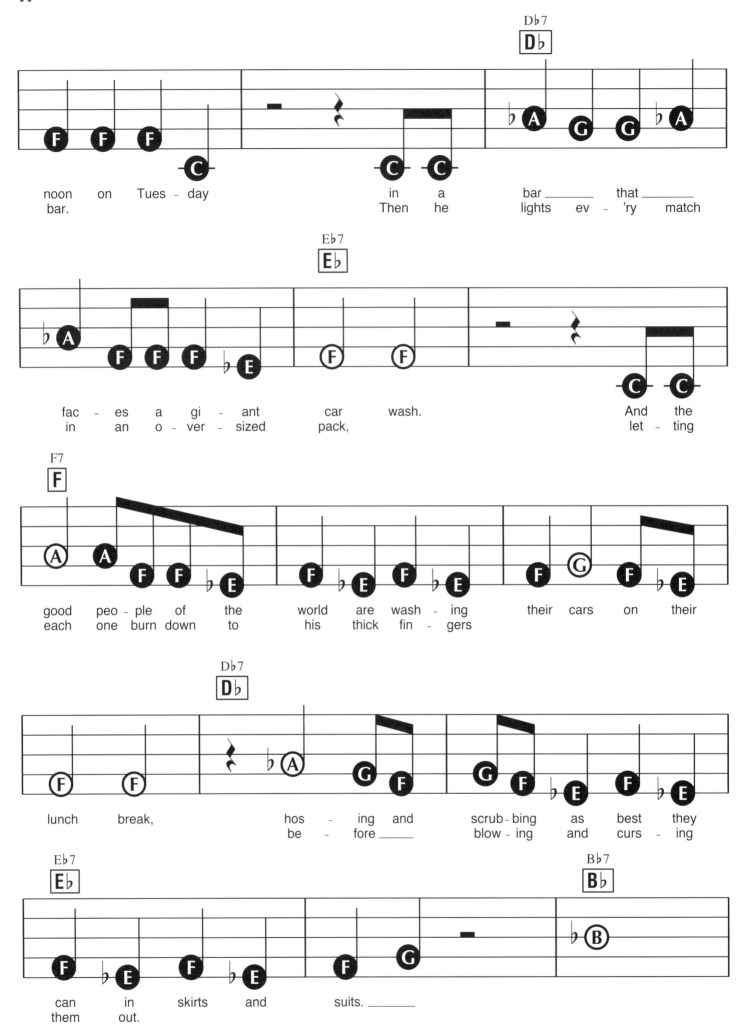

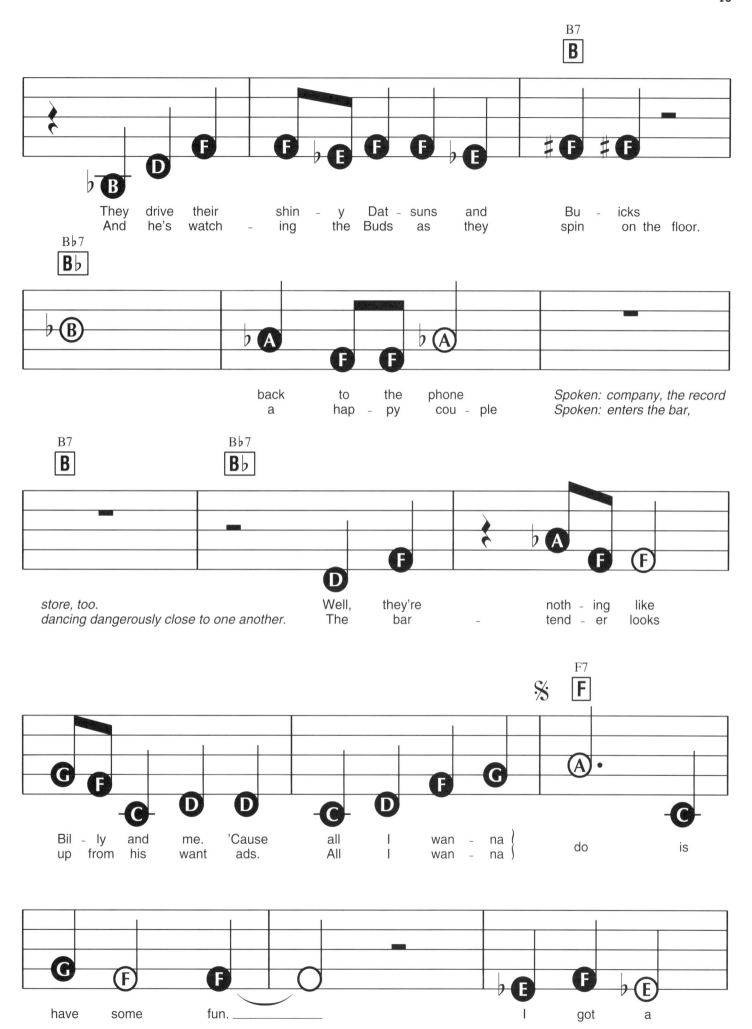

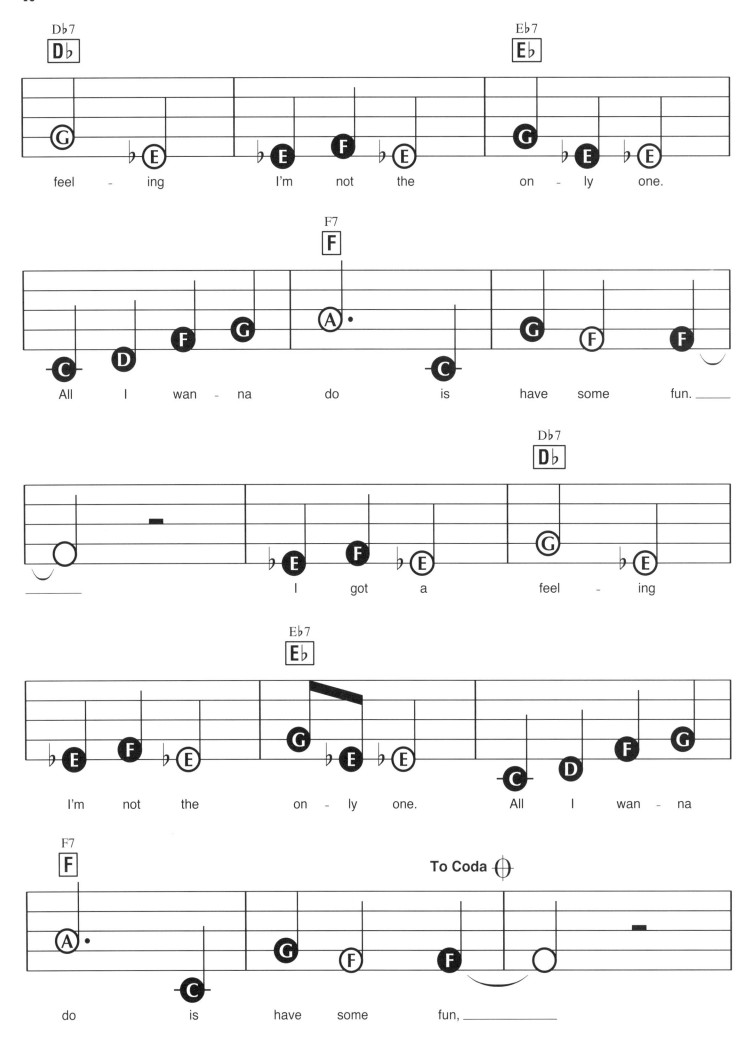

17

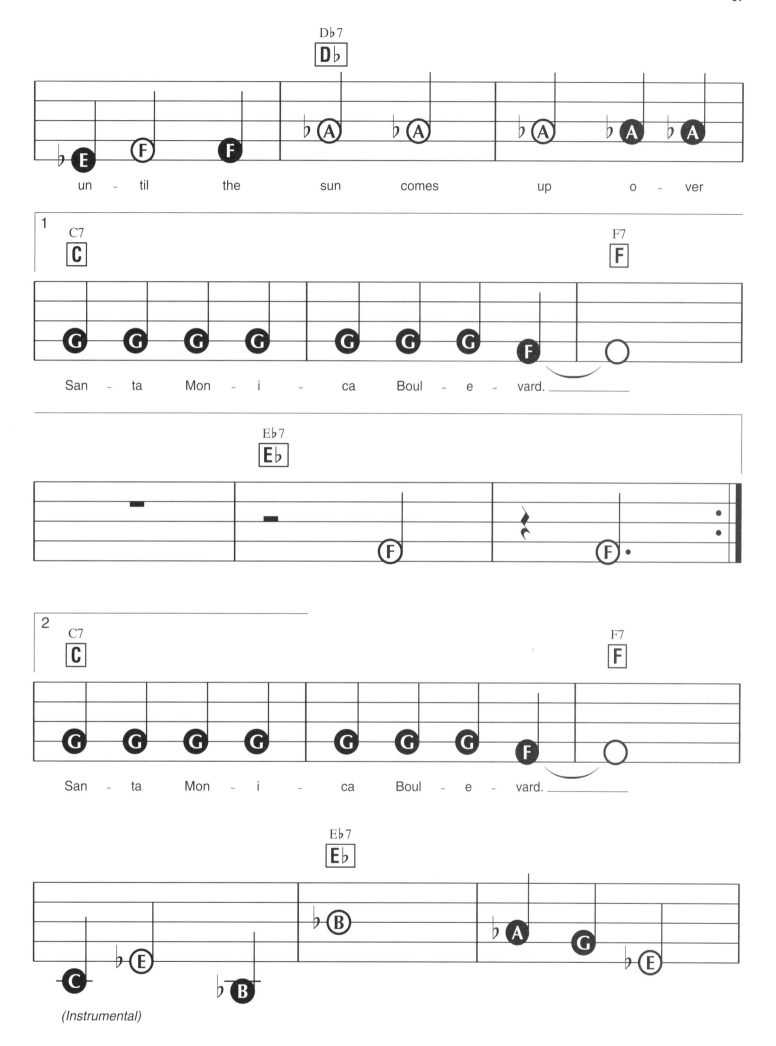

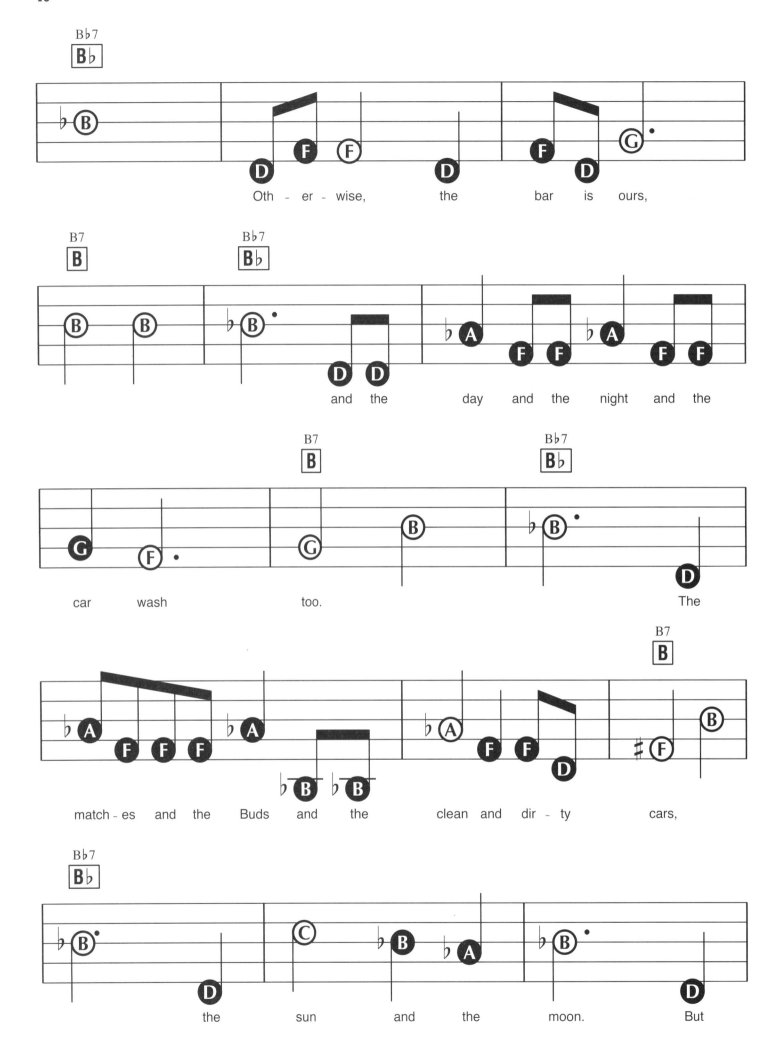

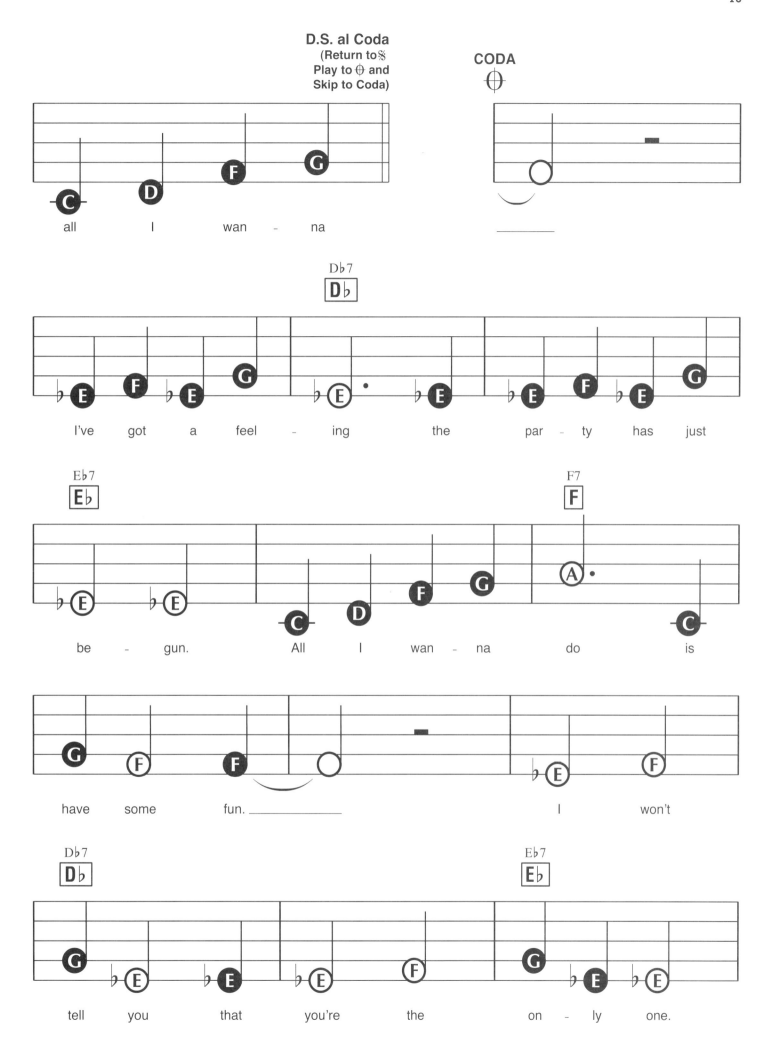

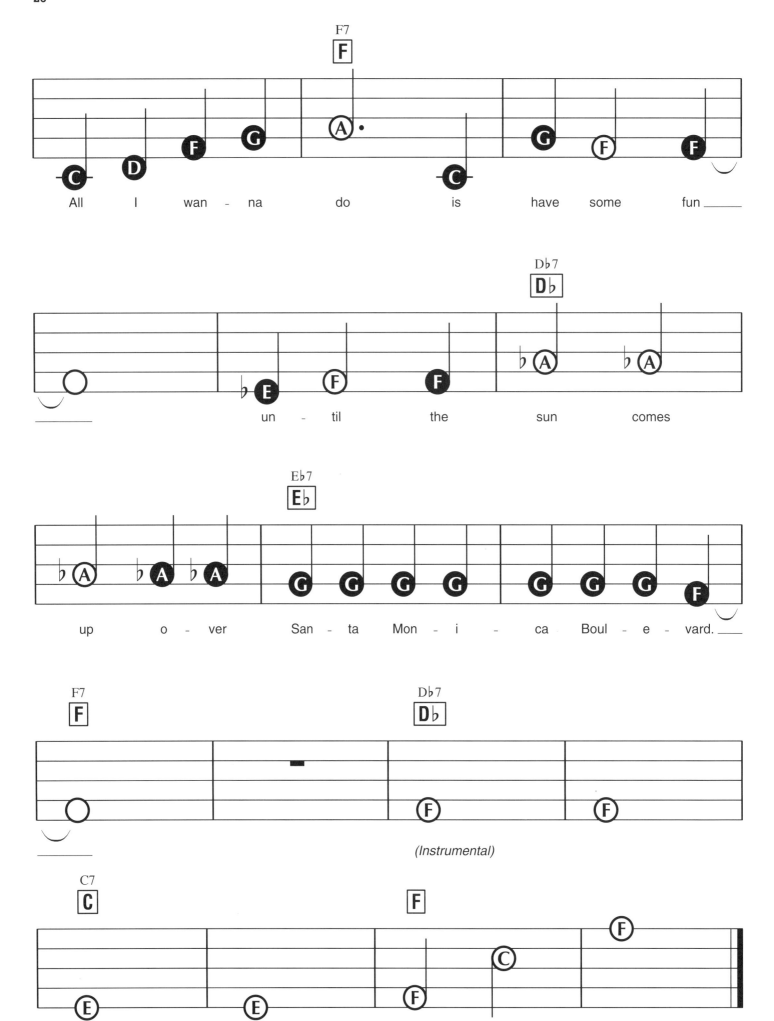

Beat It

Registration 7
Rhythm: Rock

Words and Music by
Michael Jackson

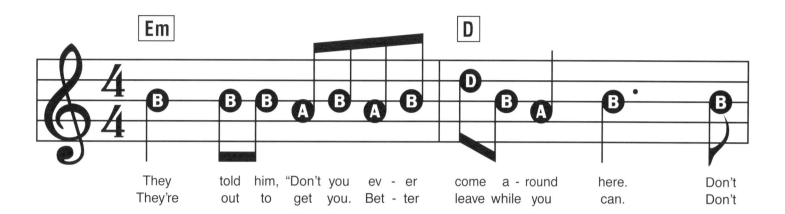

They told him, "Don't you ev - er come a - round here. Don't
They're out to get you. Bet - ter leave while you can. Don't

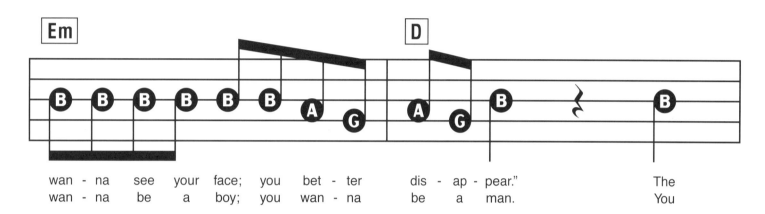

wan - na see your face; you bet - ter dis - ap - pear." The
wan - na be a boy; you wan - na be a man. You

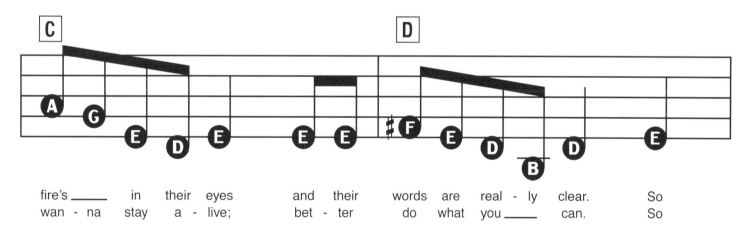

fire's ___ in their eyes and their words are real - ly clear. So
wan - na stay a - live; bet - ter do what you ___ can. So

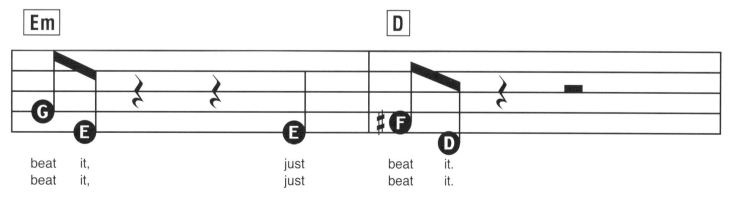

beat it, just beat it.
beat it, just beat it.

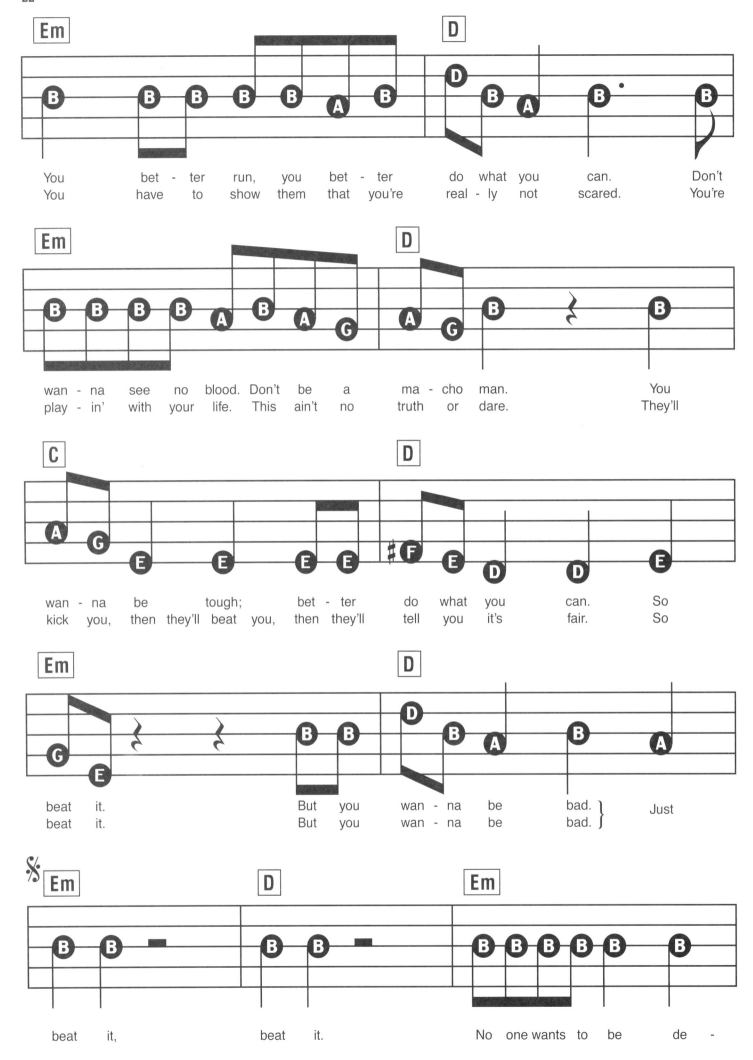

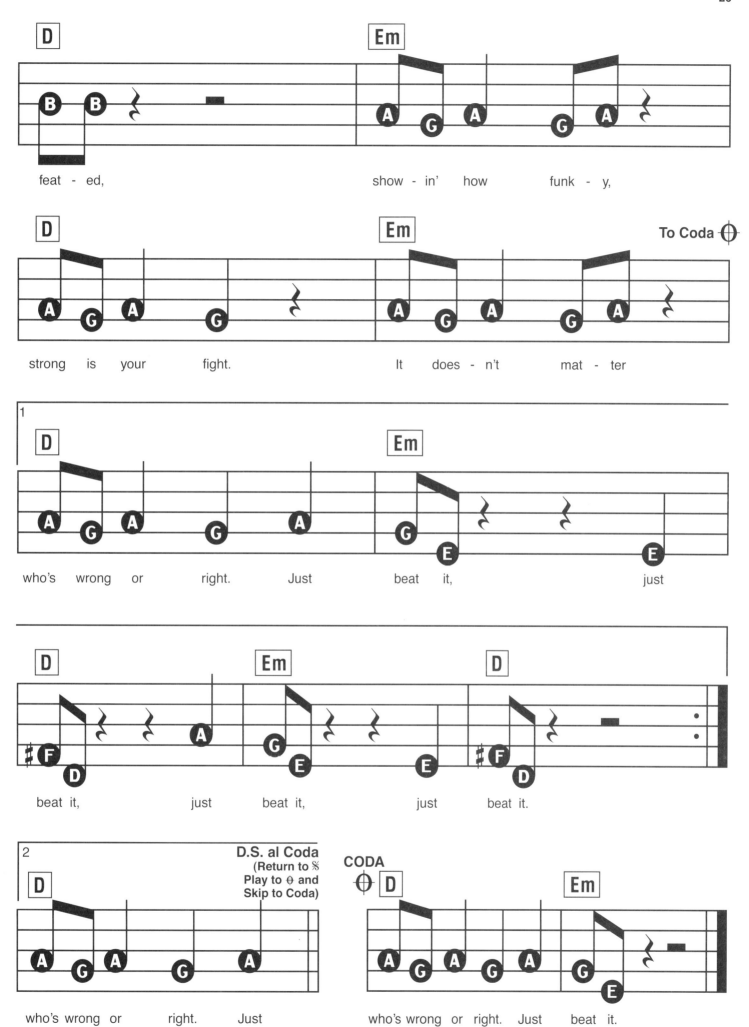

Another Day in Paradise

Registration 1
Rhythm: Rock or 8-Beat

Words and Music by
Phil Collins

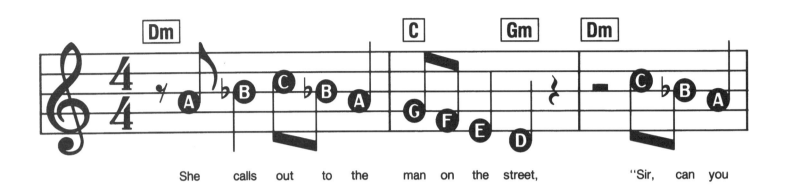

She calls out to the man on the street, "Sir, can you

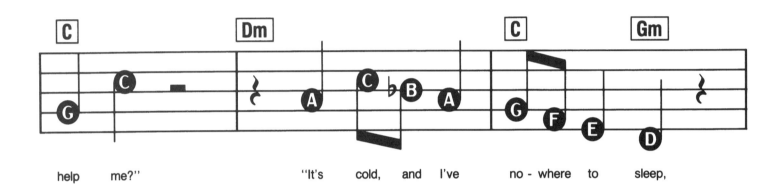

help me?" "It's cold, and I've no - where to sleep,

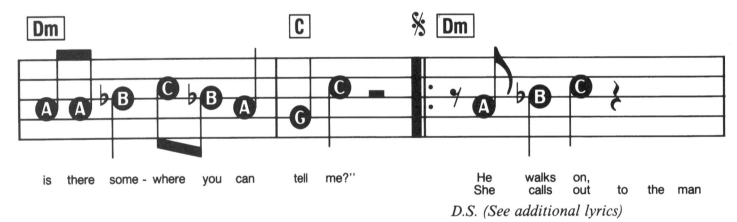

is there some - where you can tell me?"

He walks on,
She calls out to the man

D.S. (See additional lyrics)

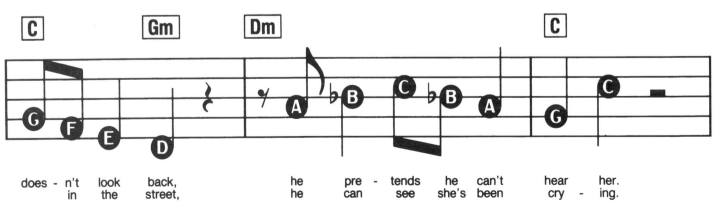

does - n't look back,
in the street,

he pre - tends he can't hear her.
he can see she's been cry - ing.

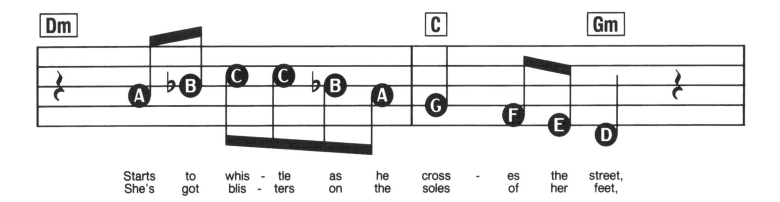

Starts to whis - tle as he cross - es the street,
She's got blis - ters on the soles of her feet,

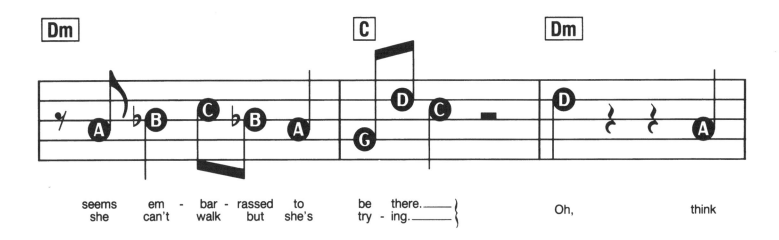

seems em - bar - rassed to be there.
she can't walk but she's try - ing.

Oh, think

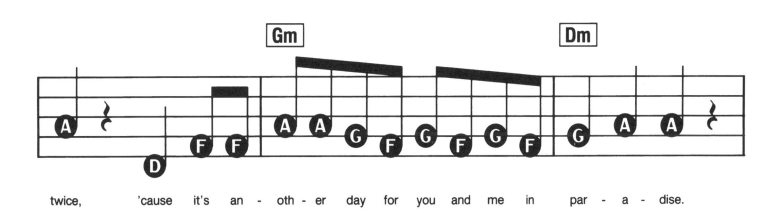

twice, 'cause it's an - oth - er day for you and me in par - a - dise.

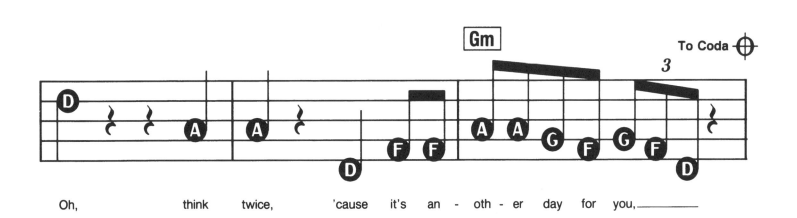

Oh, think twice, 'cause it's an - oth - er day for you,

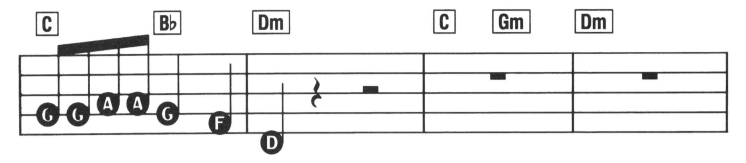

you and me in par - a - dise.

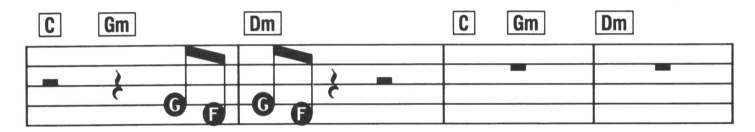

Think a - bout it.

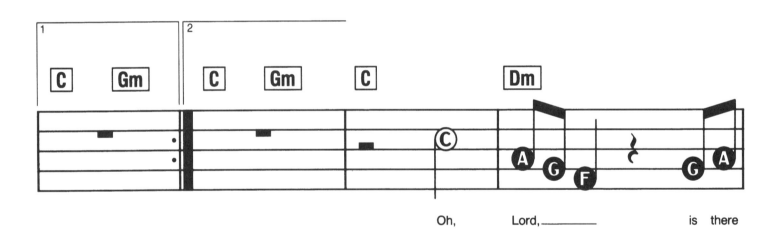

Oh, Lord,_____ is there

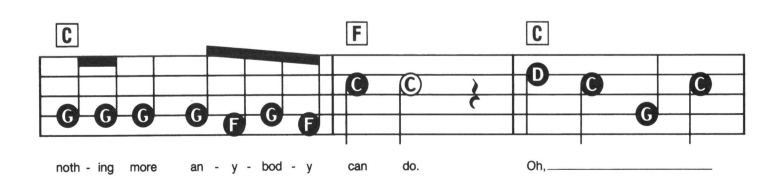

noth - ing more an - y - bod - y can do. Oh,_____

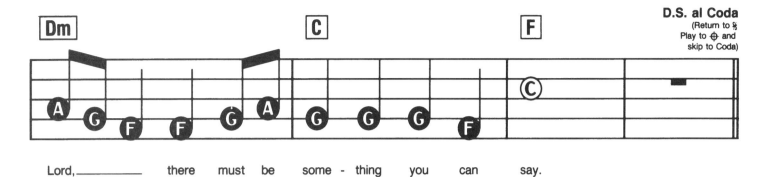

D.S. al Coda
(Return to %
Play to ⊕ and
skip to Coda)

Lord, _____ there must be some - thing you can say.

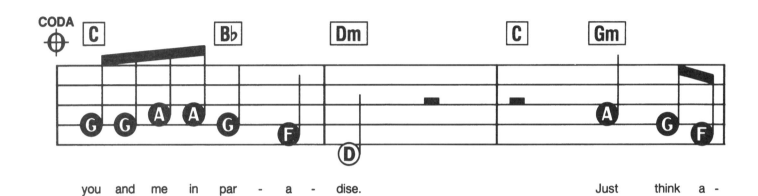

you and me in par - a - dise. Just think a -

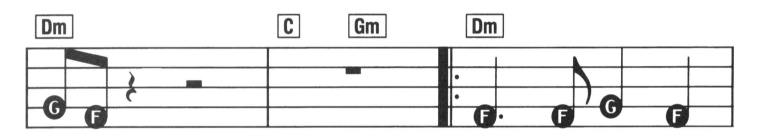

bout it.

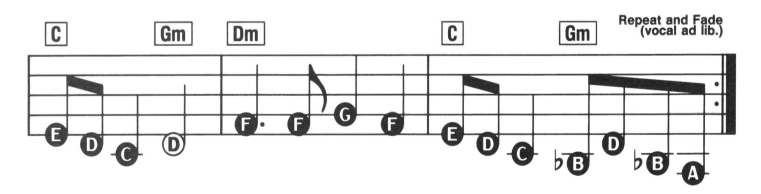

Repeat and Fade
(vocal ad lib.)

Additional Lyrics

(D.S.) You can tell from the lines, on her face,
You can see that she's been there.
Probably been moved on from every place,
'Cos she didn't fit in there.

Aquarius/Let the Sunshine In

from the Broadway Musical Production HAIR

Registration 4
Rhythm: 8-Beat or Rock

Words by James Rado and Gerome Ragni
Music by Galt MacDermot

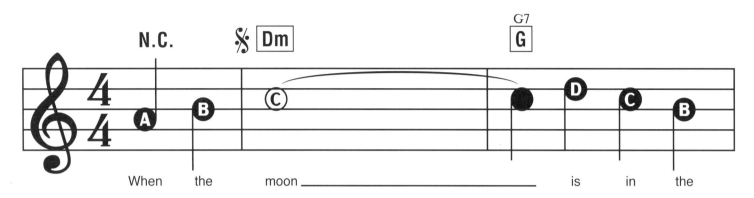

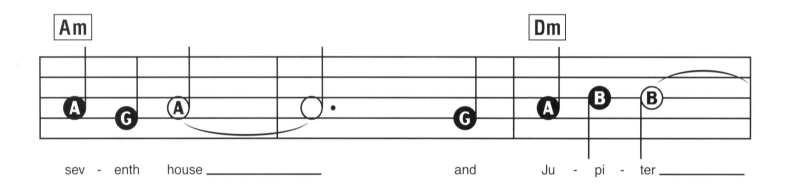

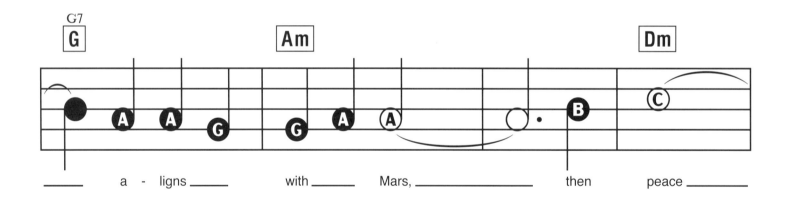

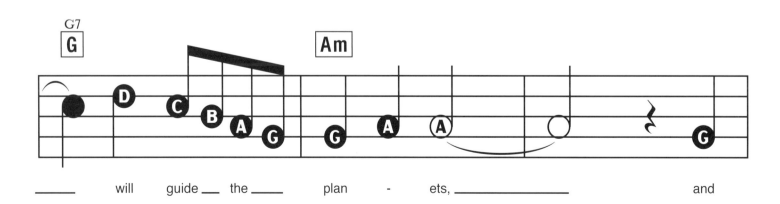

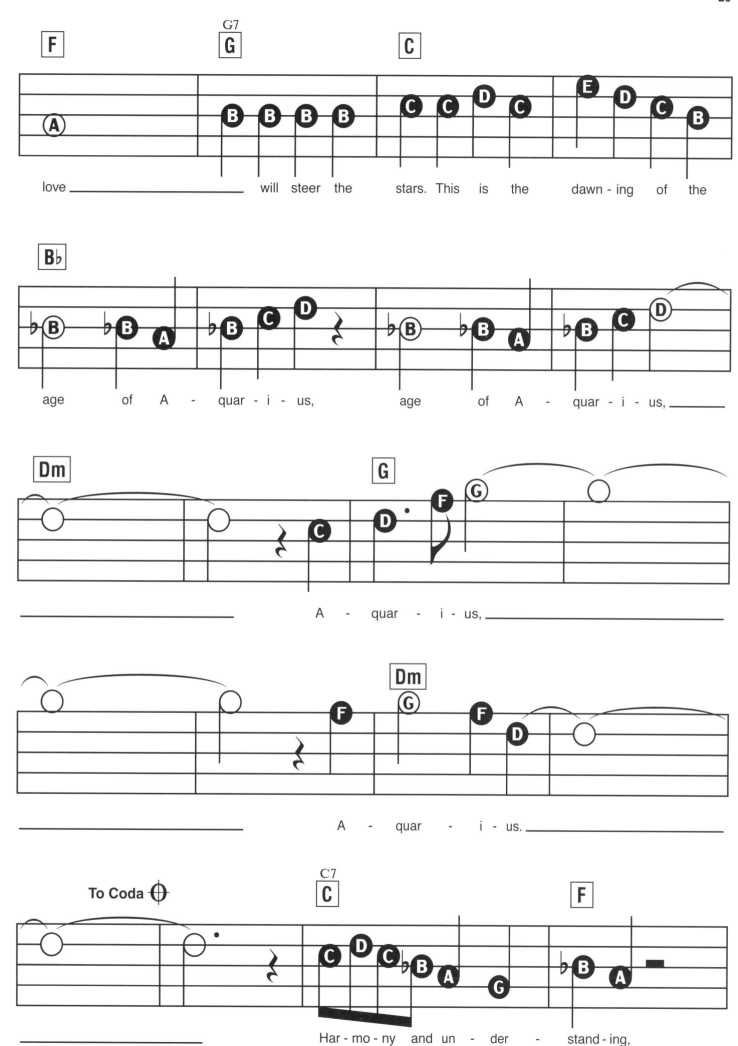

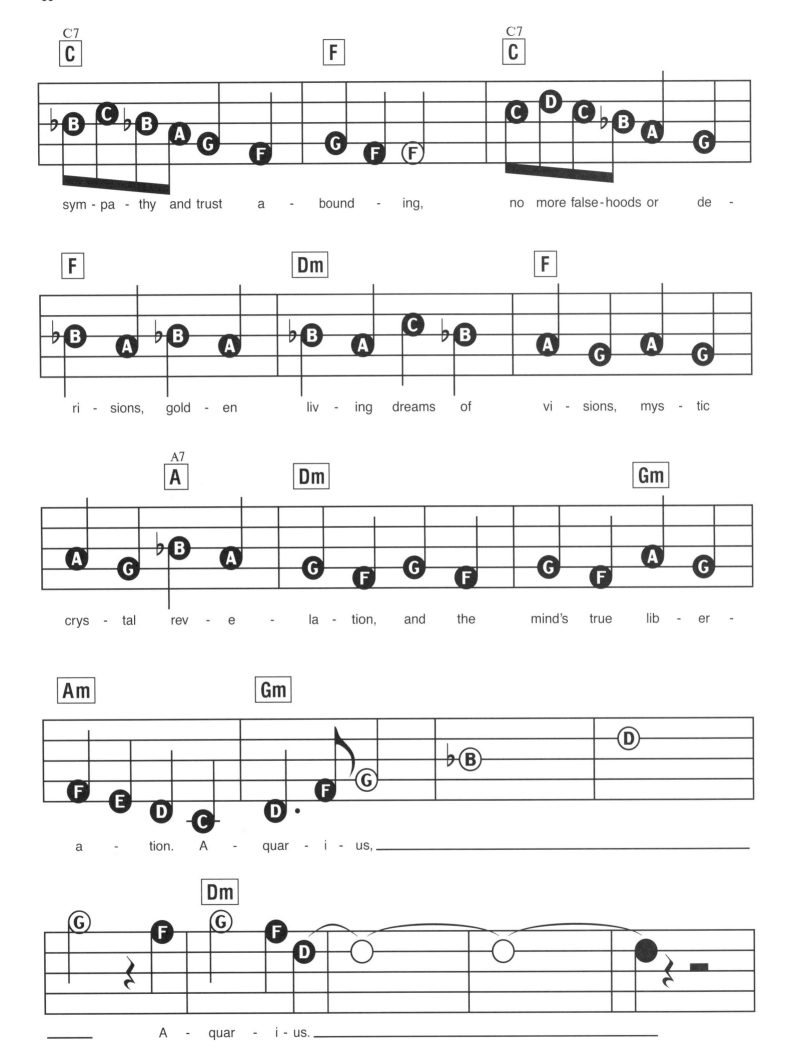

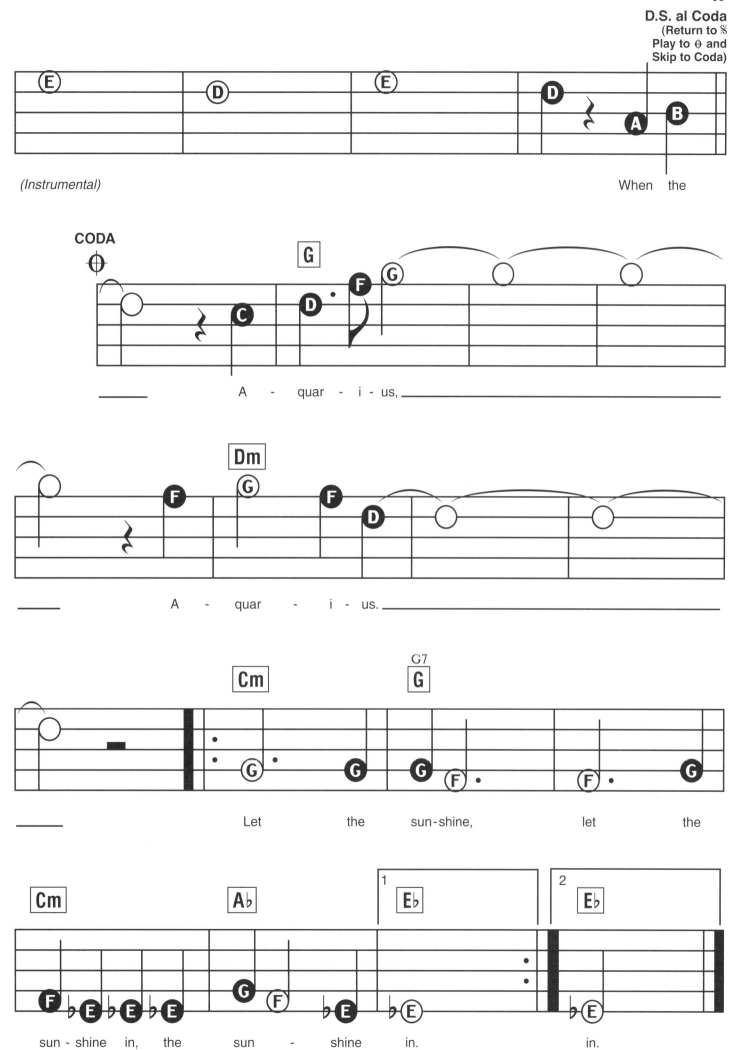

Beautiful Day

Registration 3
Rhythm: Rock

Words by Bono
Music by U2

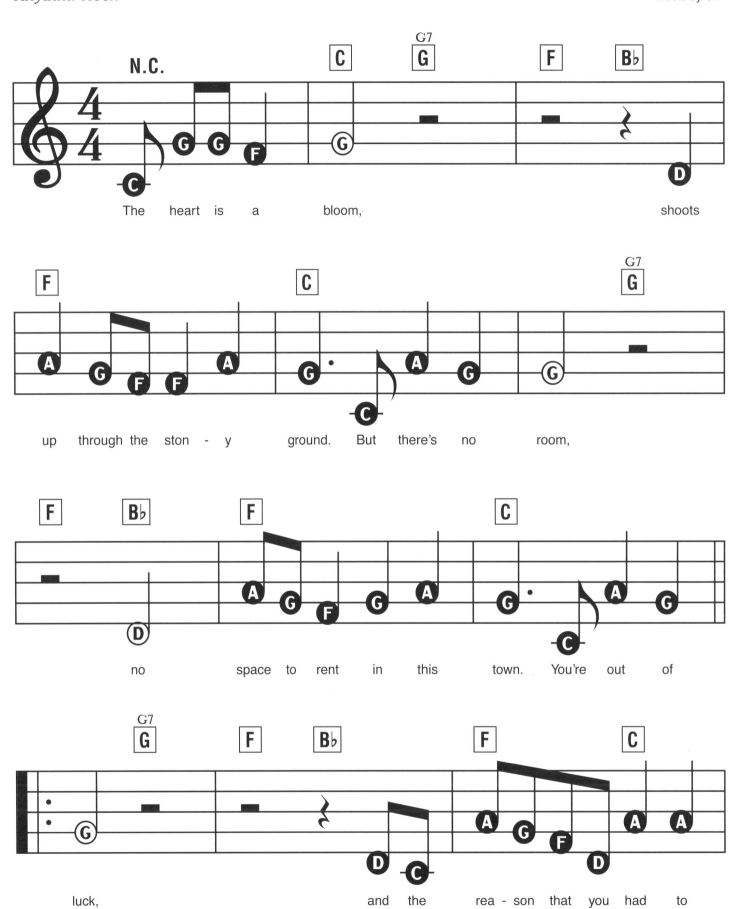

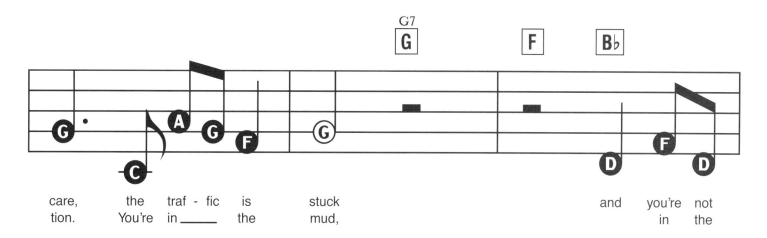

care, the traf - fic is stuck and you're not
tion. You're in _____ the mud, in the

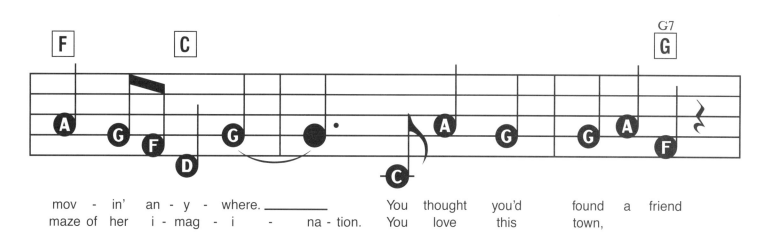

mov - in' an - y - where. _____ You thought you'd found a friend
maze of her i - mag - i - na - tion. You love this town,

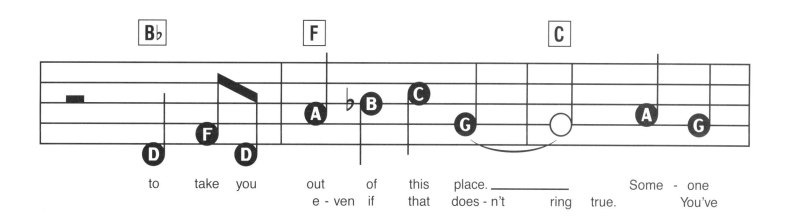

to take you out of this place. _____ Some - one
e - ven if that does - n't ring true. You've

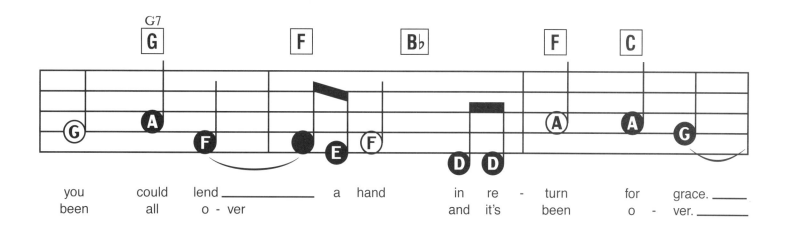

you could lend _____ a hand in re - turn for grace. _____
been all o - ver and it's been o - ver. _____

34

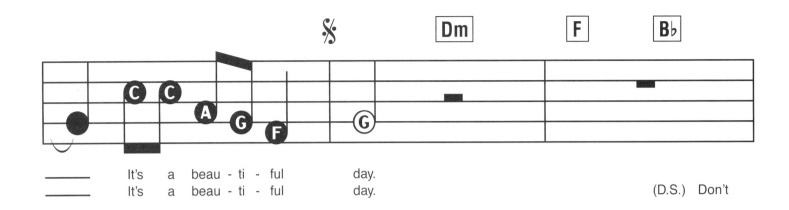

It's a beau - ti - ful day.
It's a beau - ti - ful day. (D.S.) Don't

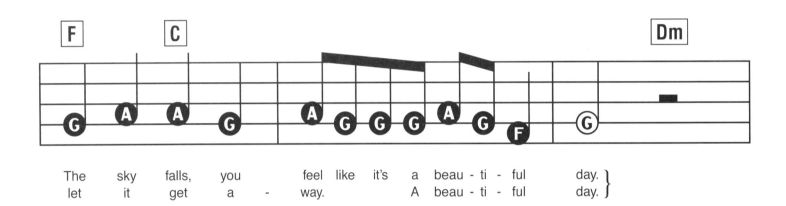

The sky falls, you feel like it's a beau - ti - ful day.
let it get a - way. A beau - ti - ful day. }

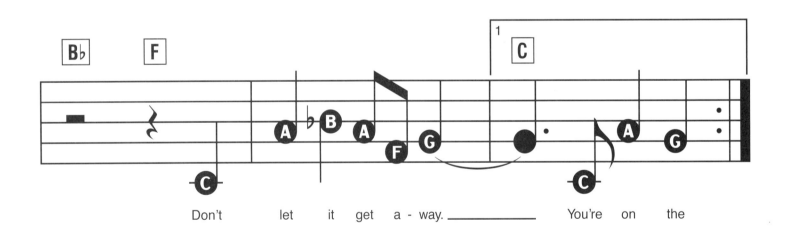

Don't let it get a - way. _____ You're on the

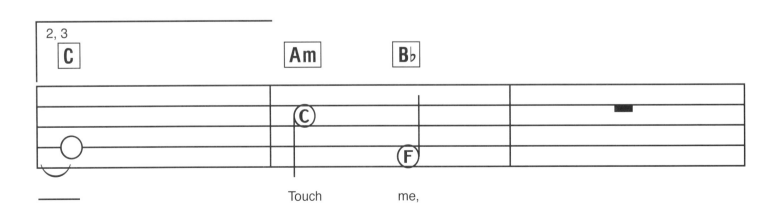

Touch me,

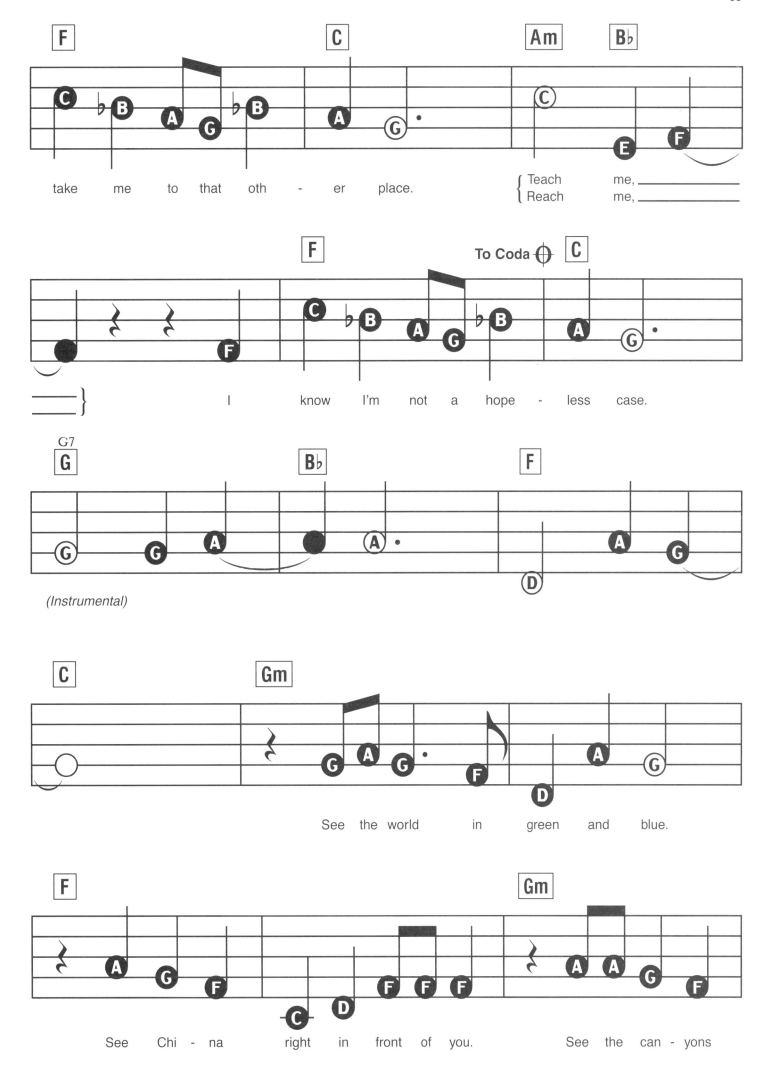

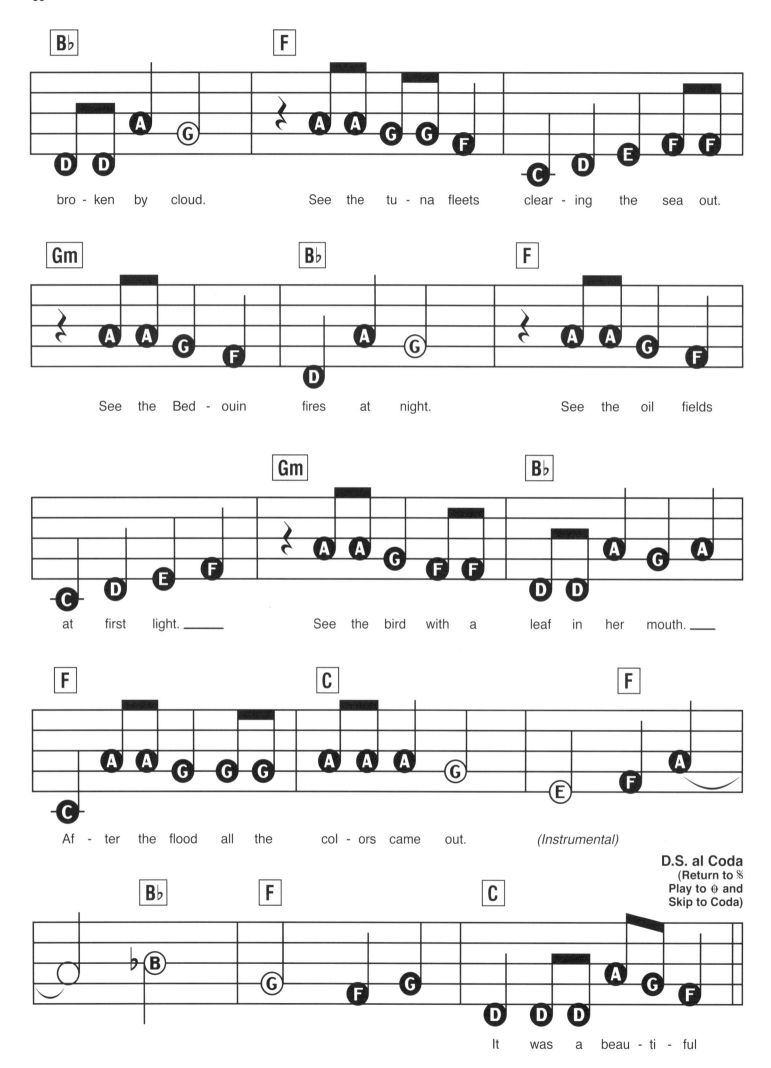

bro - ken by cloud. See the tu - na fleets clear - ing the sea out.

See the Bed - ouin fires at night. See the oil fields

at first light. _____ See the bird with a leaf in her mouth. ___

Af - ter the flood all the col - ors came out. *(Instrumental)*

D.S. al Coda
(Return to ℅
Play to ⊕ and
Skip to Coda)

It was a beau - ti - ful

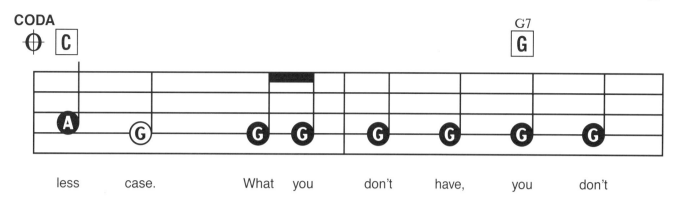

less case. What you don't have, you don't

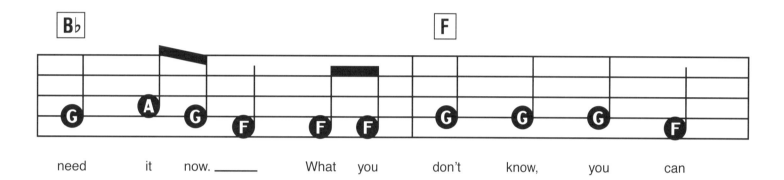

need it now. _____ What you don't know, you can

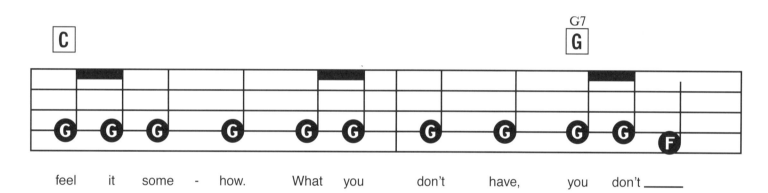

feel it some - how. What you don't have, you don't _____

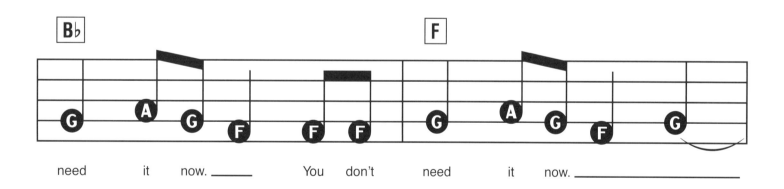

need it now. _____ You don't need it now. _____

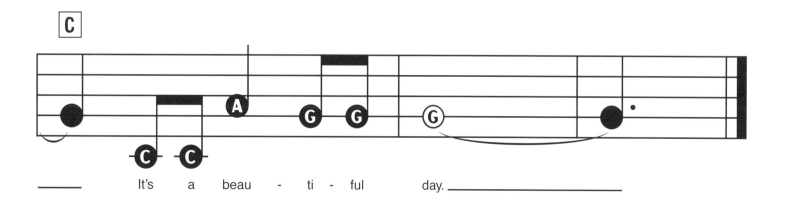

_____ It's a beau - ti - ful day. _____

Bette Davis Eyes

Registration 4
Rhythm: Rock

Words and Music by Donna Weiss
and Jackie DeShannon

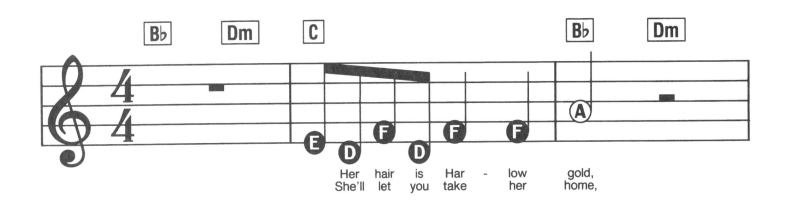

Her hair is Har - low gold,
She'll let you take her home,

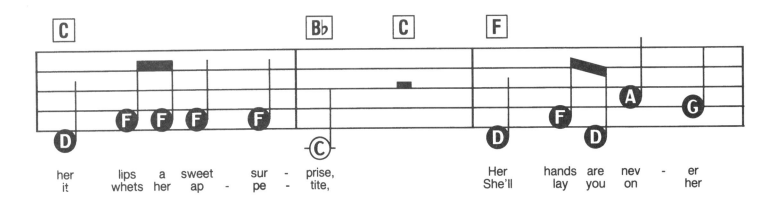

her lips a sweet sur - prise,
it whets her ap - pe - tite,

Her hands are nev - er
She'll lay you on her

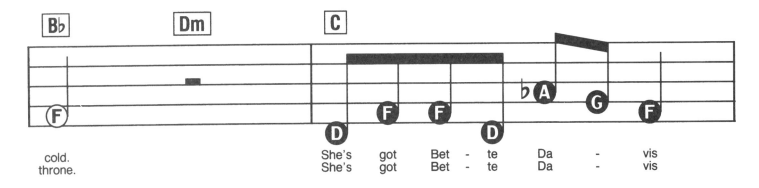

cold.
throne.

She's got Bet - te Da - vis
She's got Bet - te Da - vis

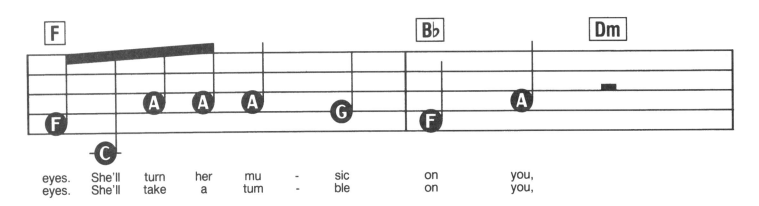

eyes. She'll turn her mu - sic on you,
eyes. She'll take a tum - ble on you,

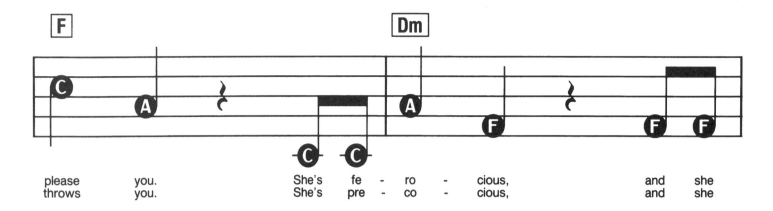

please   you.   She's   fe - ro - cious,   and   she
throws   you.   She's   pre - co - cious,   and   she

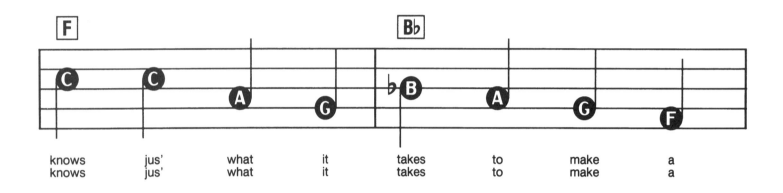

knows   jus'   what   it   takes   to   make   a
knows   jus'   what   it   takes   to   make   a

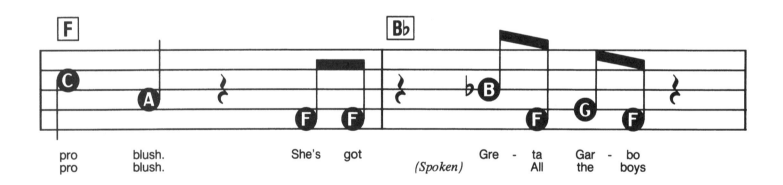

pro   blush.   She's   got   *(Spoken)*   Gre - ta   Gar - bo
pro   blush.   All   the   boys

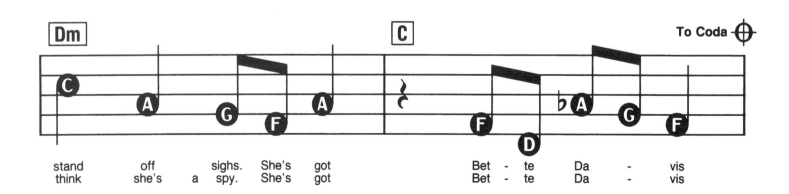

To Coda ⊕

stand   off   sighs.   She's   got   Bet - te   Da - vis
think   she's   a   spy.   She's   got   Bet - te   Da - vis

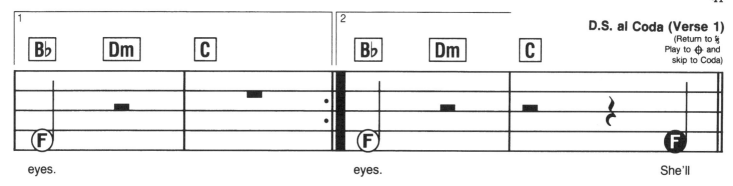

D.S. al Coda (Verse 1)
(Return to %
Play to ⊕ and
skip to Coda)

eyes.   eyes.   She'll

CODA

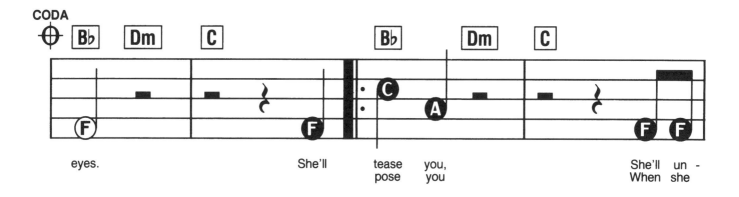

eyes.   She'll   tease you,   She'll un -
                                    pose you   When she

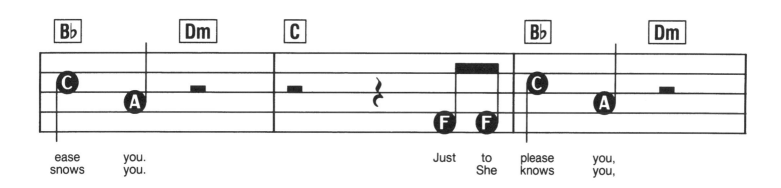

ease you.   Just to   please you,
snows you.   She   knows you,

Repeat and Fade

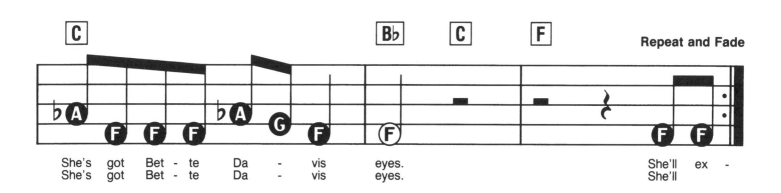

She's got Bet - te Da - vis eyes.   She'll ex -
She's got Bet - te Da - vis eyes.   She'll

Boulevard of Broken Dreams

Registration 4
Rhythm: 8-Beat or Rock

Words by Billie Joe Armstrong
Music by Green Day

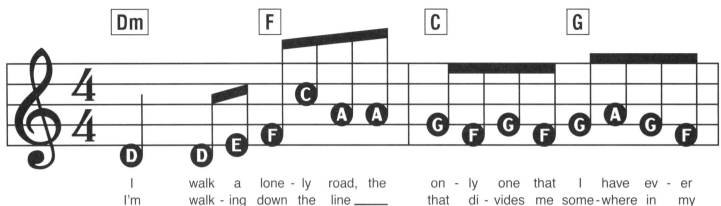

I   walk   a   lone - ly   road, the   on - ly   one   that   I   have   ev - er
I'm   walk - ing   down   the   line _____   that   di - vides   me   some - where   in   my

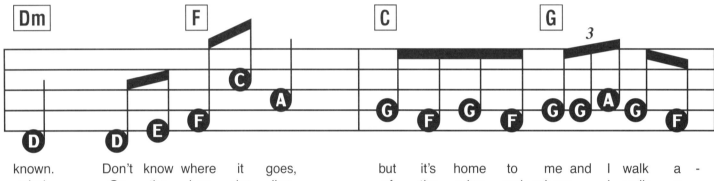

known.   Don't   know   where   it   goes,   but   it's   home   to   me   and   I   walk   a -
mind.   On   the   bor - der - line   of   the   edge   and   where   I   walk   a -

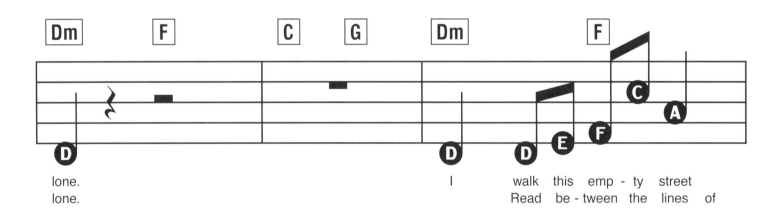

lone.   I   walk   this   emp - ty   street
lone.   Read   be - tween   the   lines   of

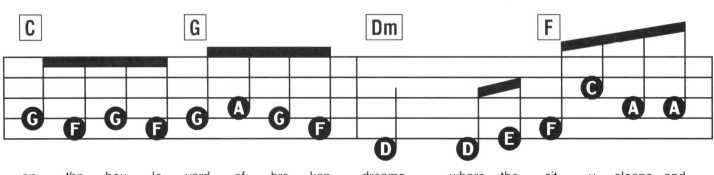

on   the   bou - le - vard   of   bro - ken   dreams,   where   the   cit - y   sleeps   and
what's _____   up   and   ev - ery - thing's   al -   right.   Check   my   vi - tal   signs   and

Change the World

Registration 7
Rhythm: Pop

Words and Music by Wayne Kirkpatrick,
Gordon Kennedy and Tommy Sims

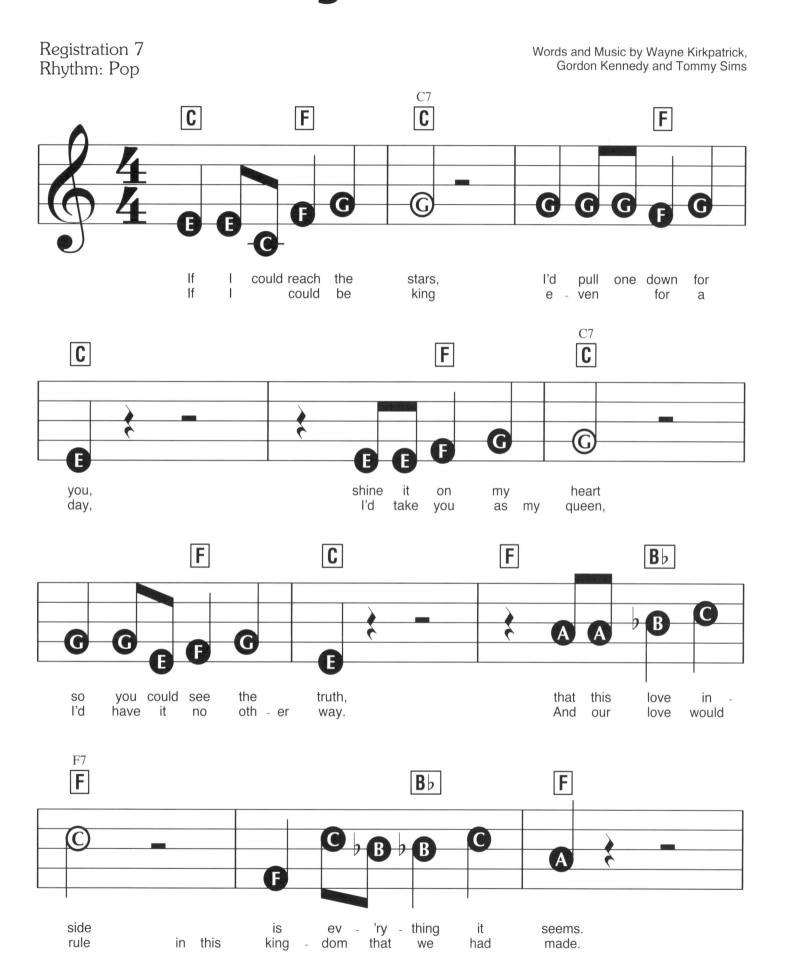

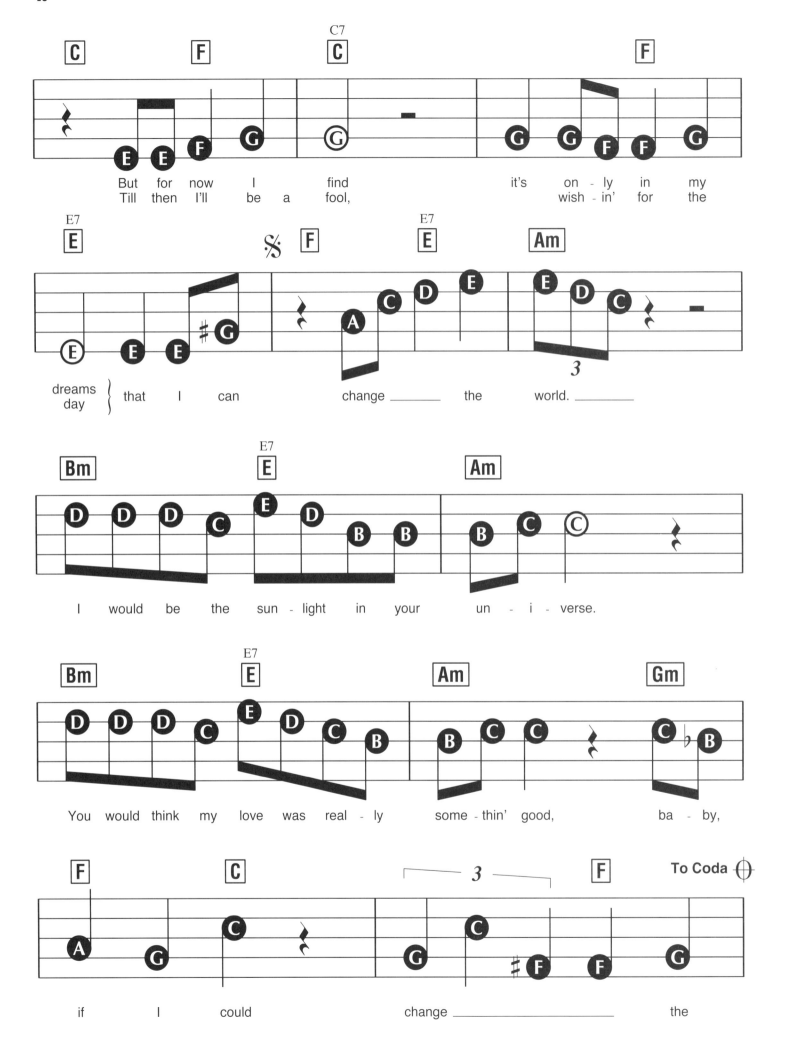

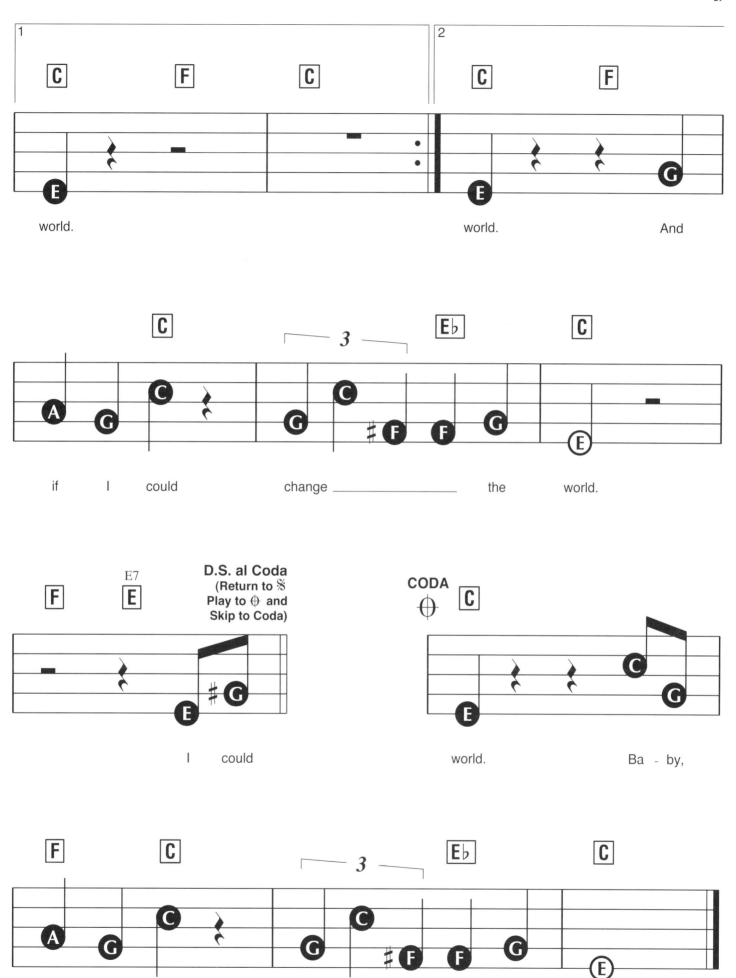

Bridge Over Troubled Water

Registration 3
Rhythm: Slow Rock or Ballad

Words and Music by
Paul Simon

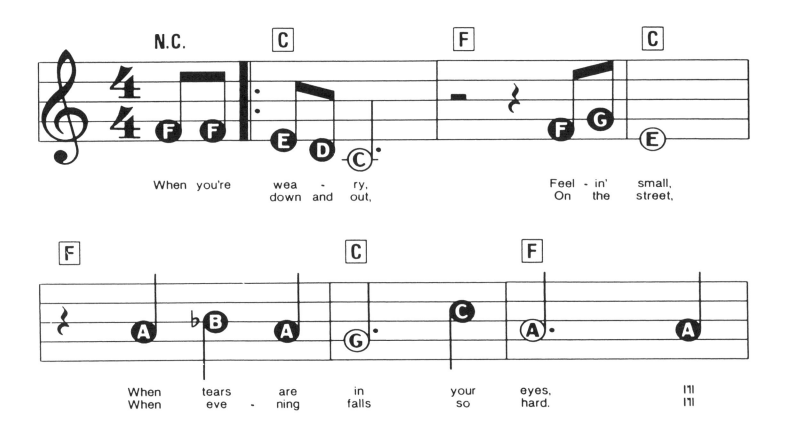

When you're wea - ry,
down and out,

Feel - in' small,
On the street,

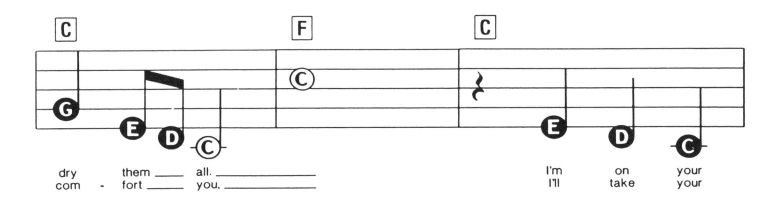

When tears are in your eyes,
When eve - ning falls so hard.

I'll
I'll

dry them _____ all. _____
com - fort _____ you, _____

I'm on your
I'll take your

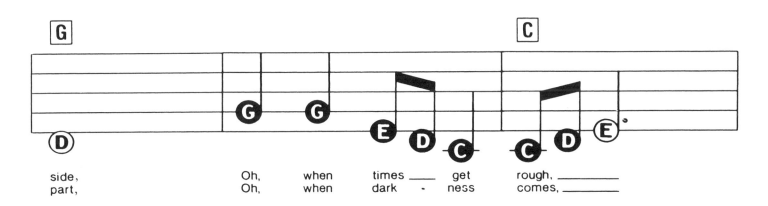

side,
part,

Oh, when times _____ get rough, _____
Oh, when dark - ness comes, _____

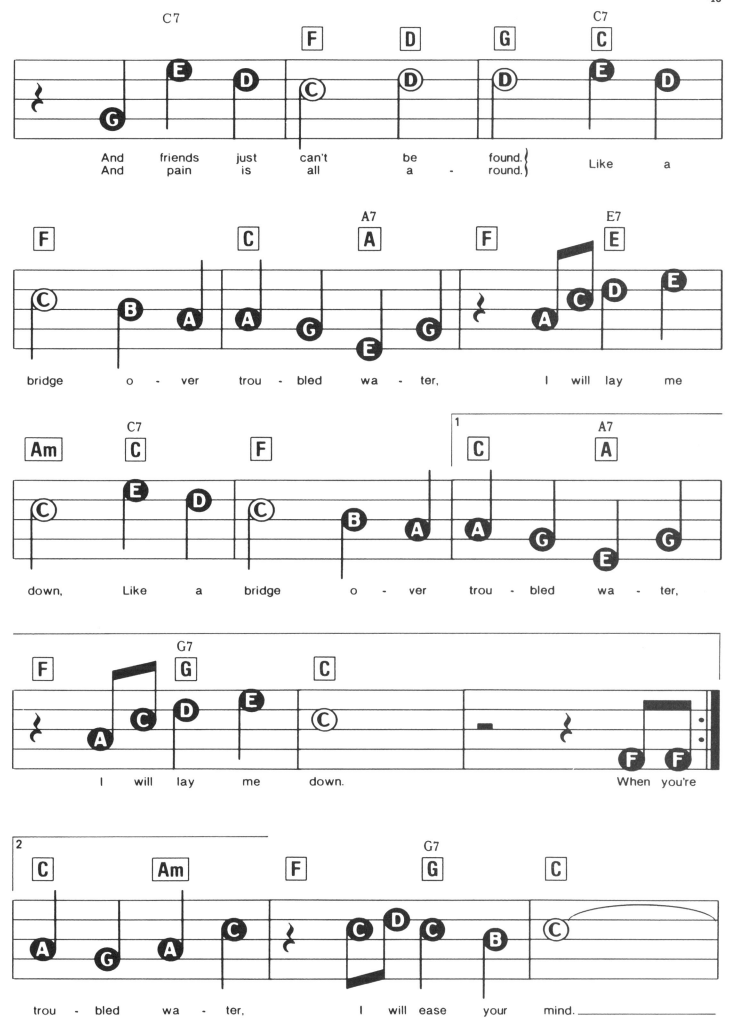

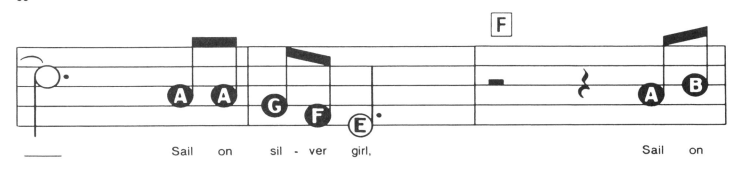

Sail on sil - ver girl, Sail on

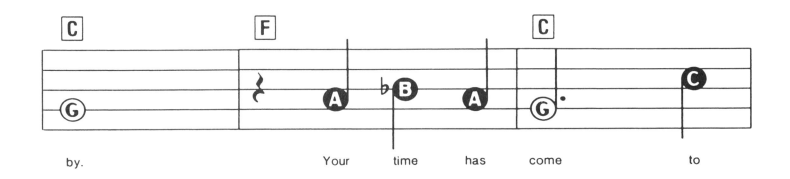

by. Your time has come to

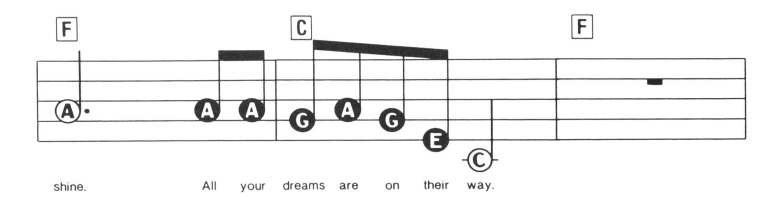

shine. All your dreams are on their way.

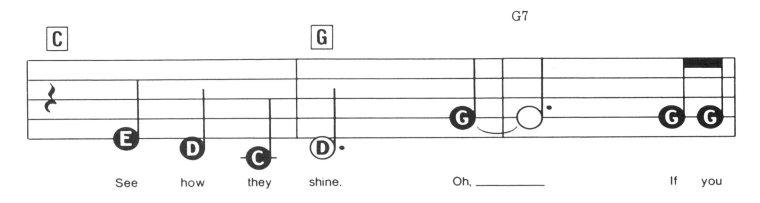

See how they shine. Oh, _____ If you

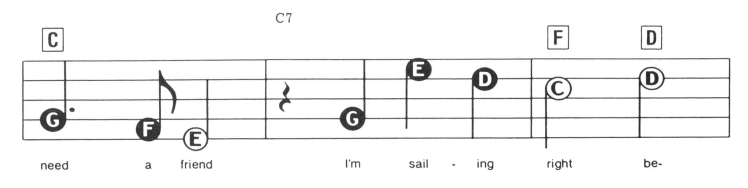

need a friend I'm sail - ing right be-

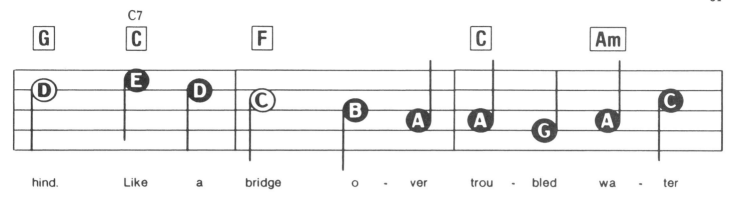

hind. Like a bridge o - ver trou - bled wa - ter

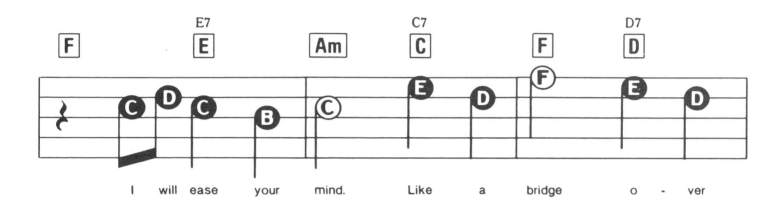

I will ease your mind. Like a bridge o - ver

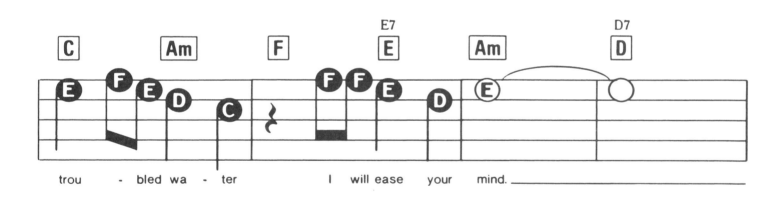

trou - bled wa - ter I will ease your mind._____

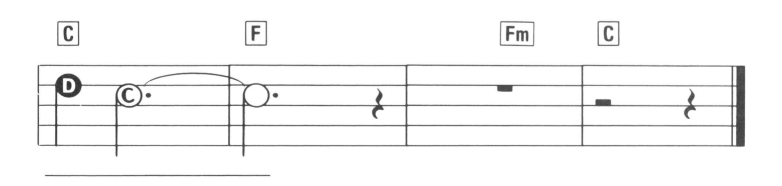

Clocks

Registration 5
Rhythm: Rock

Words and Music by Guy Berryman,
Jon Buckland, Will Champion
and Chris Martin

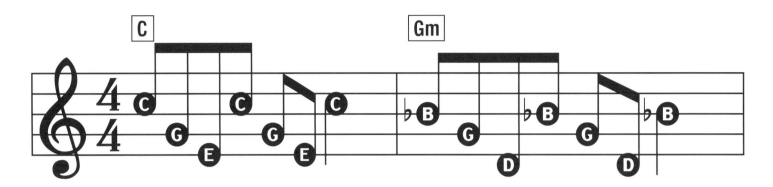

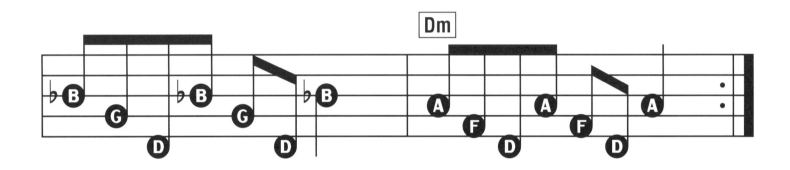

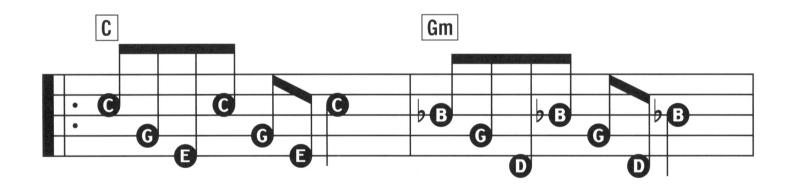

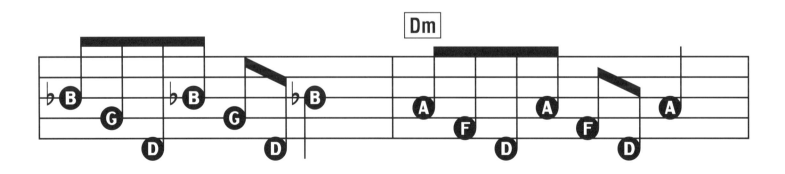

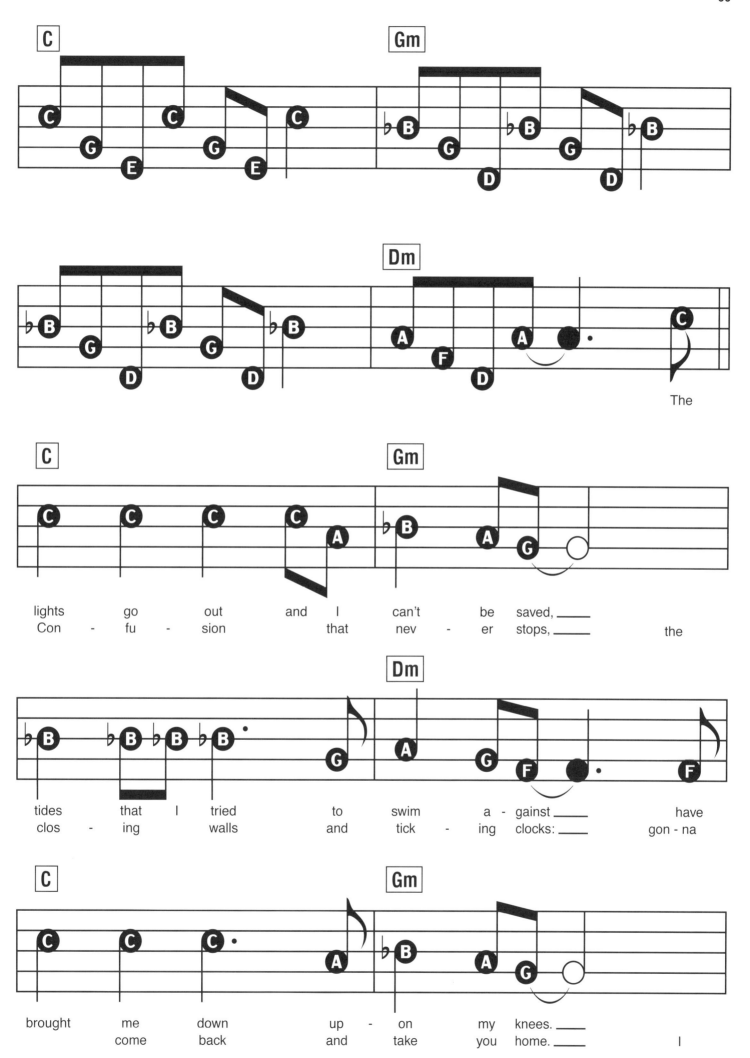

The

lights   go   out   and   I   can't   be   saved, _____
Con - fu - sion   that   nev - er   stops, _____   the

tides   that   I   tried   to   swim   a - gainst _____   have
clos - ing   walls   and   tick - ing   clocks: _____   gon - na

brought   me   down   up - on   my   knees. _____
come   back   down   and   take   you   home. _____   I

54

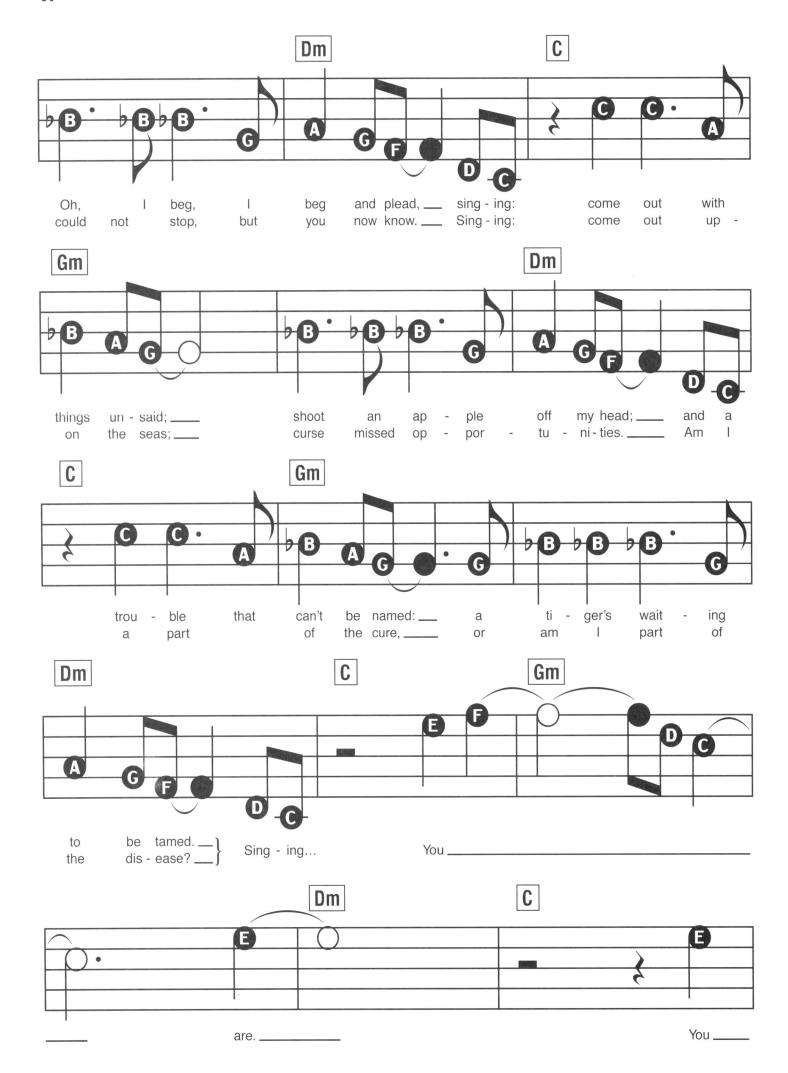

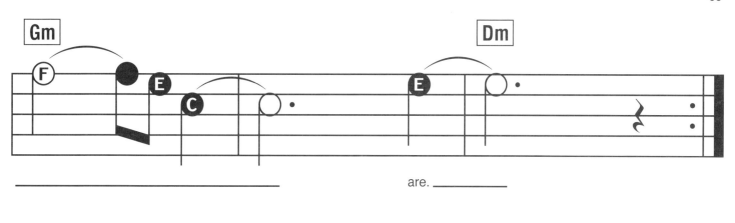

are.

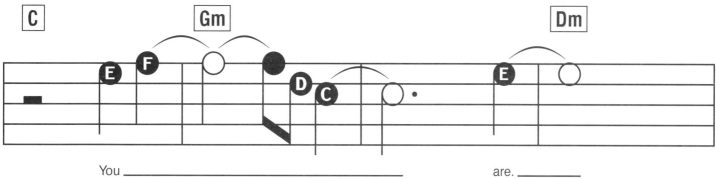

You _____ are. _____

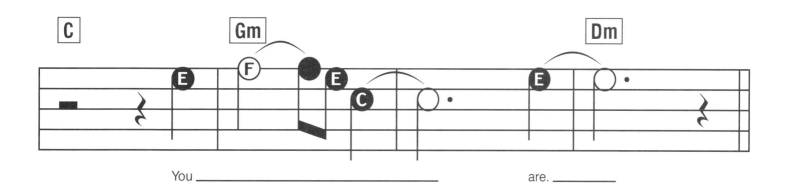

You _____ are. _____

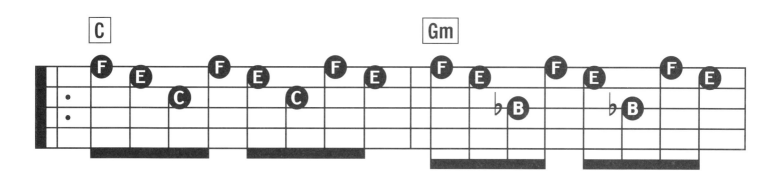

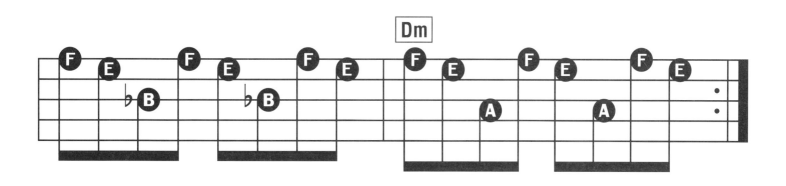

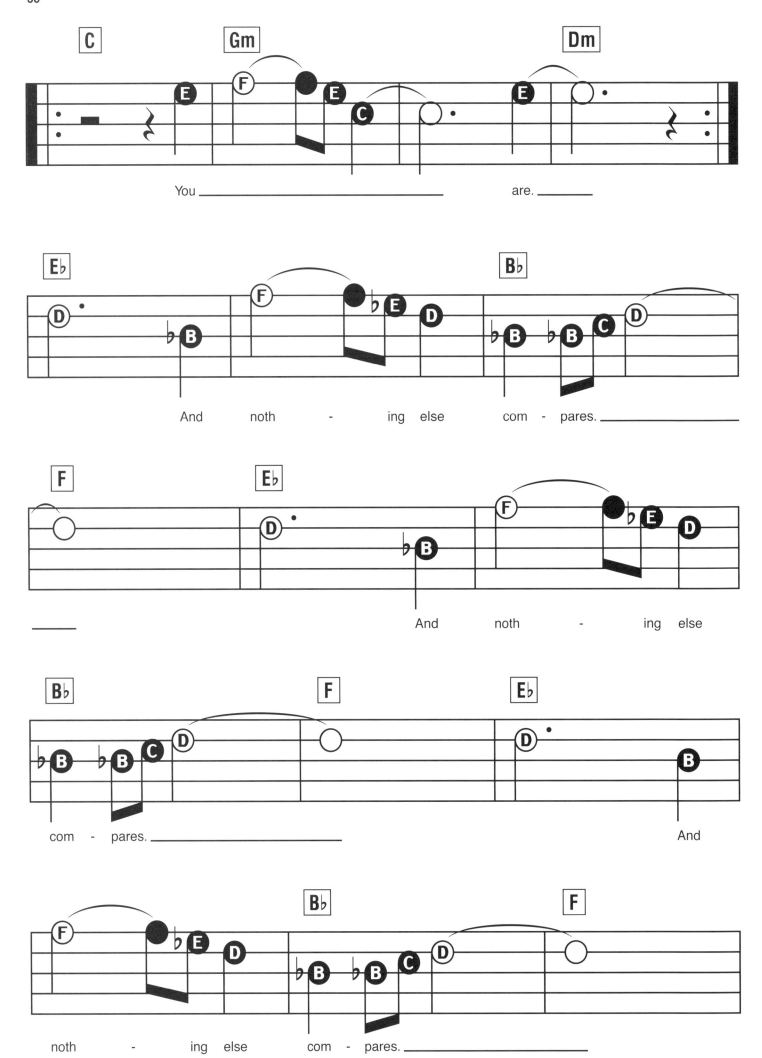

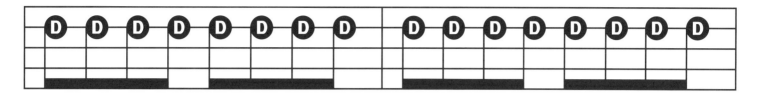

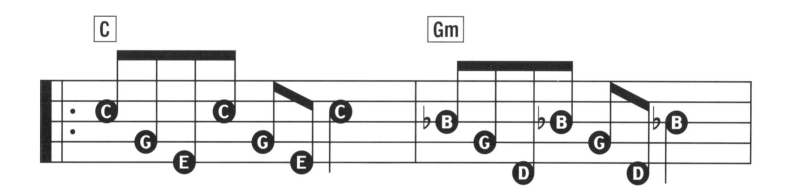

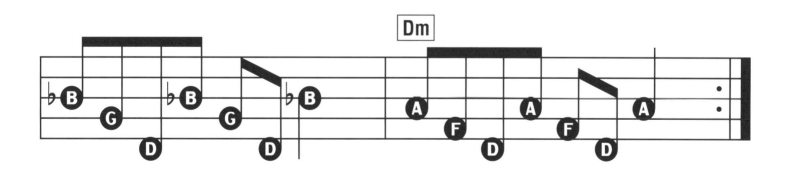

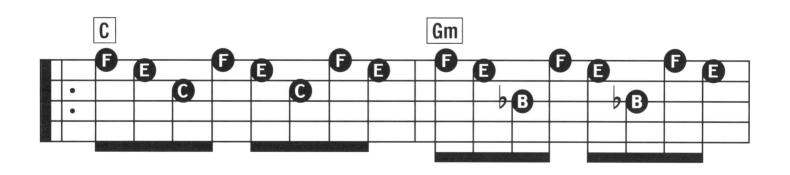

58

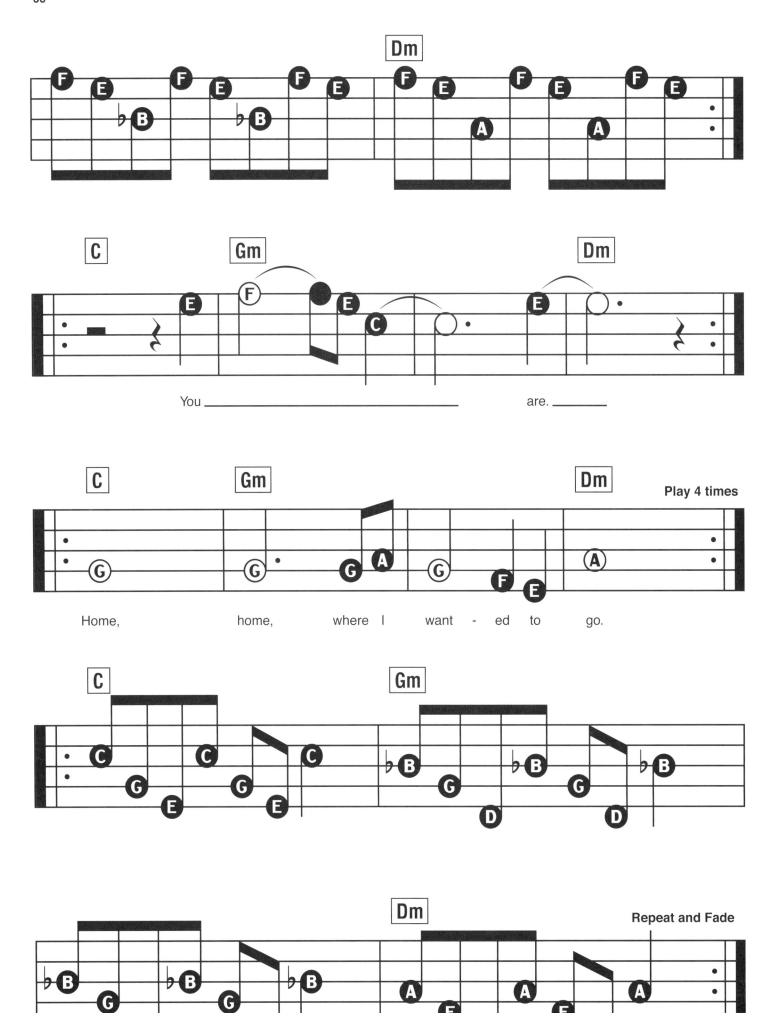

You _____ are. _____

Home, home, where I want - ed to go.

Don't Worry, Be Happy

Registration 5
Rhythm: Calypso

Words and Music by
Bobby McFerrin

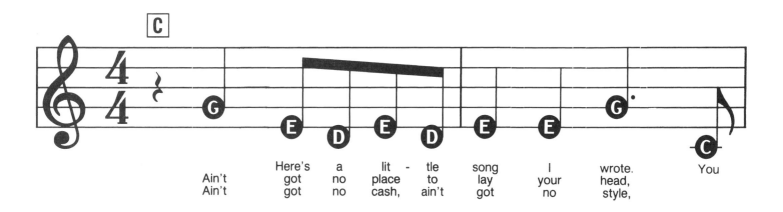

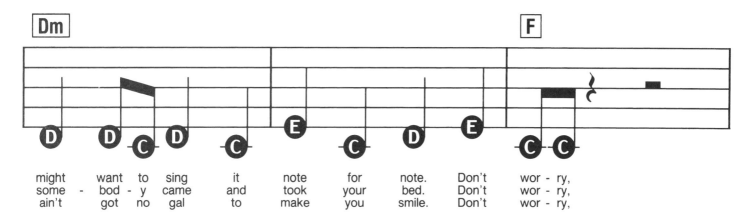

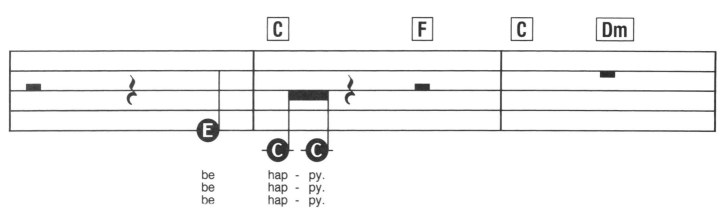

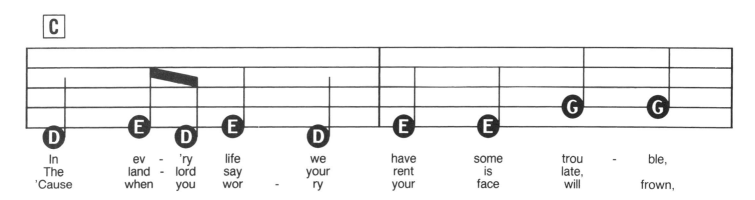

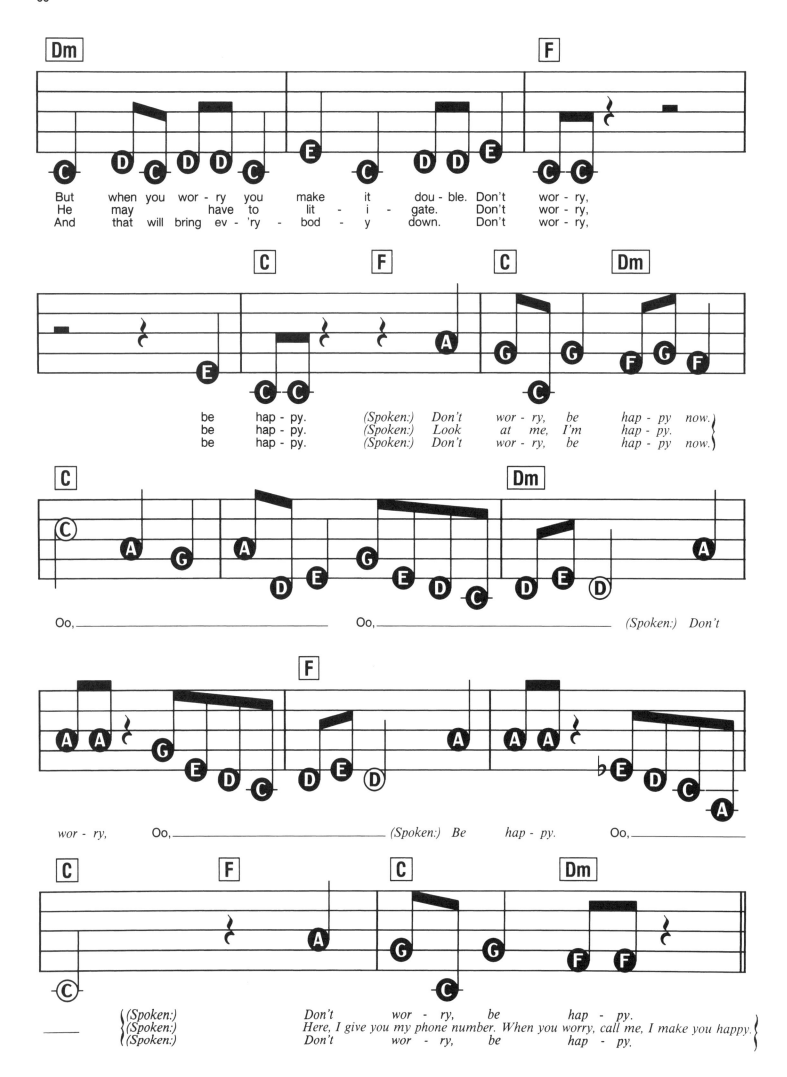

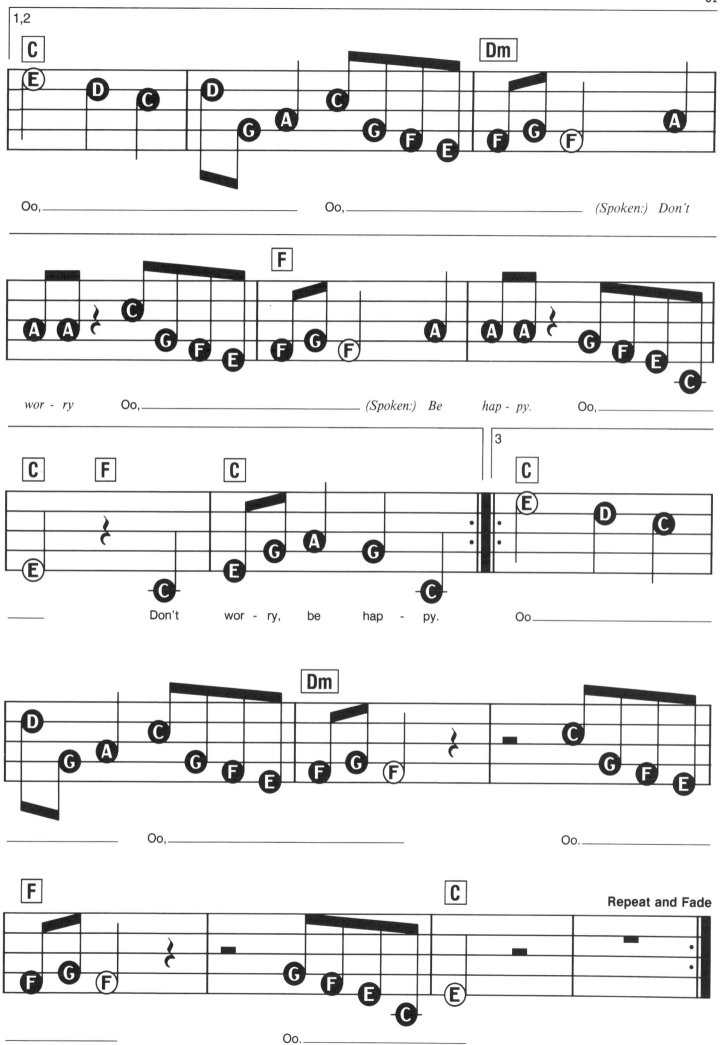

Days of Wine and Roses
from DAYS OF WINE AND ROSES

Registration 2
Rhythm: Swing

Lyrics by Johnny Mercer
Music by Henry Mancini

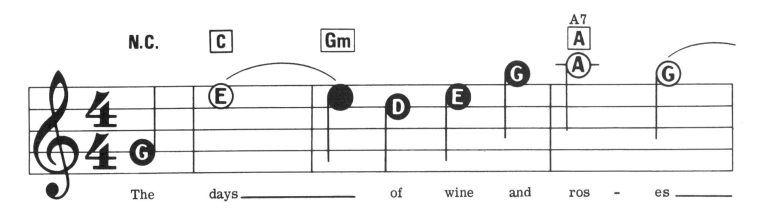

The days _____ of wine and ros - es _____

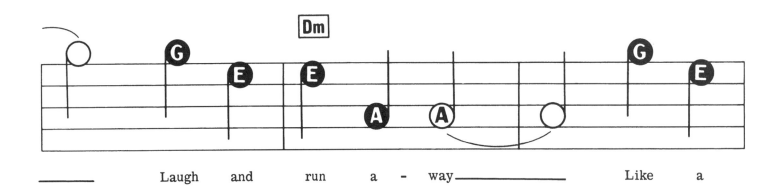

_____ Laugh and run a - way _____ Like a

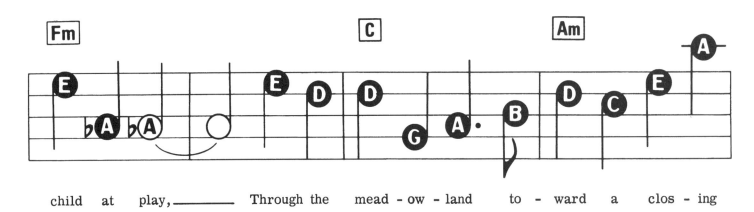

child at play, _____ Through the mead - ow - land to - ward a clos - ing

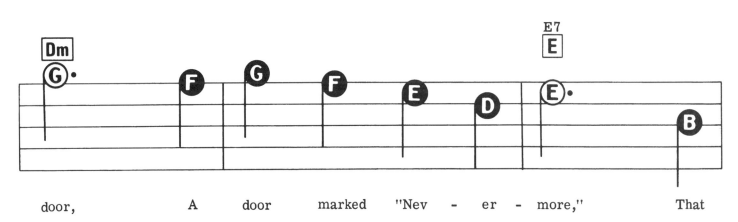

door, A door marked "Nev - er - more," That

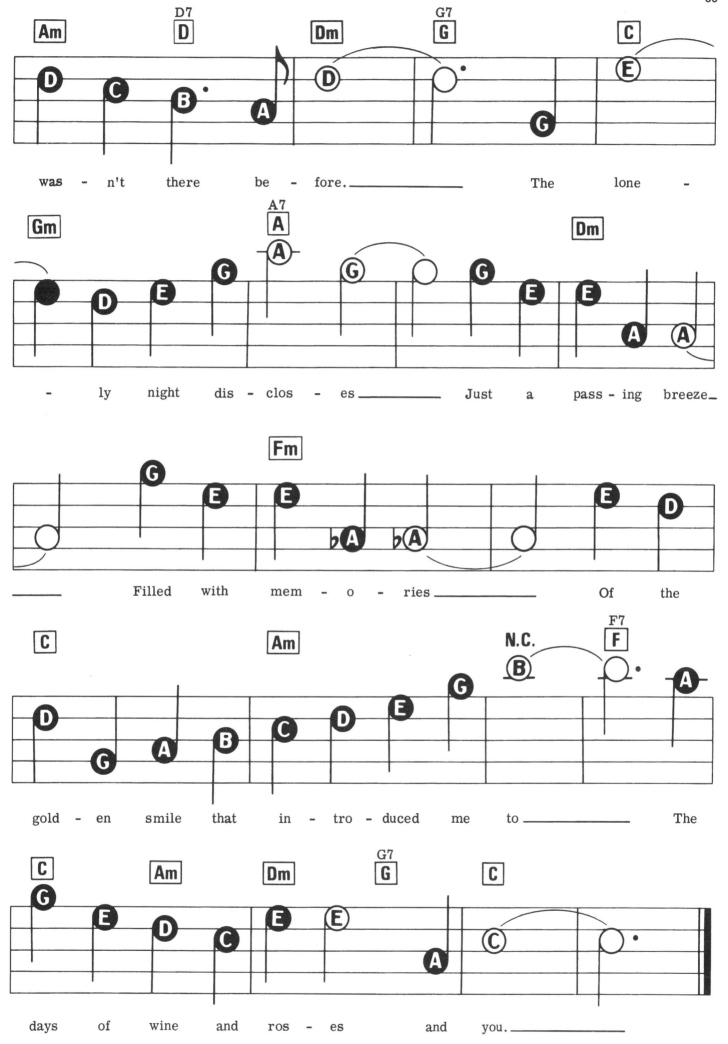

was - n't there be - fore.____ The lone -

- ly night dis - clos - es ____ Just a pass - ing breeze____

____ Filled with mem - o - ries ____ Of the

gold - en smile that in - tro - duced me to ____ The

days of wine and ros - es and you.____

Don't Know Why

Registration 8
Rhythm: 8-Beat or Bossa Nova

Words and Music by
Jesse Harris

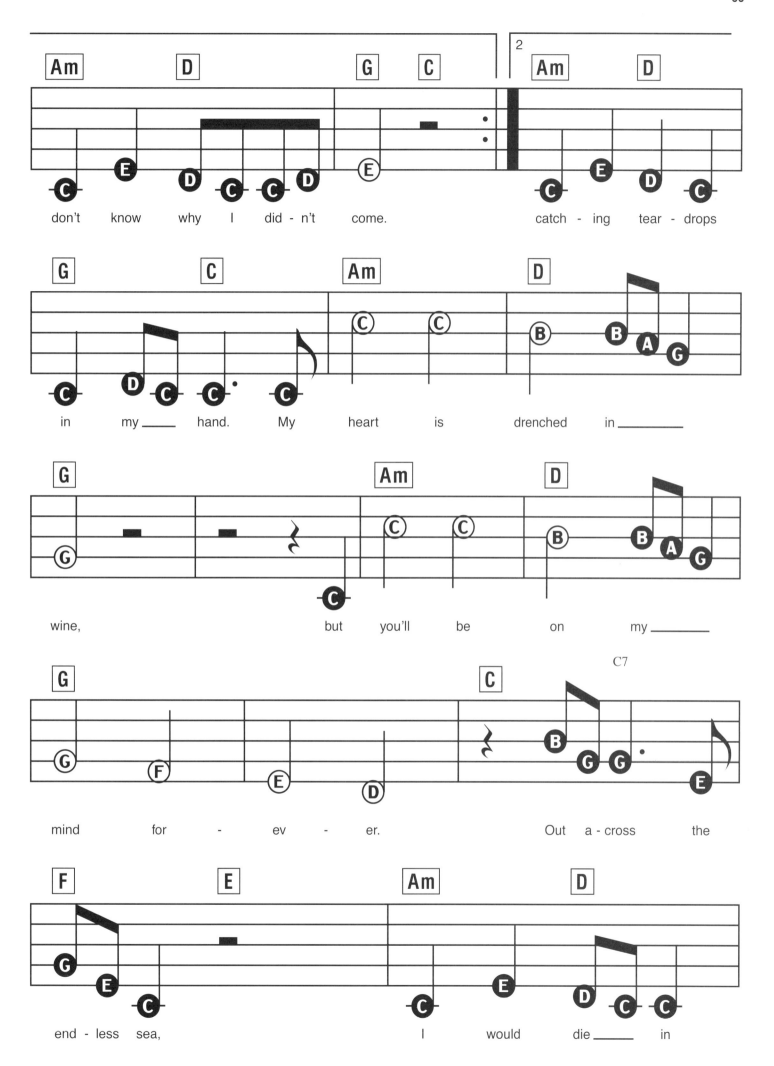

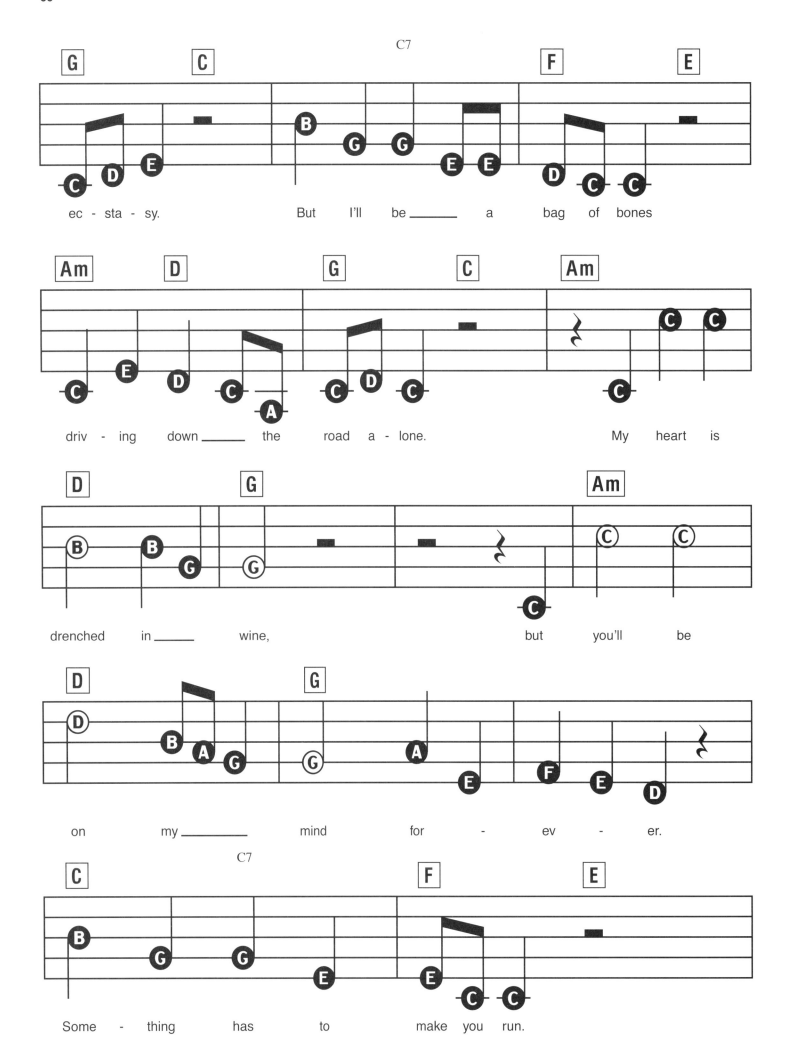

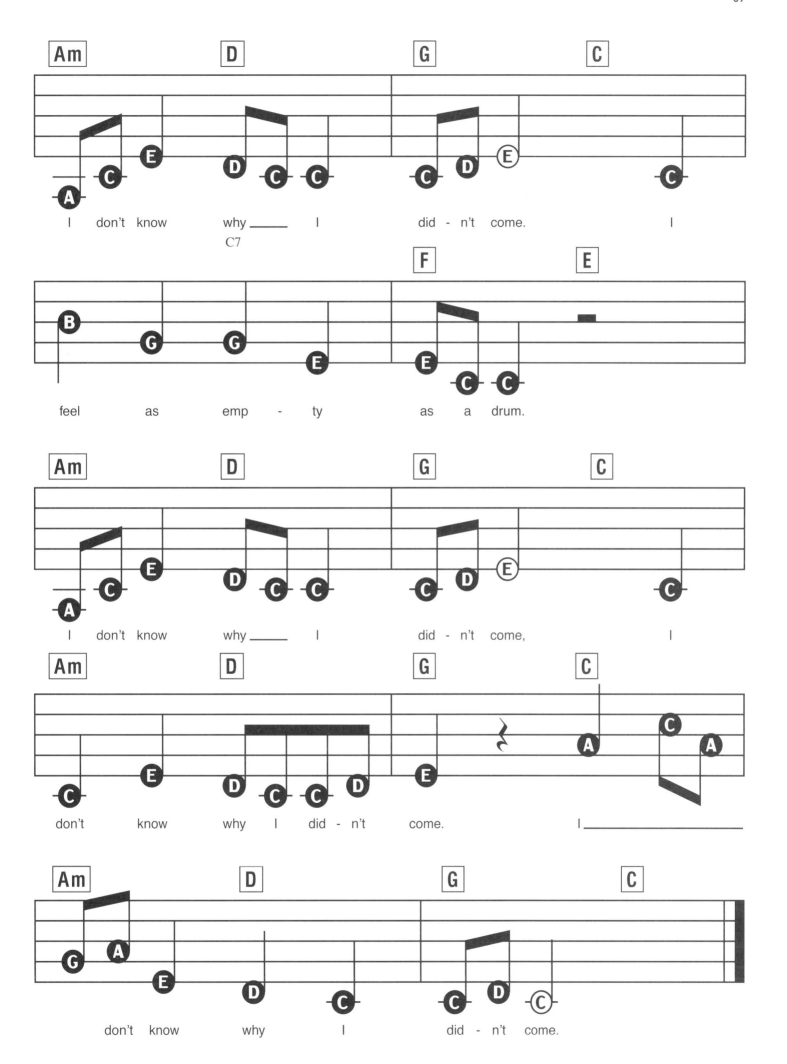

The First Time Ever I Saw Your Face

Registration 9
Rhythm: Ballad

Words and Music by
Ewan MacColl

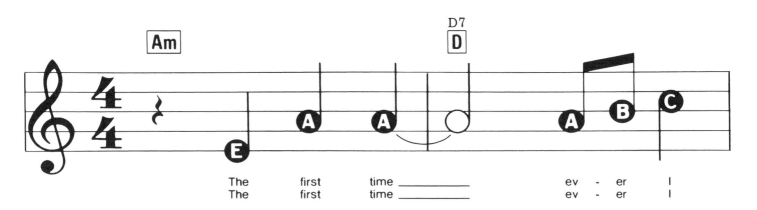

The first time _____ ev - er I
The first time _____ ev - er I

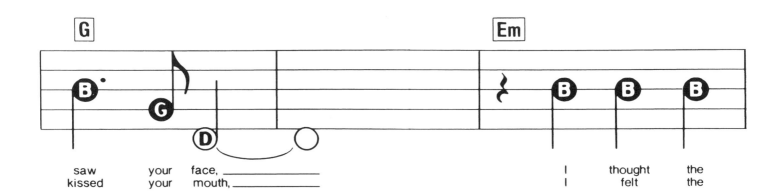

saw your face, _____
kissed your mouth, _____

I thought the
I felt the

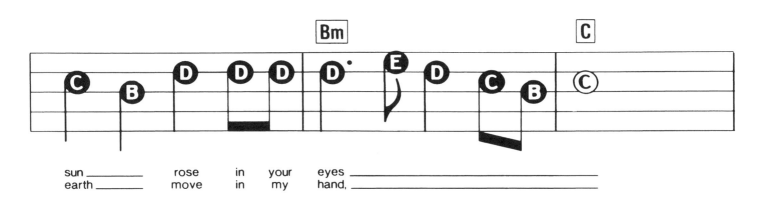

sun _____ rose in your eyes _____
earth _____ move in my hand, _____

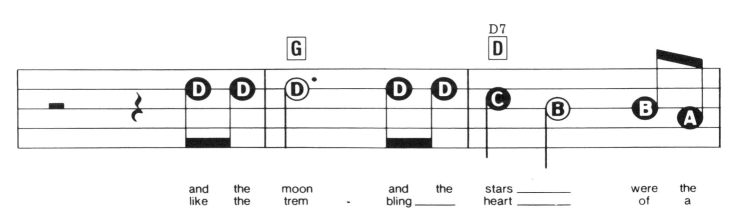

and the moon _____ and the stars _____ were the
like the trem - bling _____ heart _____ of a

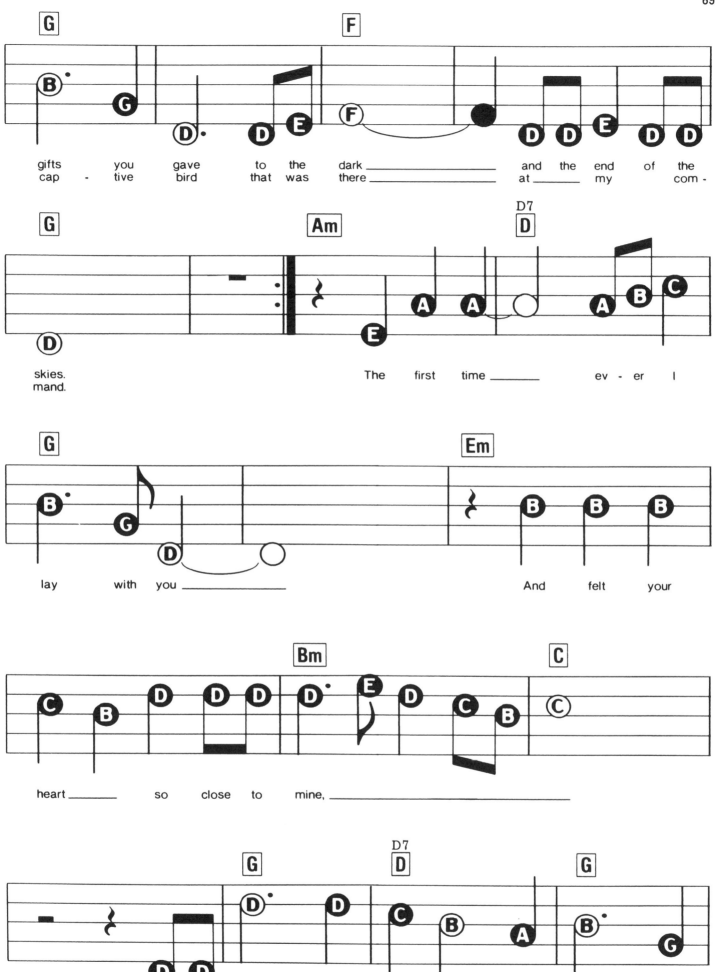

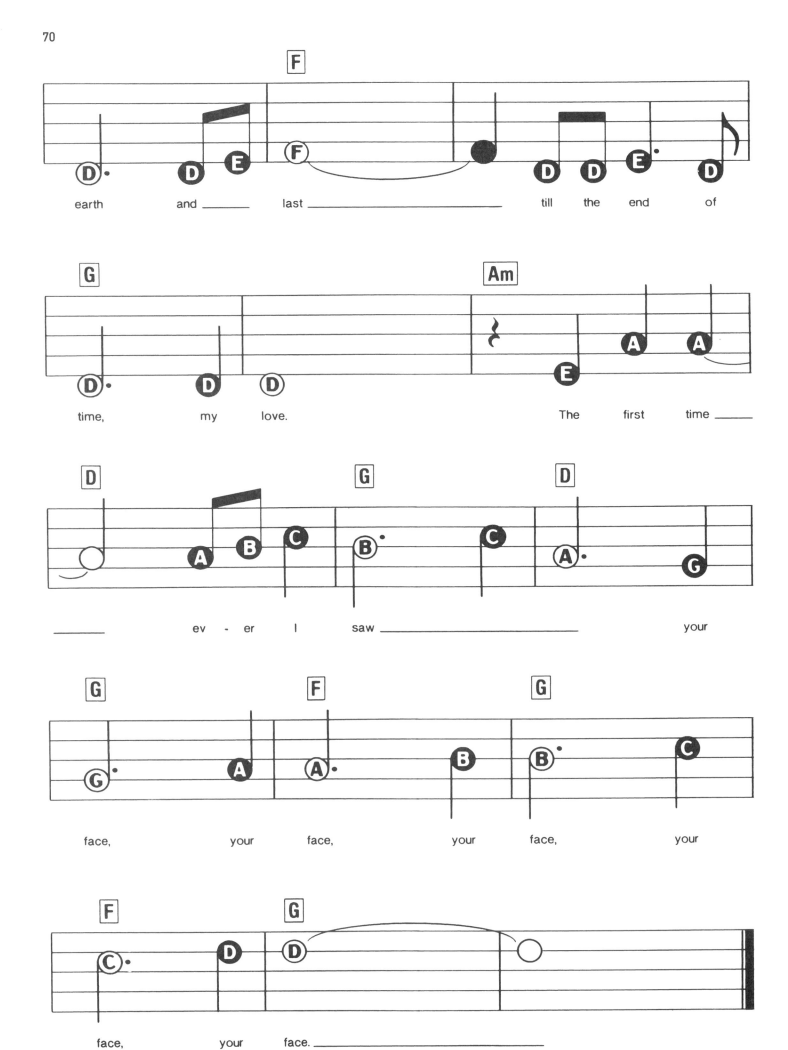

Graceland

Registration 4
Rhythm: 16-Beat or Rock

Words and Music by
Paul Simon

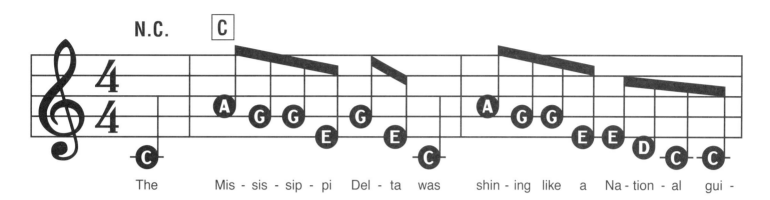

The Mis - sis - sip - pi Del - ta was shin - ing like a Na - tion - al gui -

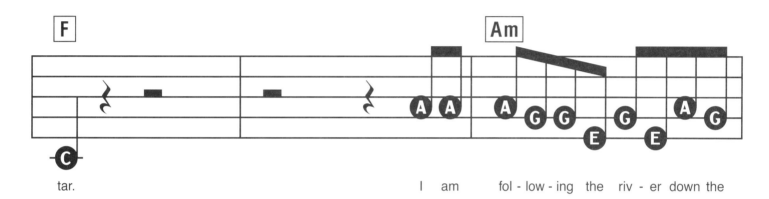

tar. I am fol - low - ing the riv - er down the

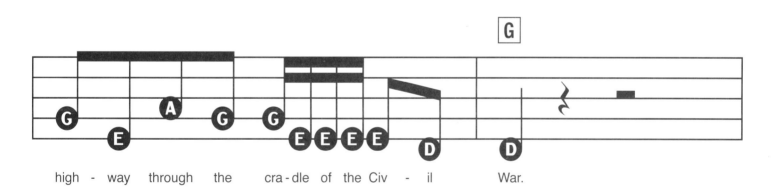

high - way through the cra - dle of the Civ - il War.

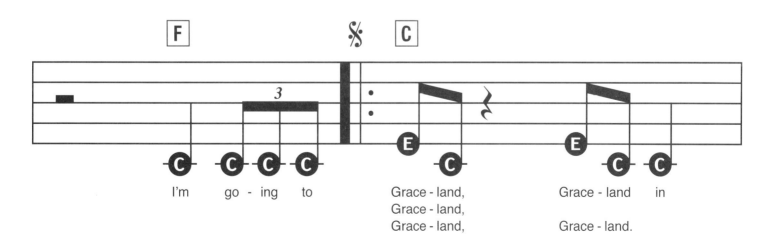

I'm go - ing to Grace - land, Grace - land in
Grace - land, Grace - land,
Grace - land.

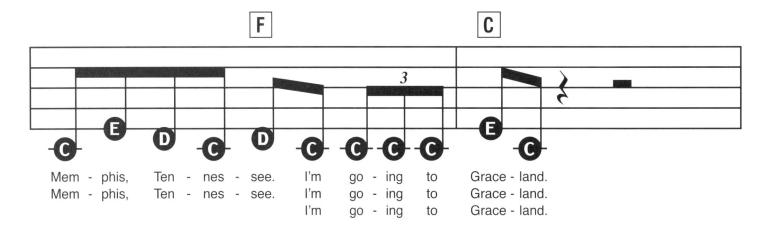

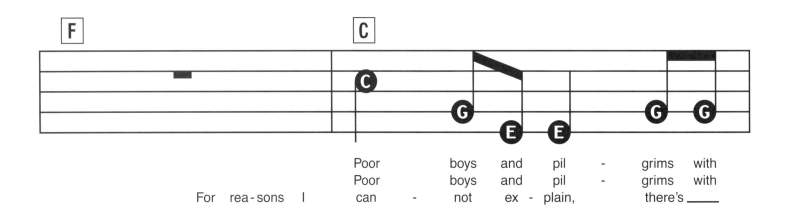

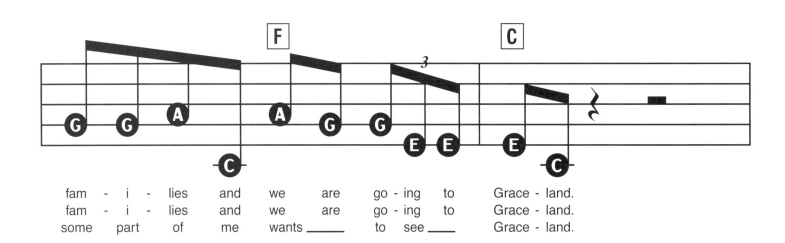

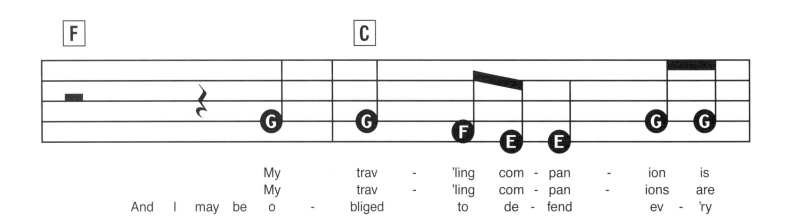

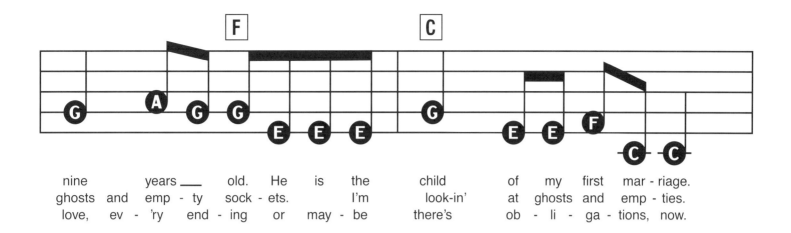

nine   years ___ old. He   is   the   child   of   my first mar - riage.
ghosts and emp - ty sock - ets.   I'm   look-in'   at ghosts and emp - ties.
love, ev - 'ry end - ing or may - be   there's   ob - li - ga - tions, now.

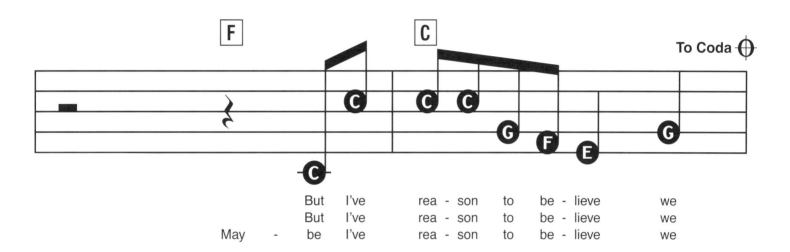

To Coda

But I've rea - son to be - lieve   we
But I've rea - son to be - lieve   we
May - be I've rea - son to be - lieve   we

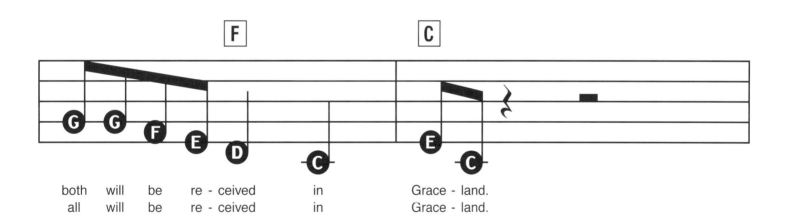

both will be re - ceived   in   Grace - land.
all   will be re - ceived   in   Grace - land.

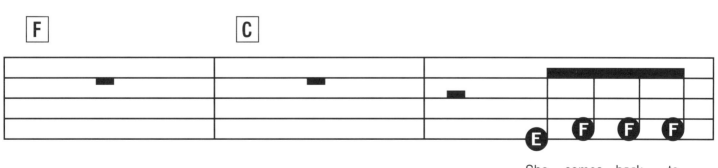

She comes back to
There is   a

74

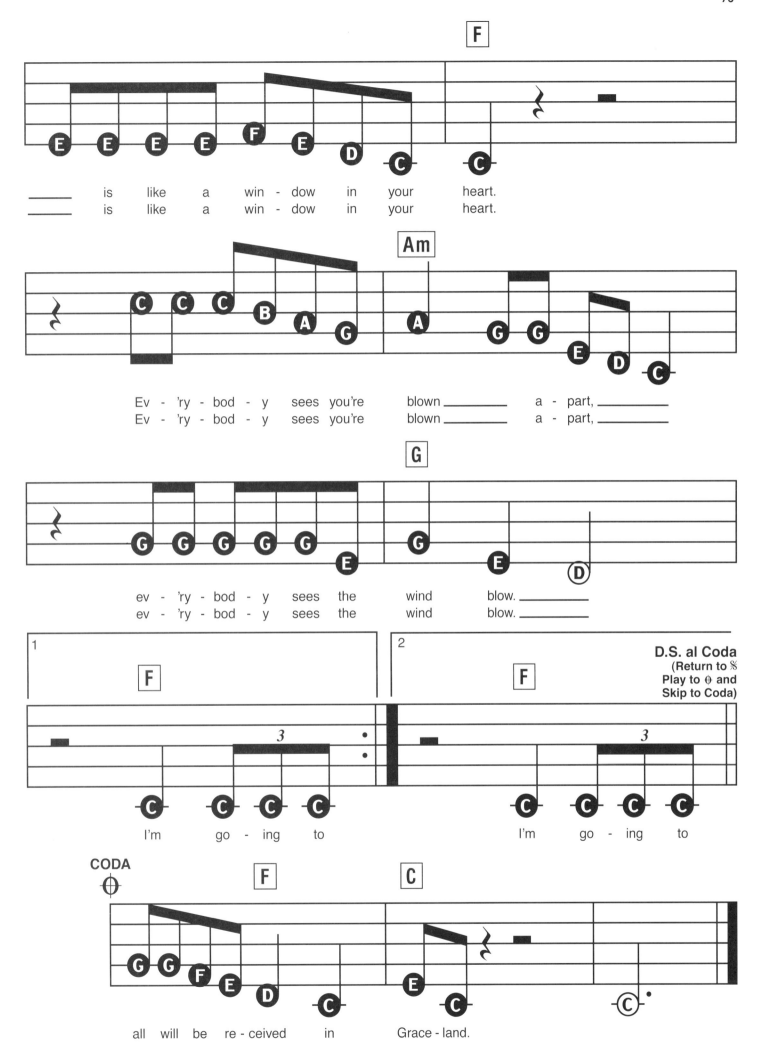

The Girl from Ipanema
(Garôta de Ipanema)

Registration 4
Rhythm: Latin or Bossa Nova

Music by Antonio Carlos Jobim
English Words by Norman Gimbel
Original Words by Vinicius de Moraes

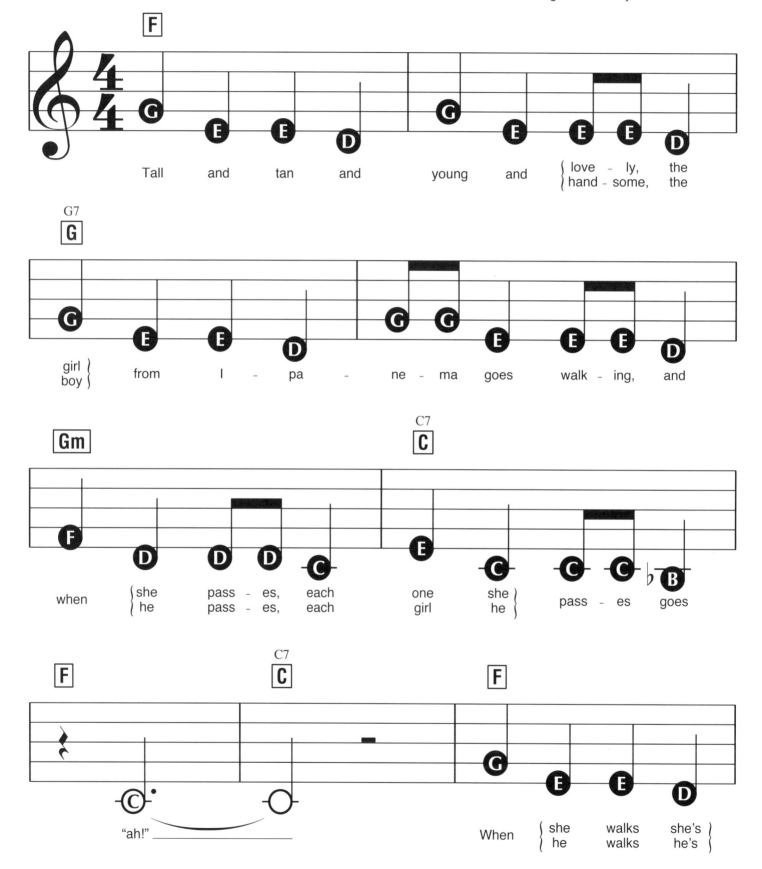

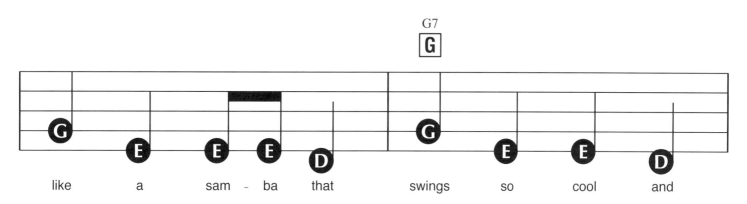

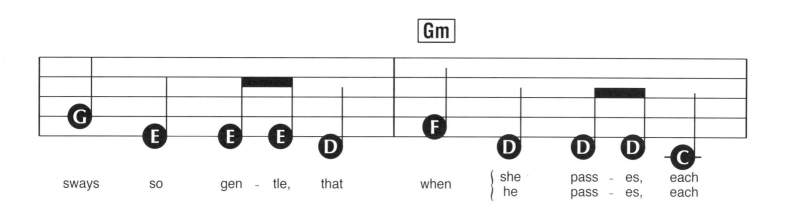

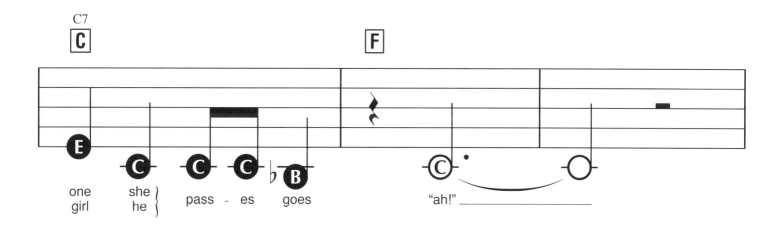

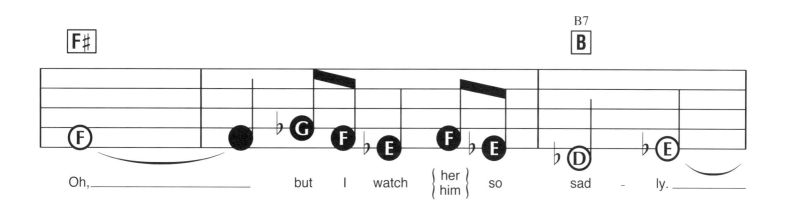

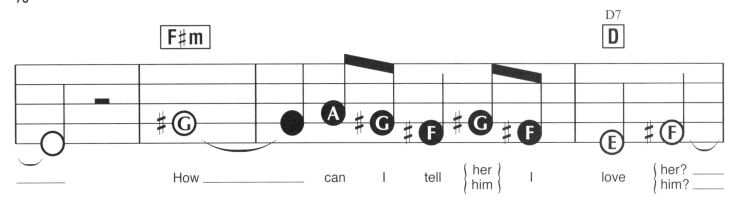

How _____ can I tell { her / him } I love { her? / him? } _____

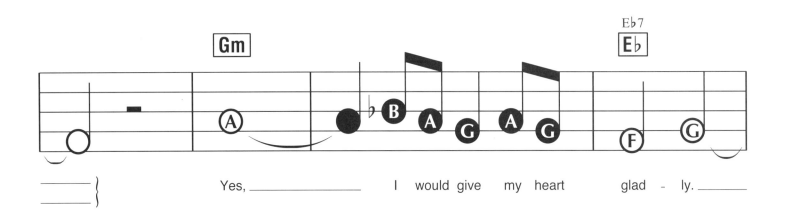

Yes, _____ I would give my heart glad - ly. _____

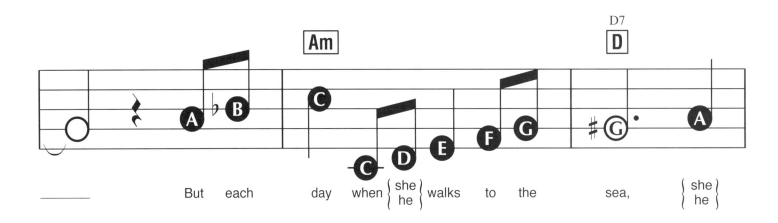

But each day when { she / he } walks to the sea, { she / he }

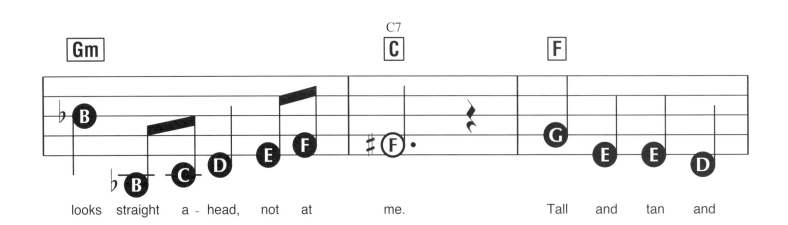

looks straight a - head, not at me. Tall and tan and

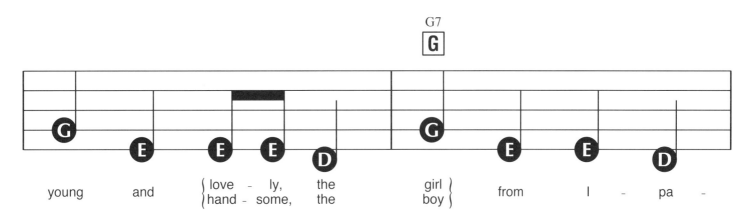

young and { love - ly, the   { girl } from I - pa -
          { hand - some, the { boy }

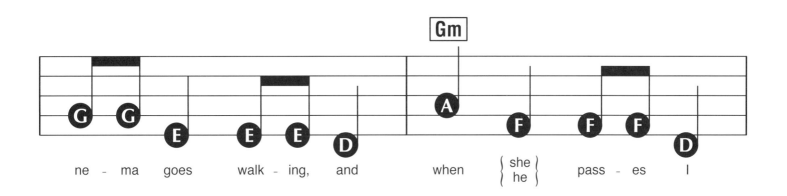

ne - ma goes walk - ing, and   when { she } pass - es   I
                                     { he }

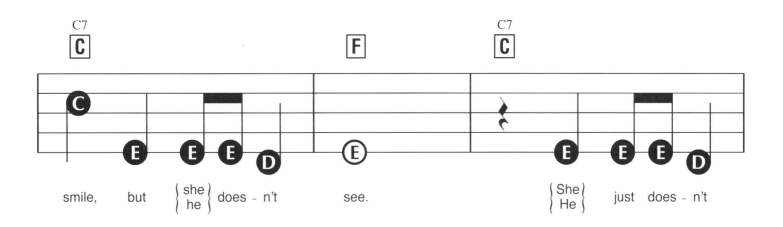

smile, but { she } does - n't   see.   { She } just does - n't
           { he }   { He }

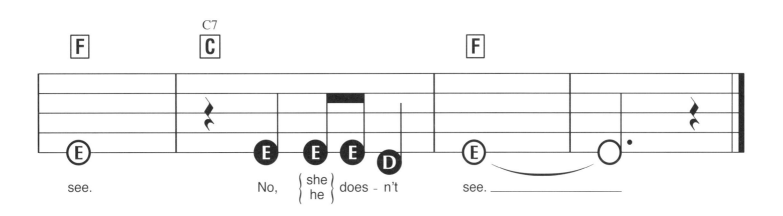

see.   No, { she } does - n't   see. _____
           { he }

Here We Go Again

Registration 8
Rhythm: Slow Rock or Rock

Words and Music by Red Steagall
and Donnie Lanier

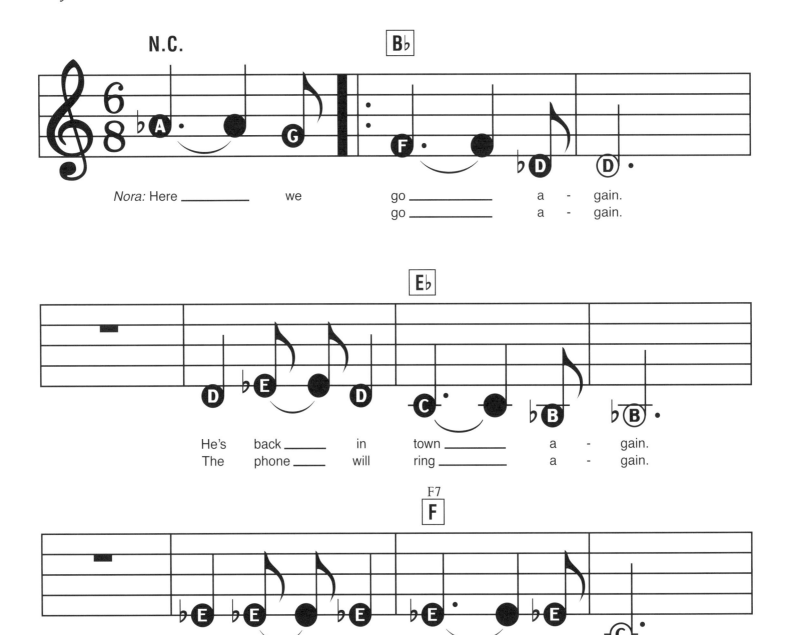

Nora: Here _____ we go _____ a - gain.
go _____ a - gain.

He's back _____ in town _____ a - gain.
The phone _____ will ring _____ a - gain.

I'll take _____ him back _____ a - gain,
I'll be _____ her fool _____ a - gain,

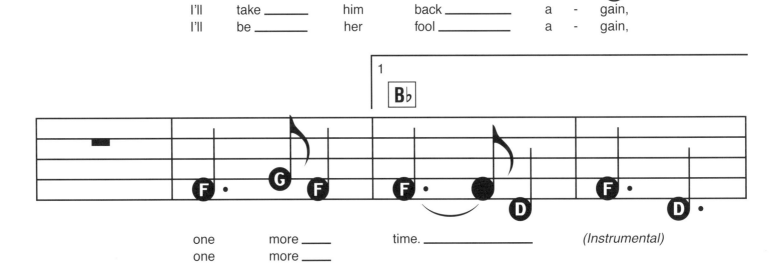

one more _____ time. _____ (Instrumental)
one more _____

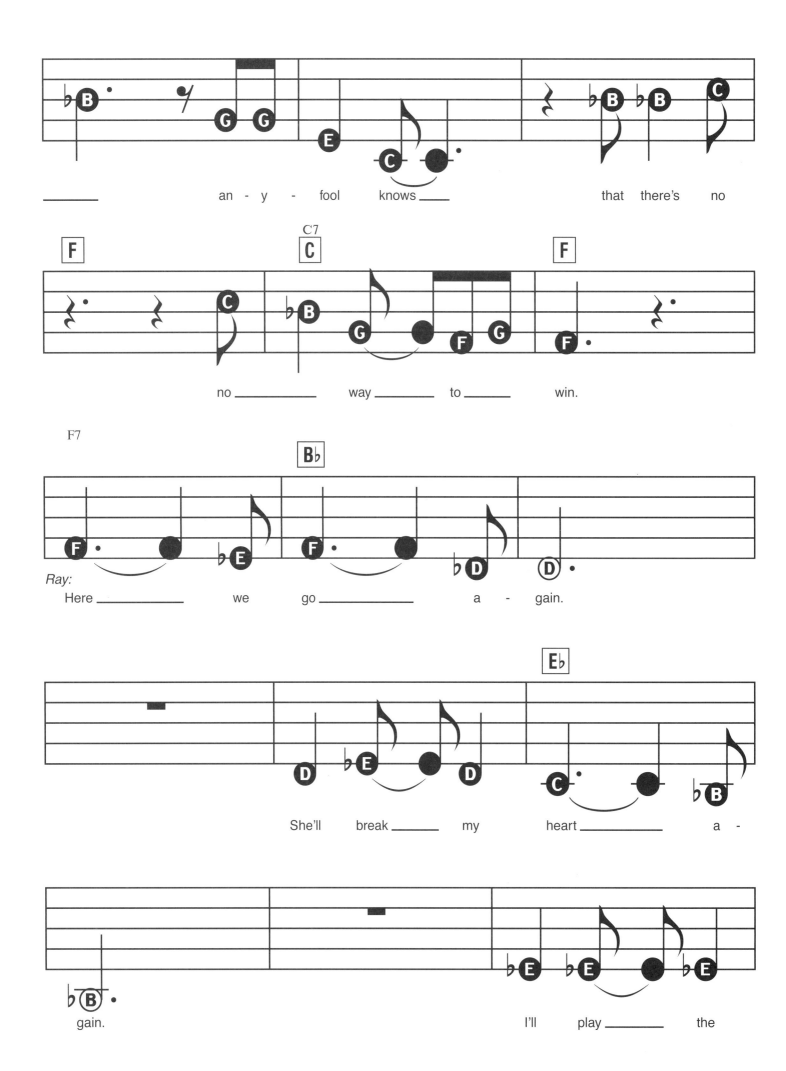

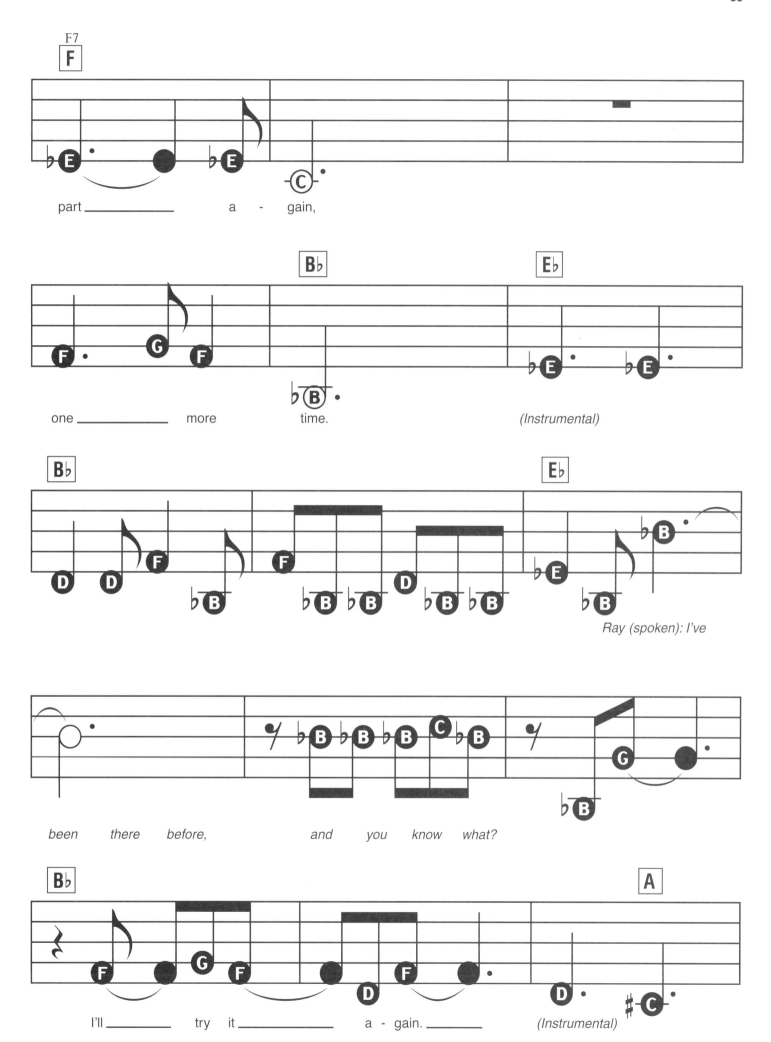

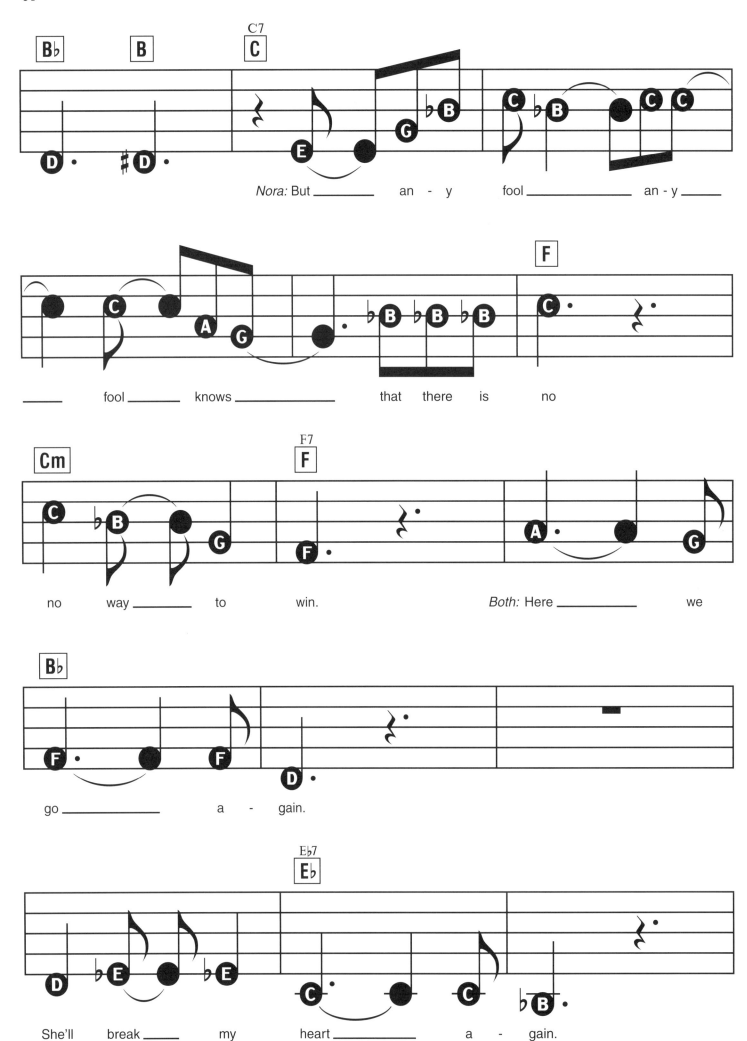

85

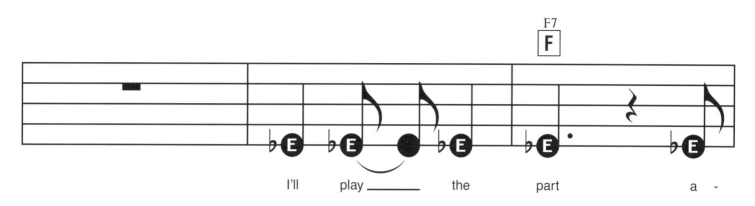

I'll play _____ the part a -

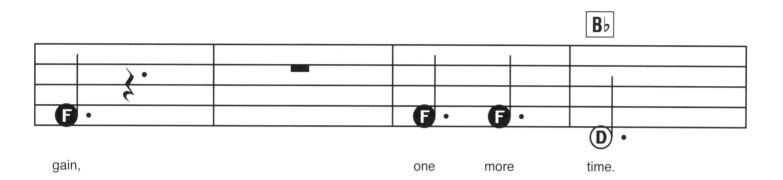

gain, one more time.

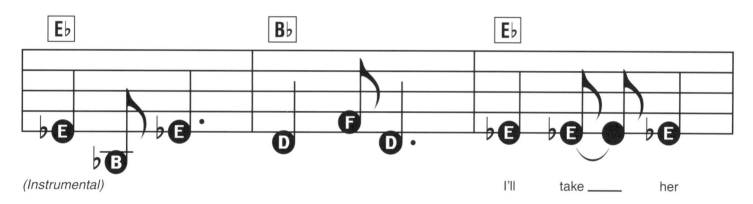

(Instrumental) I'll take _____ her

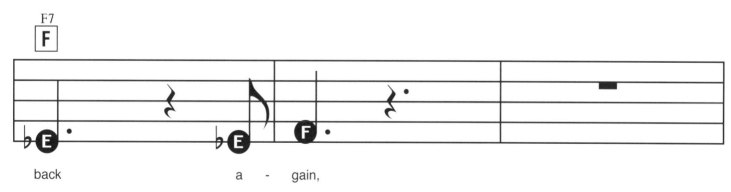

back a - gain,

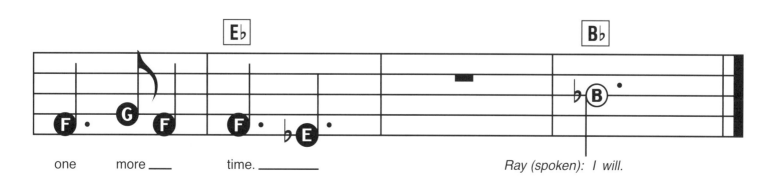

one more _____ time. _____ Ray (spoken): I will.

Higher Love

Registration 2
Rhythm: Rock or Disco

Words and Music by Will Jennings
and Steve Winwood

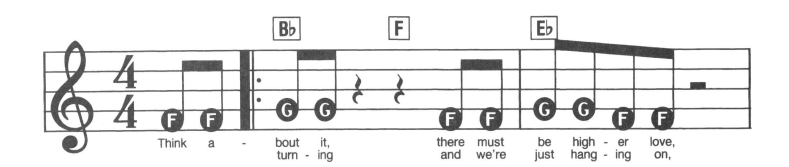

Think a - bout it, there must be high - er love,
turn - ing and we're just hang - ing on,

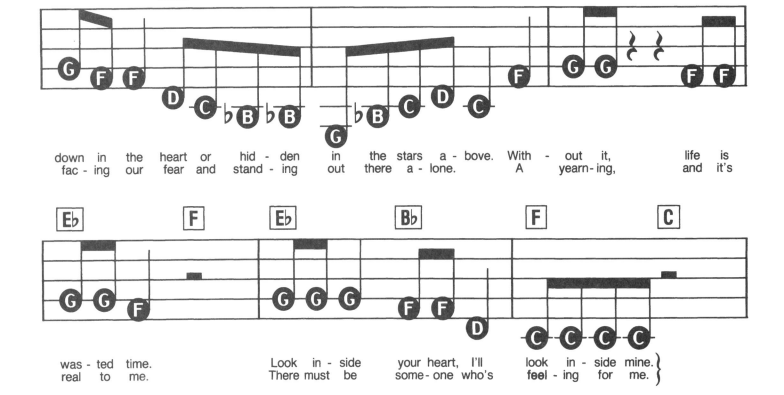

down in the heart or hid - den in the stars a - bove. With - out it, life is
fac - ing our fear and stand - ing out there a - lone. A yearn - ing, and it's

was - ted time.
real to me.

Look in - side your heart, I'll look in - side mine.
There must be some - one who's feel - ing for me.

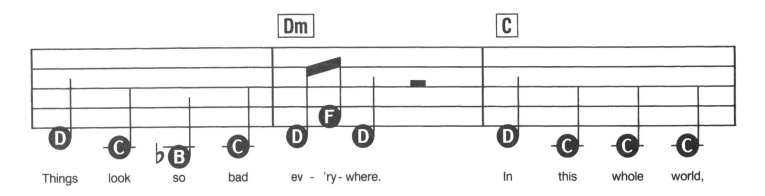

Things look so bad ev - 'ry - where. In this whole world,

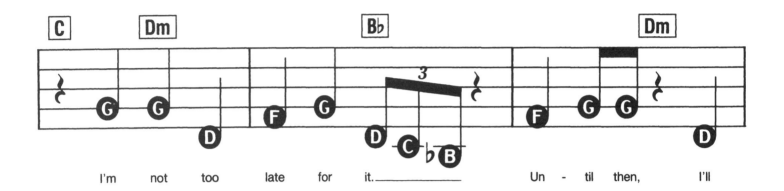

high - er love.   I will wait for it.

I'm not too late for it._____ Un - til then, I'll

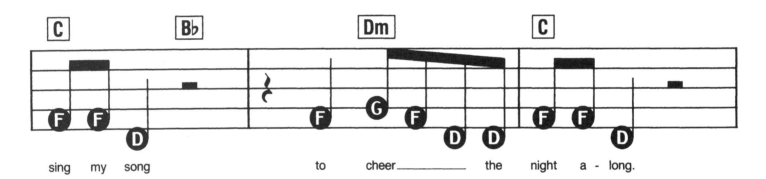

sing my song   to cheer_____ the night a - long.

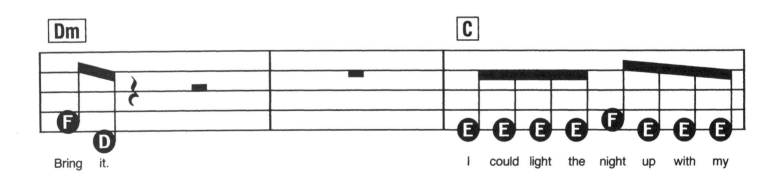

Bring it.   I could light the night up with my

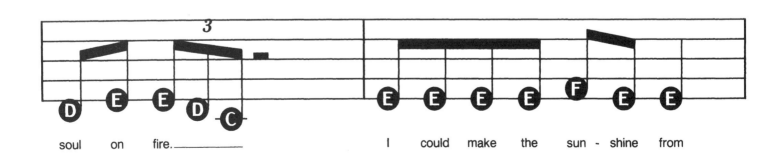

soul on fire._____   I could make the sun - shine from

Hotel California

Registration 9
Rhythm: Rock or Disco

Words and Music by Don Henley,
Glenn Frey and Don Felder

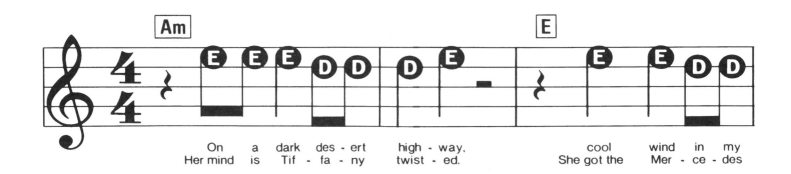

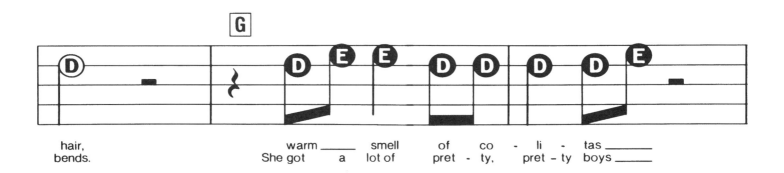

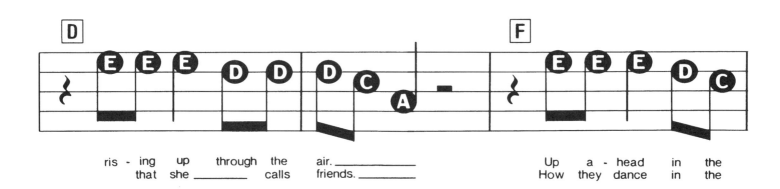

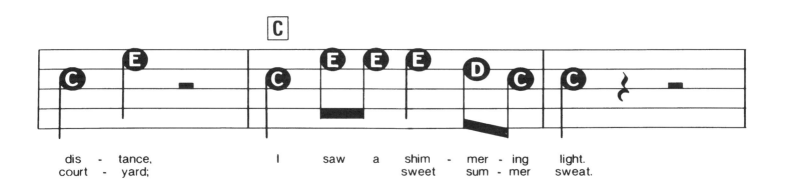

91

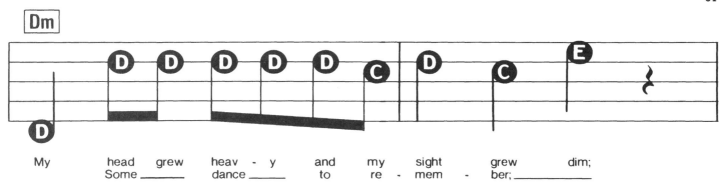

My head grew heav - y and my sight grew dim;
Some _____ dance _____ to re - mem - ber; _____

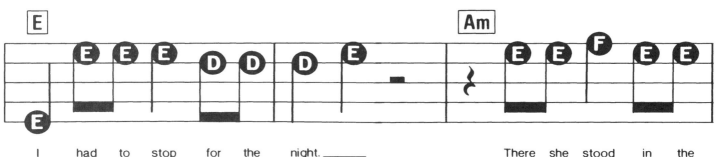

I had to stop for the night. _____ There she stood in the
some _____ dance to for - get. _____ So I called up the

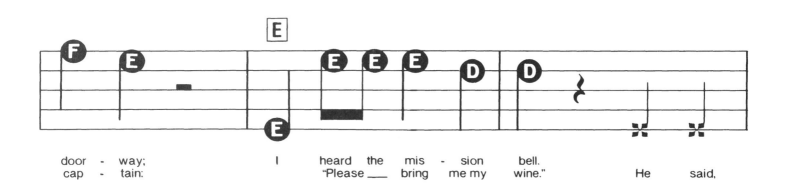

door - way; I heard the mis - sion bell.
cap - tain: "Please ___ bring me my wine." He said,

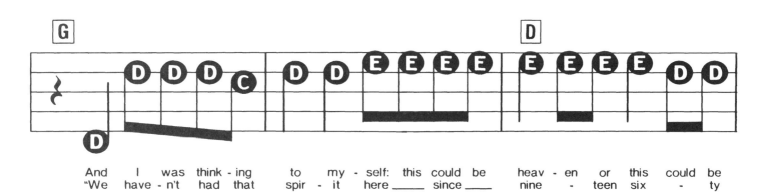

And I was think - ing to my - self: this could be heav - en or this could be
"We have - n't had that spir - it here _____ since _____ nine - teen six - ty

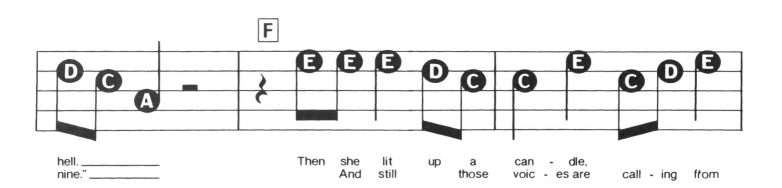

hell. _____ Then she lit up a can - dle,
nine." _____ And still those voic - es are call - ing from

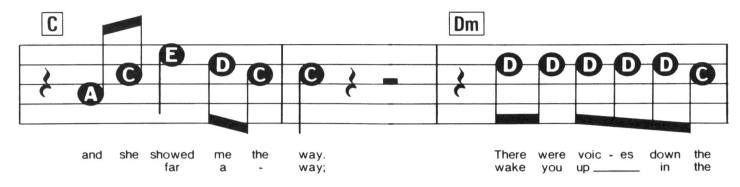

and she showed me the way.
far a - way;
There were voic - es down the
wake you up _____ in the

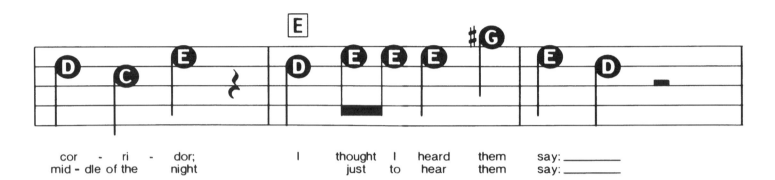

cor - ri - dor;
mid - dle of the night
I thought I heard them say: _____
just to hear them say: _____

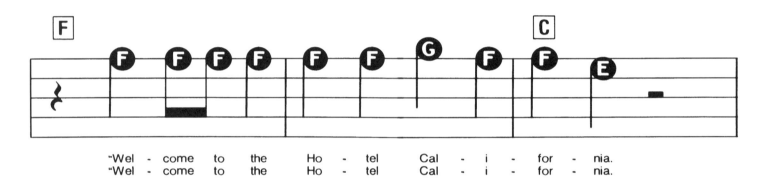

"Wel - come to the Ho - tel Cal - i - for - nia.
"Wel - come to the Ho - tel Cal - i - for - nia.

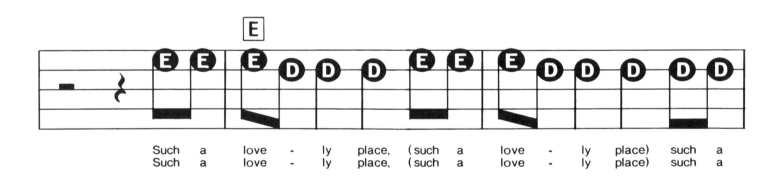

Such a love - ly place, (such a love - ly place) such a
Such a love - ly place, (such a love - ly place) such a

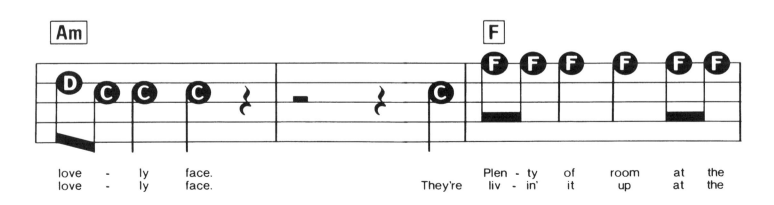

love - ly face.
love - ly face.
Plen - ty of room at the
They're liv - in' it up at the

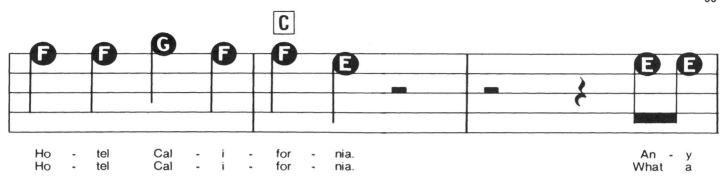

Ho - tel Cal - i - for - nia. An - y
Ho - tel Cal - i - for - nia. What a

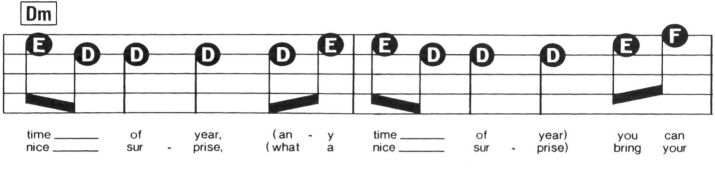

time ____ of year, (an - y time ____ of year) you can
nice ____ sur - prise, (what a nice ____ sur - prise) bring your

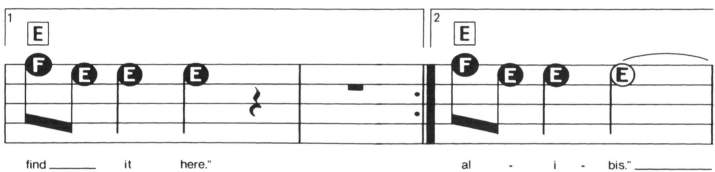

find ____ it here." al - i - bis." ____

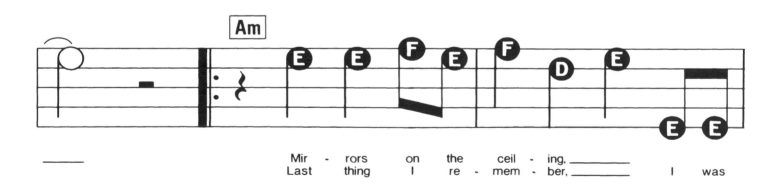

____ Mir - rors on the ceil - ing, ____ I was
Last thing I re - mem - ber, ____ I was

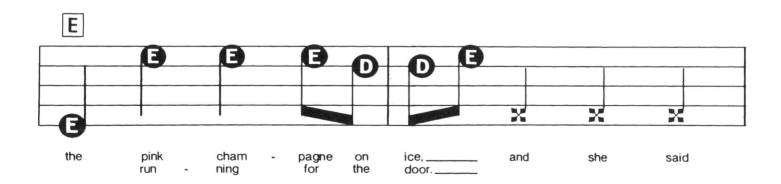

the pink cham - pagne on ice, ____ and she said
run - ning for the door. ____

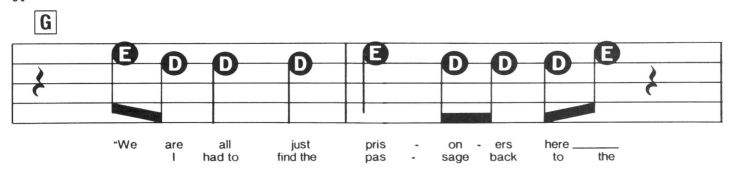

"We   are   all   just   pris - on - ers   here _____
I   had to   just   find the   pas - sage   back   to   the

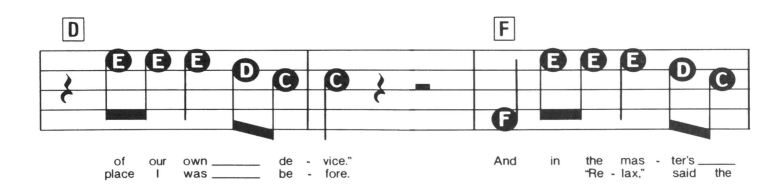

of   our   own _____ de - vice."   And   in   the   mas - ter's _____
place   I   was _____ be - fore.   "Re - lax,"   said   the

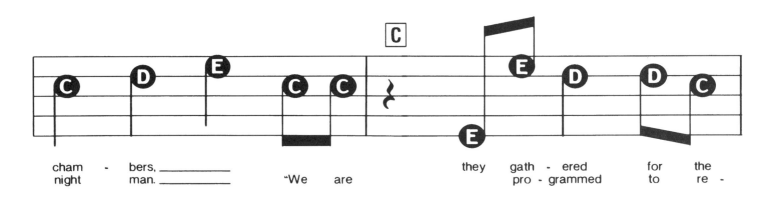

cham - bers, _____   "We   are   they   gath - ered   for   the
night   man. _____   pro - grammed   to   re -

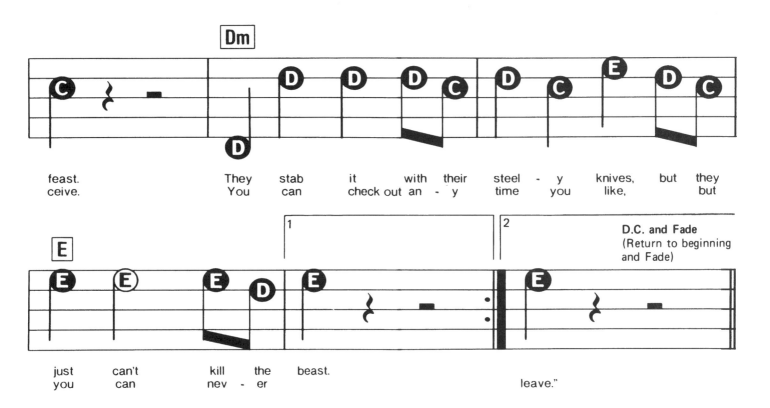

feast.   They   stab   it   with their   steel - y   knives, but   they
ceive.   You   can   check out an - y   time   you   like,   but

just   can't   kill   the   beast.
you   can   nev - er   leave."

I Honestly Love You

Registration 1
Rhythm: 8-Beat or Pops

Words and Music by Jeff Barry
and Peter Allen

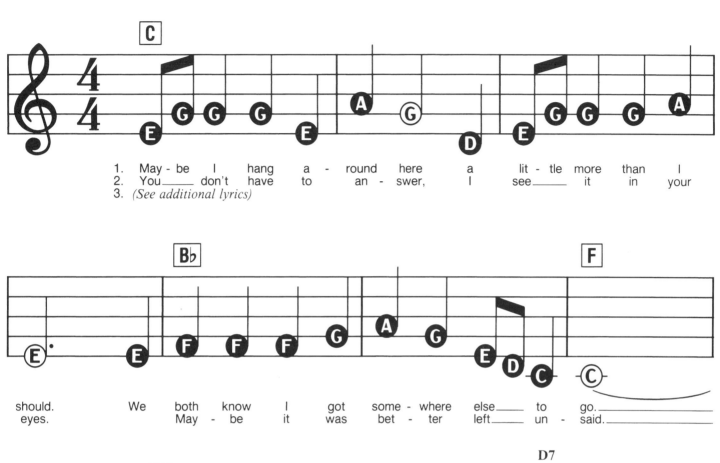

1. May-be I hang a - round here a lit-tle more than I
2. You___ don't have to an - swer, I see___ it in your
3. *(See additional lyrics)*

should. We both know I got some - where else___ to go.
eyes. May - be it was bet - ter left___ un - said.

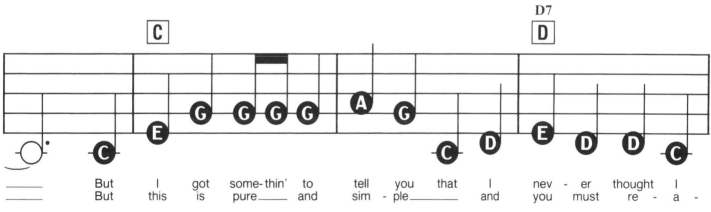

But I got some-thin' to tell you that I nev - er thought I
But this is pure___ and sim - ple___ and you must re - a -

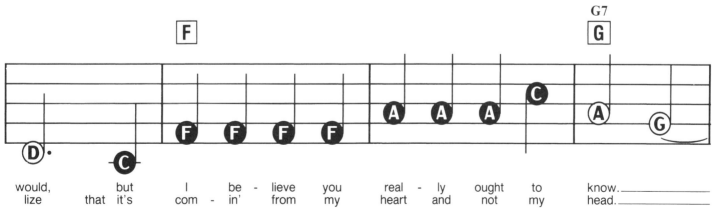

would, but I be - lieve you real - ly ought to know.___
lize that it's com - in' from my heart and not my head.___

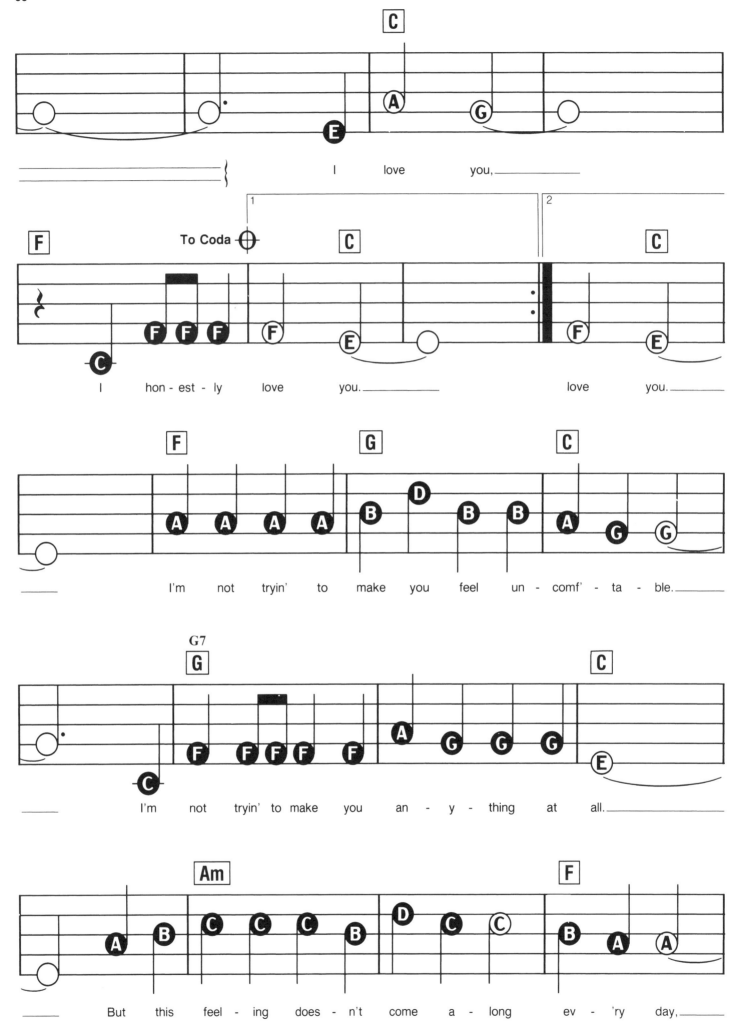

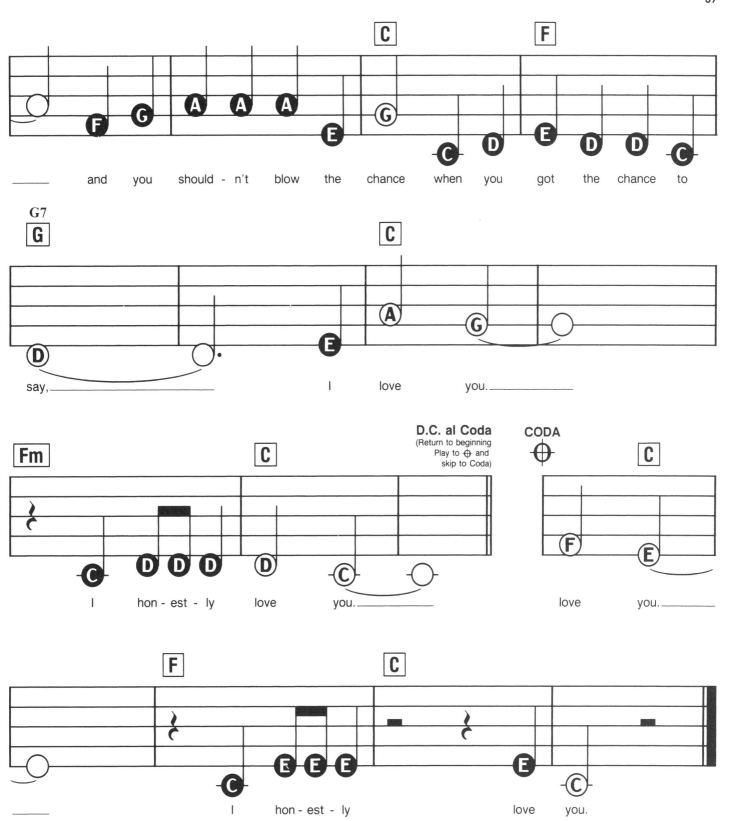

Additional Lyrics

3. If we were both born
   In another place and time,
   This moment might be ending with a kiss,
   But there you are with yours
   And here am I with mine.
   So I guess we'll just be leaving it at this,
   I love you.
   I honestly love you.
   I honestly love you.

I Left My Heart in San Francisco

Registration 9
Rhythm: Fox Trot

Words by Douglass Cross
Music by George Cory

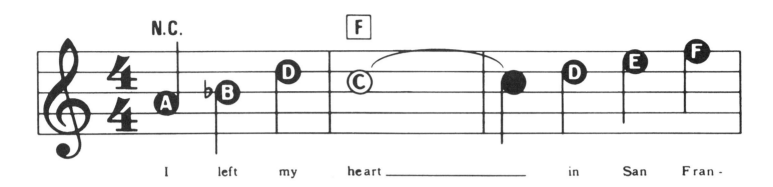

I left my heart _____ in San Fran -

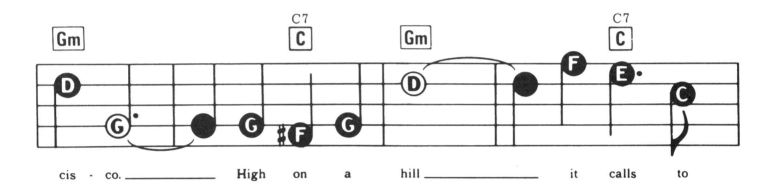

cis - co. _____ High on a hill _____ it calls to

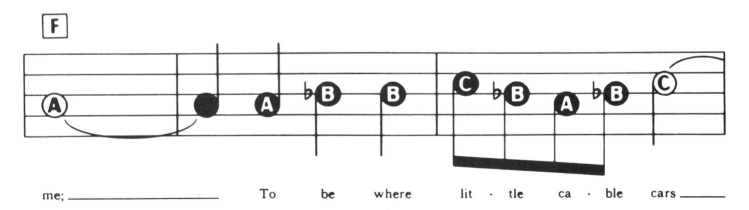

me; _____ To be where lit - tle ca - ble cars _____

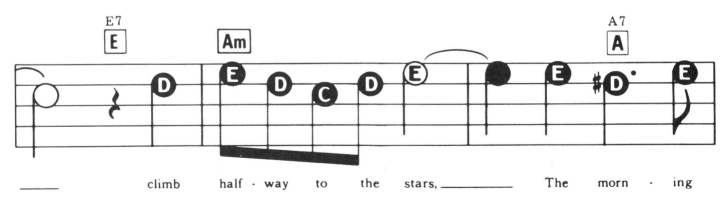

_____ climb half - way to the stars, _____ The morn - ing

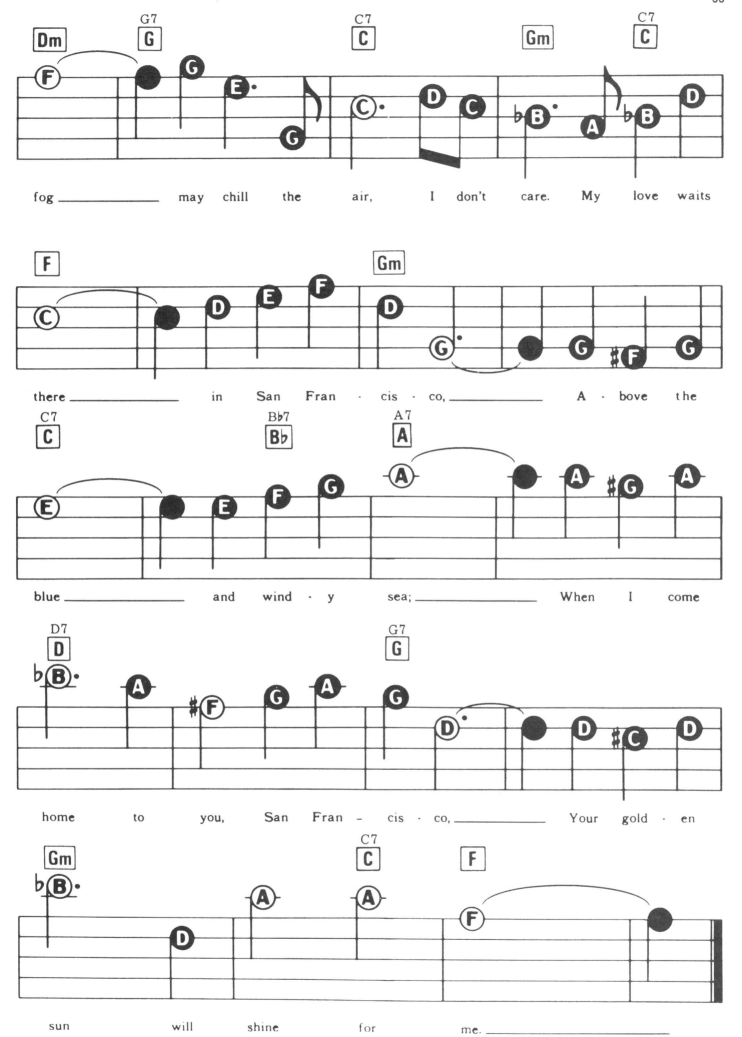

I Will Always Love You

Registration 3
Rhythm: Pops or 8-Beat

Words and Music by
Dolly Parton

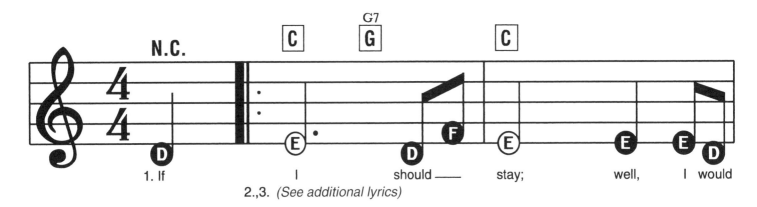

1. If I should ___ stay; well, I would

2.,3. *(See additional lyrics)*

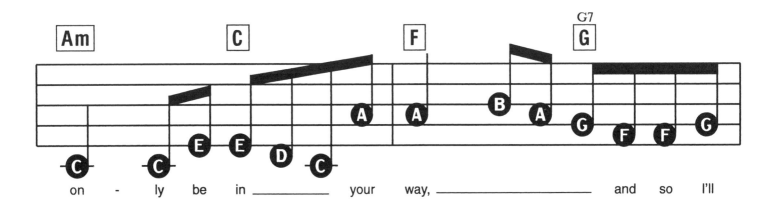

on - ly be in _____ your way, _____ and so I'll

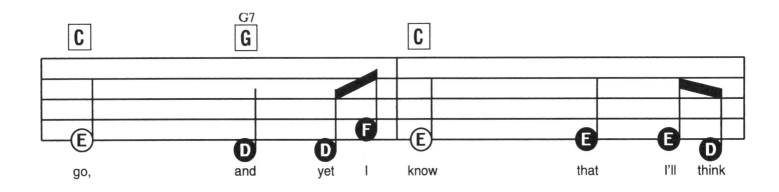

go, and yet I know that I'll think

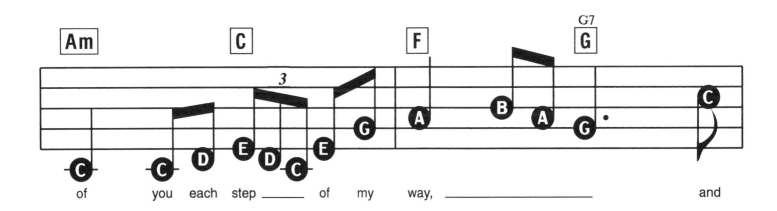

of you each step ___ of my way, _____ and

Chorus

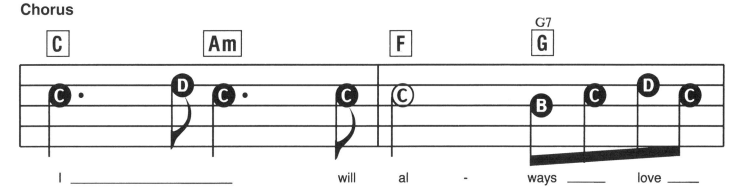

I _____ will al - ways _____ love _____

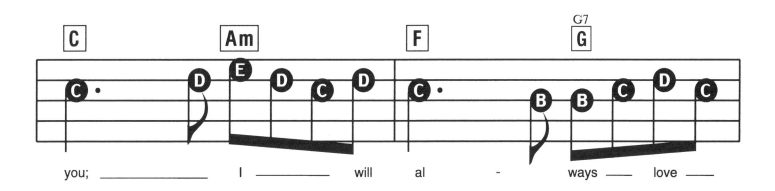

you; _____ I _____ will al - ways ____ love ____

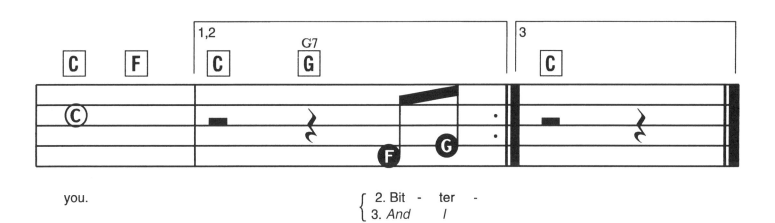

you.

2. Bit - ter -
3. *And I*

Additional Lyrics

2. Bittersweet memories, that's all I have and all I'm taking with me.
   Good-bye, oh please don't cry, 'cause we both know that I'm not what you need. But…
   Chorus

   (Spoken:)
3. *And I hope life will treat you kind, and I hope that you have all that you ever dreamed of.*
   Oh, I do wish you joy, and I wish you happiness, but above all this, I wish you love. And…
   Chorus

It's Too Late

Registration 8
Rhythm: 8-Beat or Rock

Words and Music by Carole King
and Toni Stern

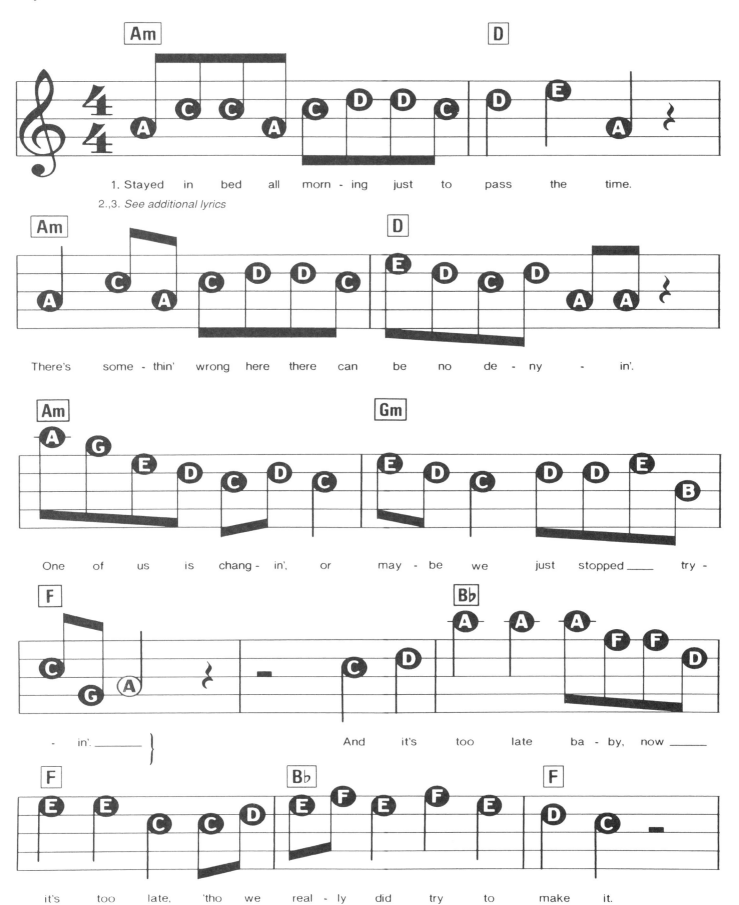

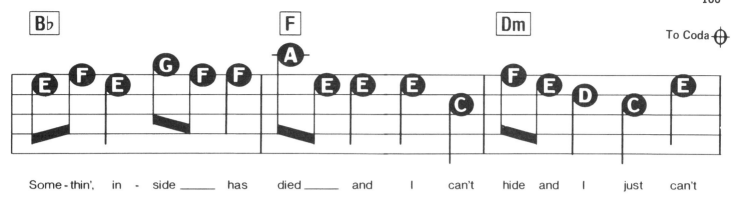

Some-thin', in - side _____ has died _____ and I can't hide and I just can't

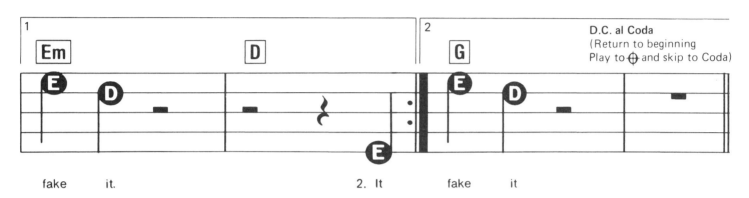

fake it.   2. It fake it

fake it It's too late   ba - by, it's too _____

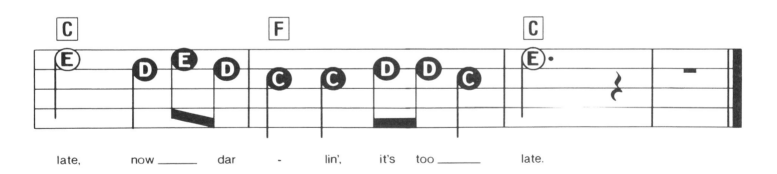

late, now _____ dar - lin', it's too _____ late.

Additional Lyrics

2. It used to be so easy living here with you;
   You were light and breezy and
   I knew just what to do.
   Now you look so unhappy and I feel like a fool.

3. There'll be good times again for me and you;
   But we just can't stay together,
   Don't you feel it too?
   Still I'm glad for what we had and how I once loved you.

Just the Way You Are

Registration 4
Rhythm: Rock or Jazz Rock

Words and Music by
Billy Joel

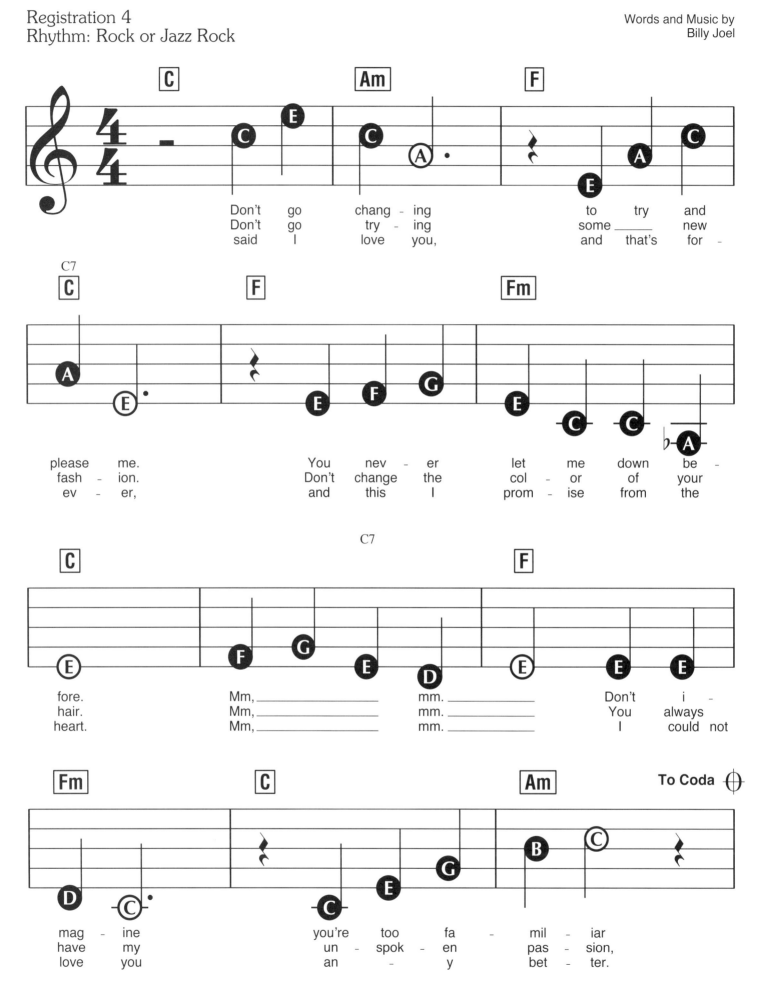

105

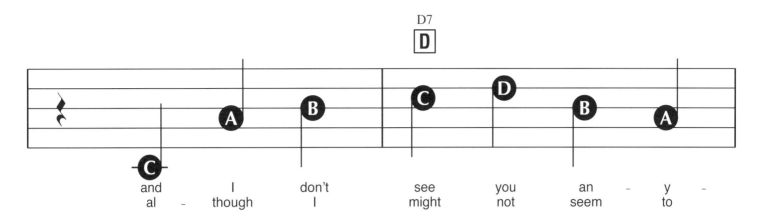

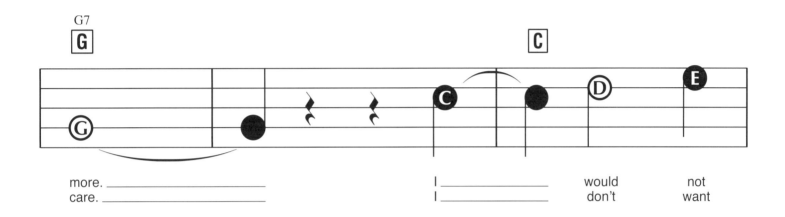

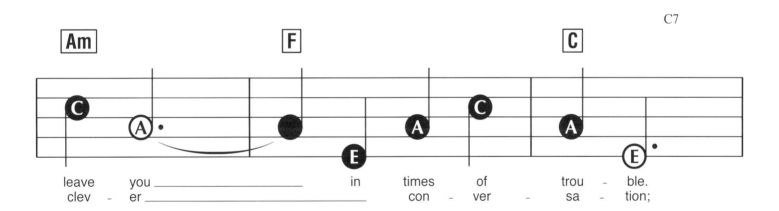

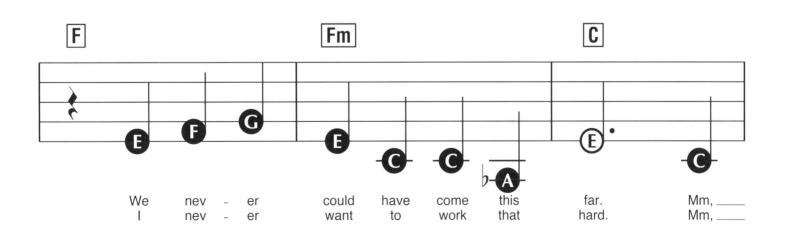

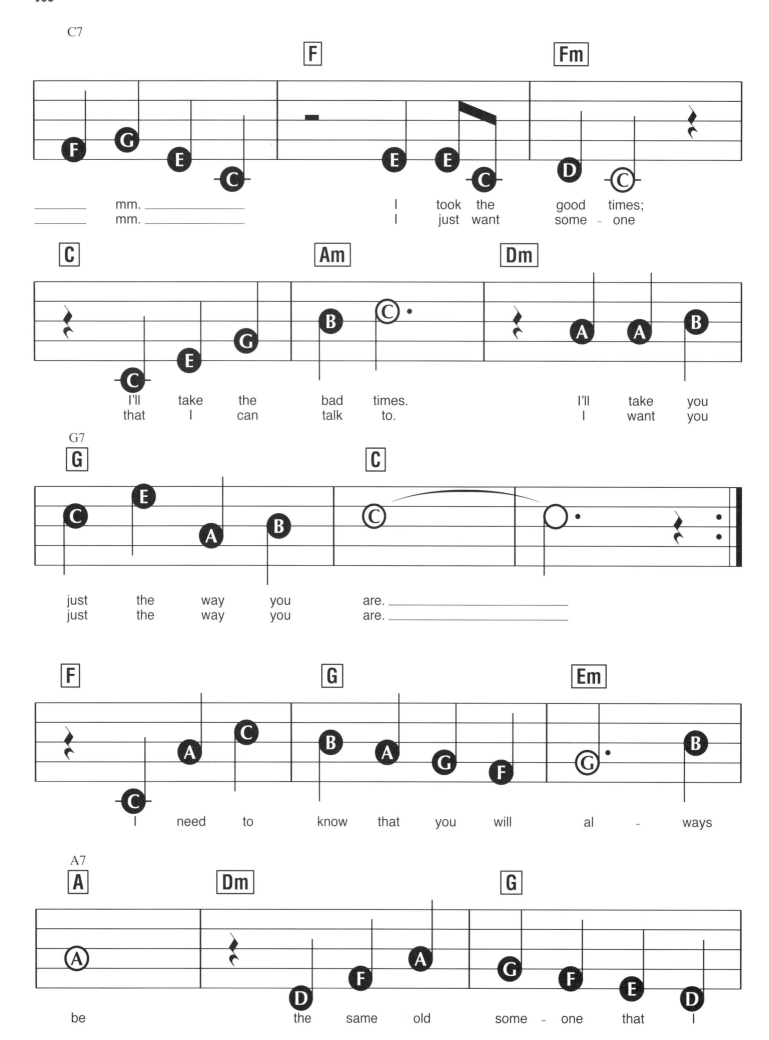

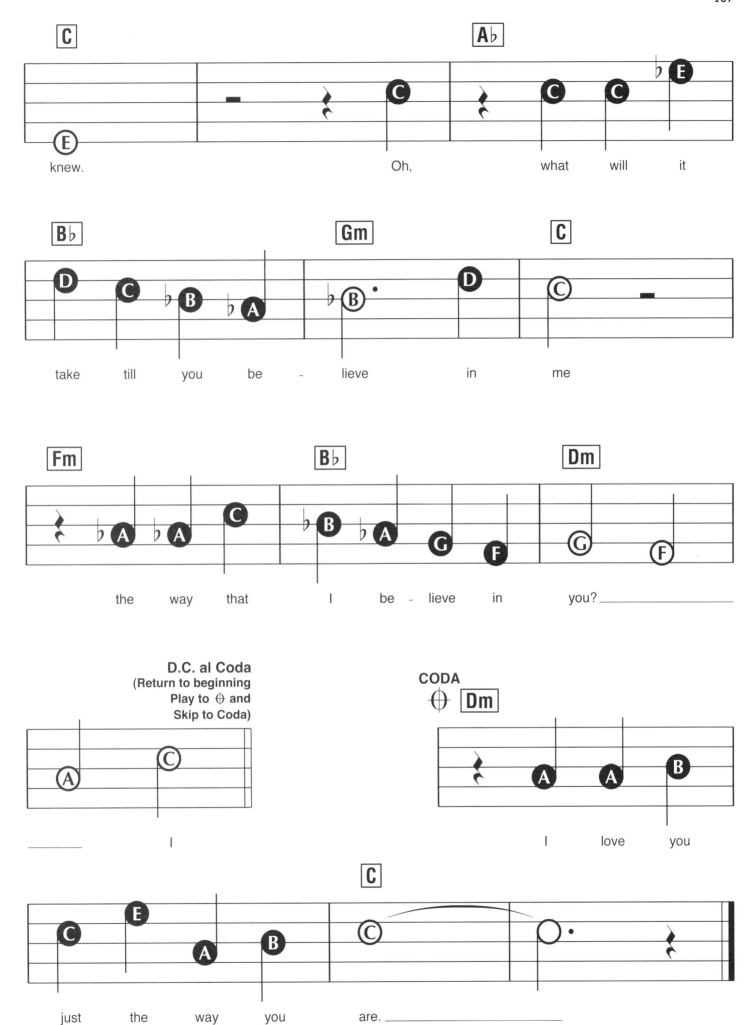

Killing Me Softly With His Song

Registration 2
Rhythm: Rock

Words by Norman Gimbel
Music by Charles Fox

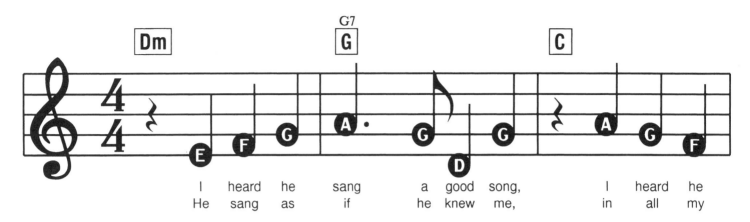

I heard he sang a good song, I heard he
He sang as if he knew me, in all my

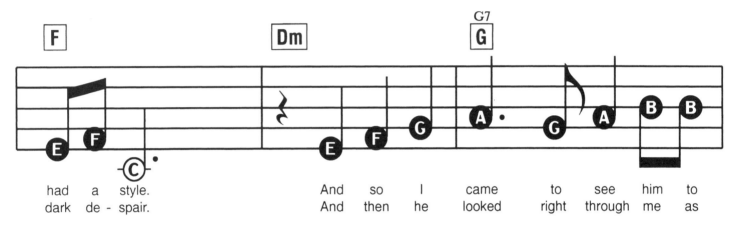

had a style.
dark de - spair.
And so I came to see him to
And then he looked right through me as

lis - ten for a while. _____
if I was - n't there. _____
And there he
But he was

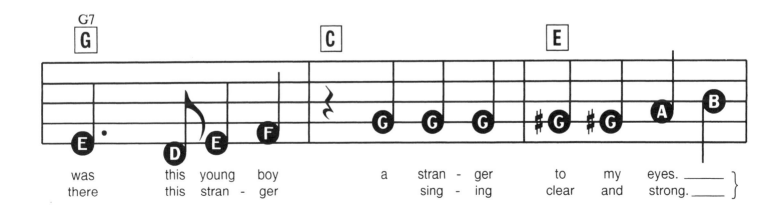

was this young boy a stran - ger to my eyes. _____
there this stran - ger sing - ing clear and strong. _____

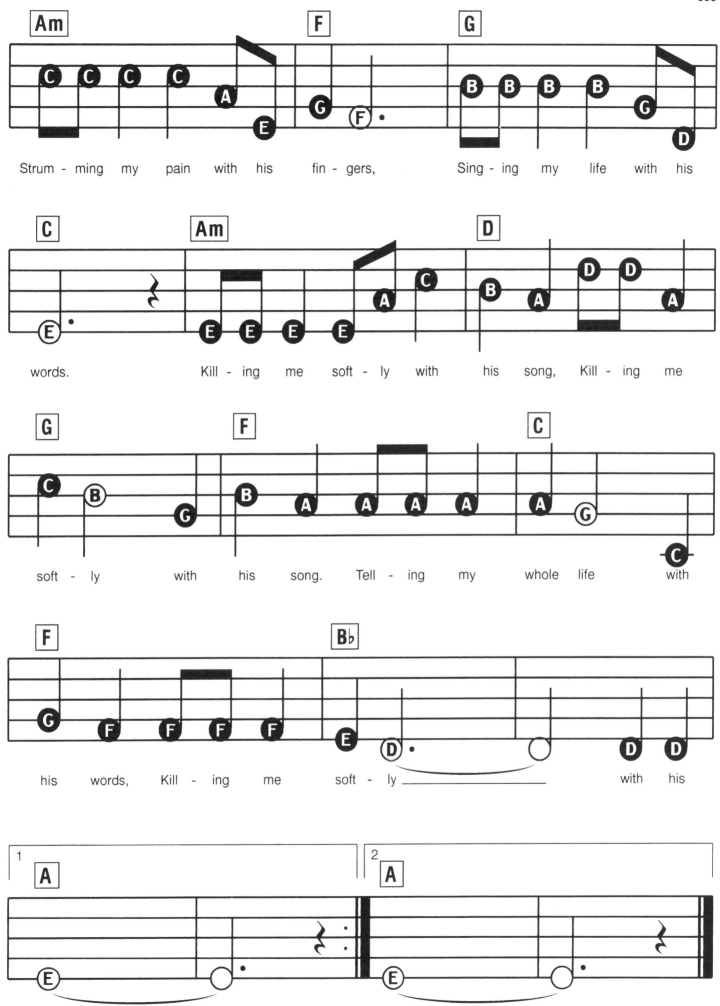

Kiss from a Rose

Registration 4
Rhythm: Slow Rock

Words and Music by
Seal

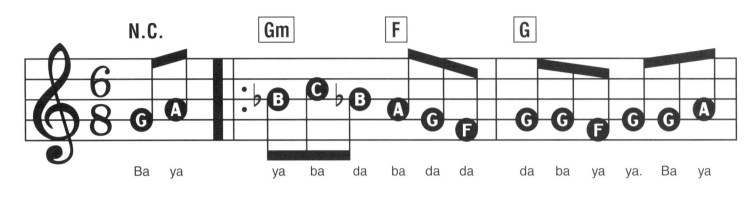

Ba ya ya ba da ba da da da ba ya ya. Ba ya

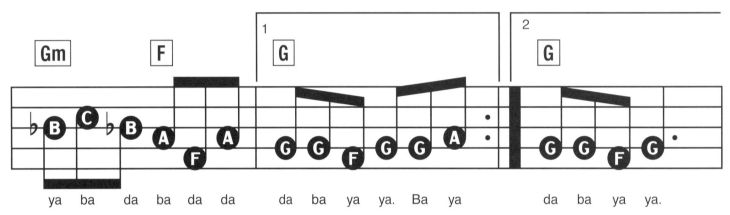

ya ba da ba da da da ba ya ya. Ba ya da ba ya ya.

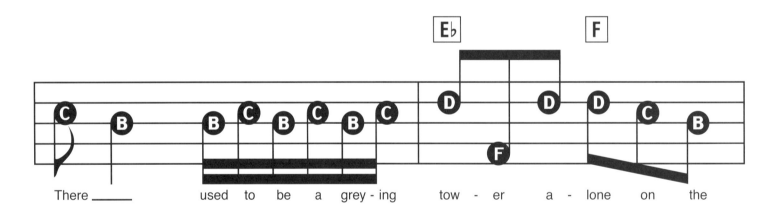

There ____ used to be a grey-ing tow-er a-lone on the

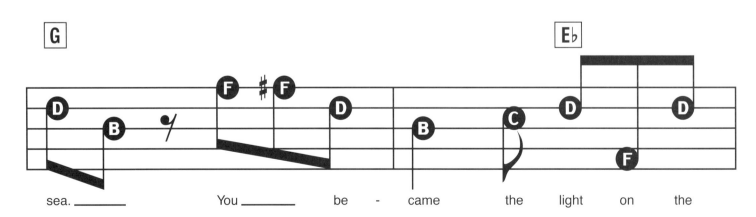

sea. ____ You ____ be - came the light on the

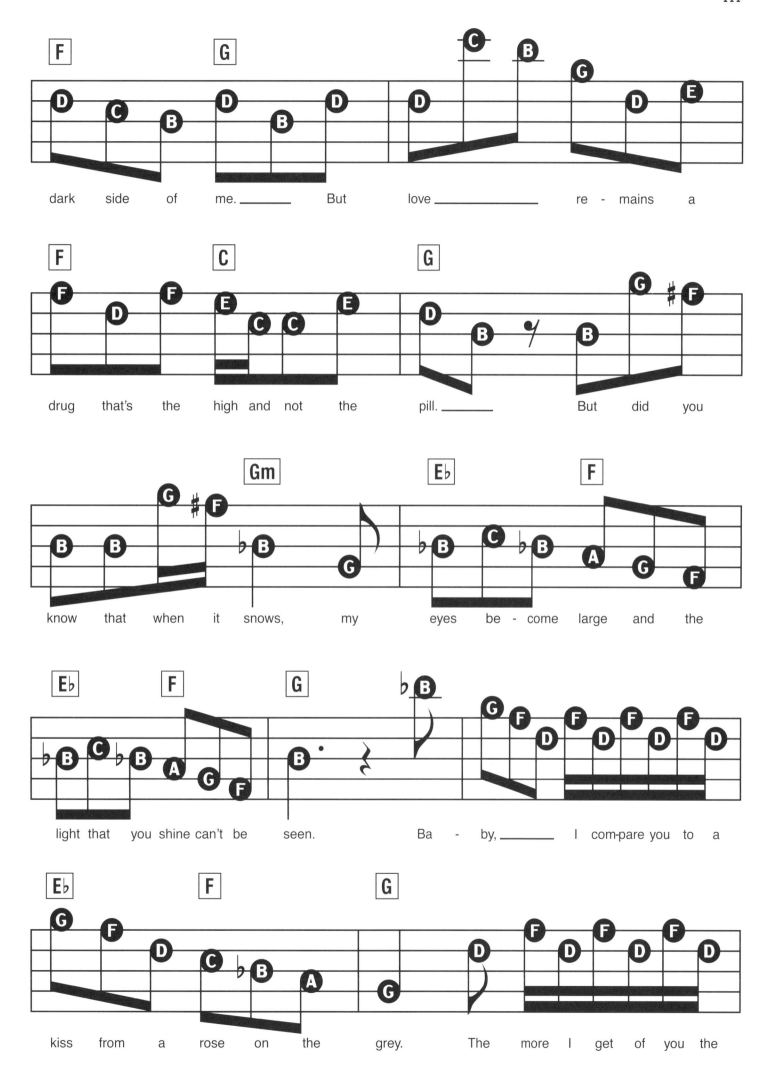

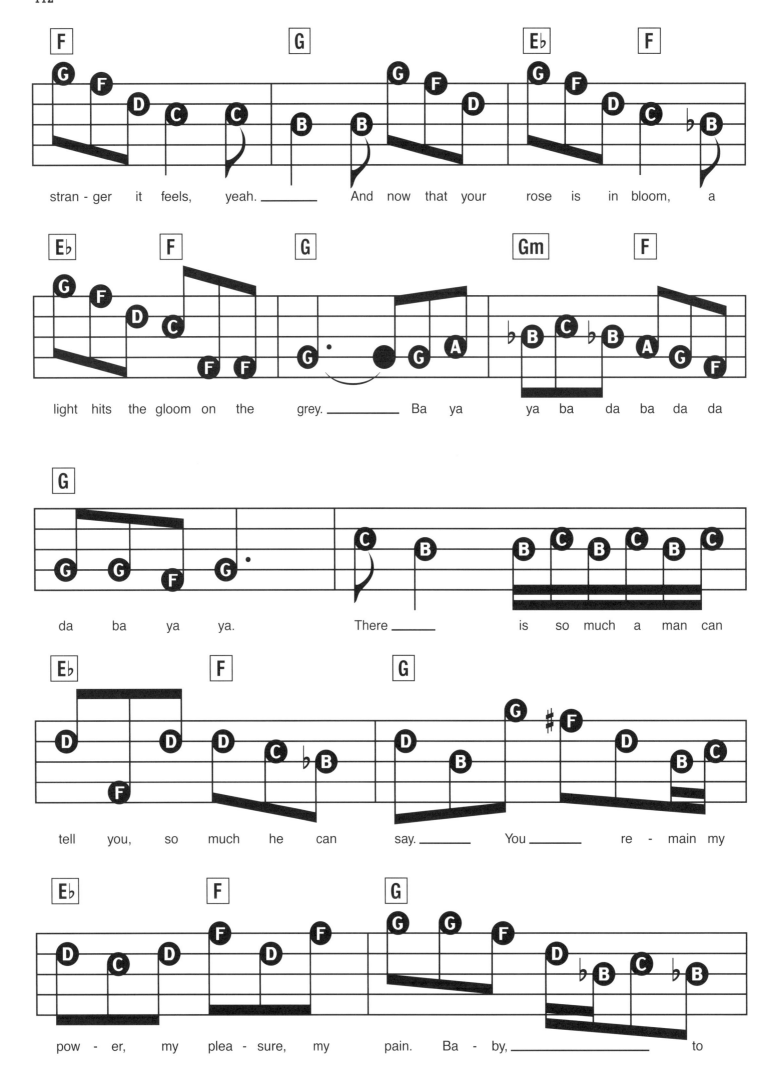

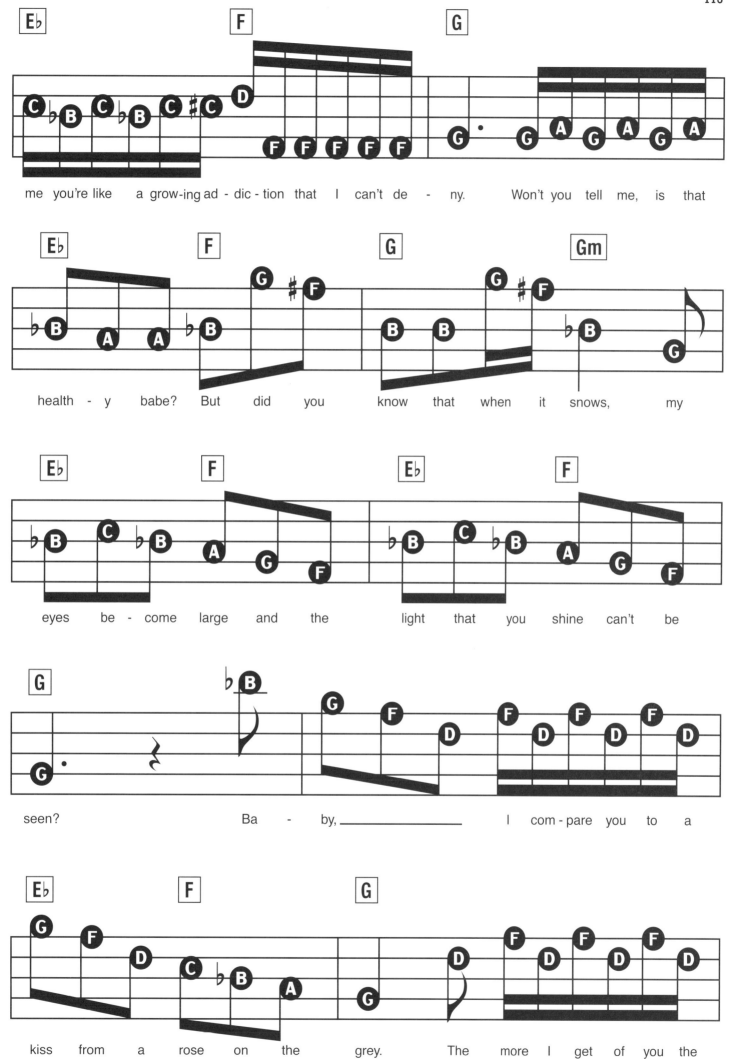

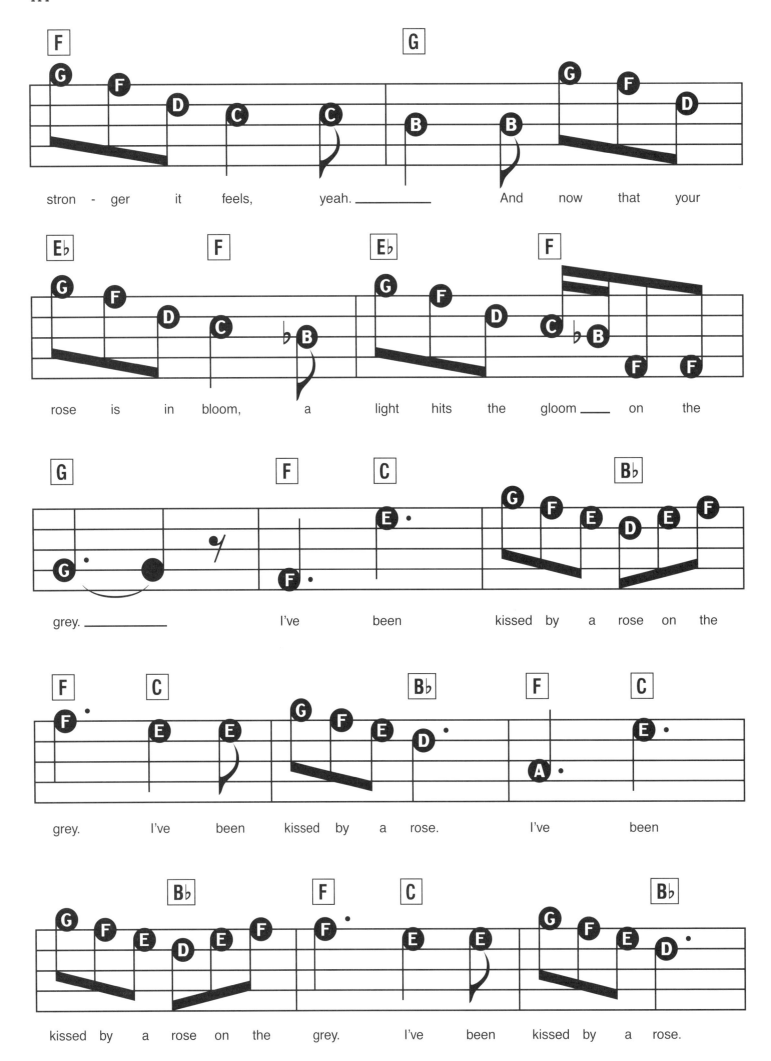

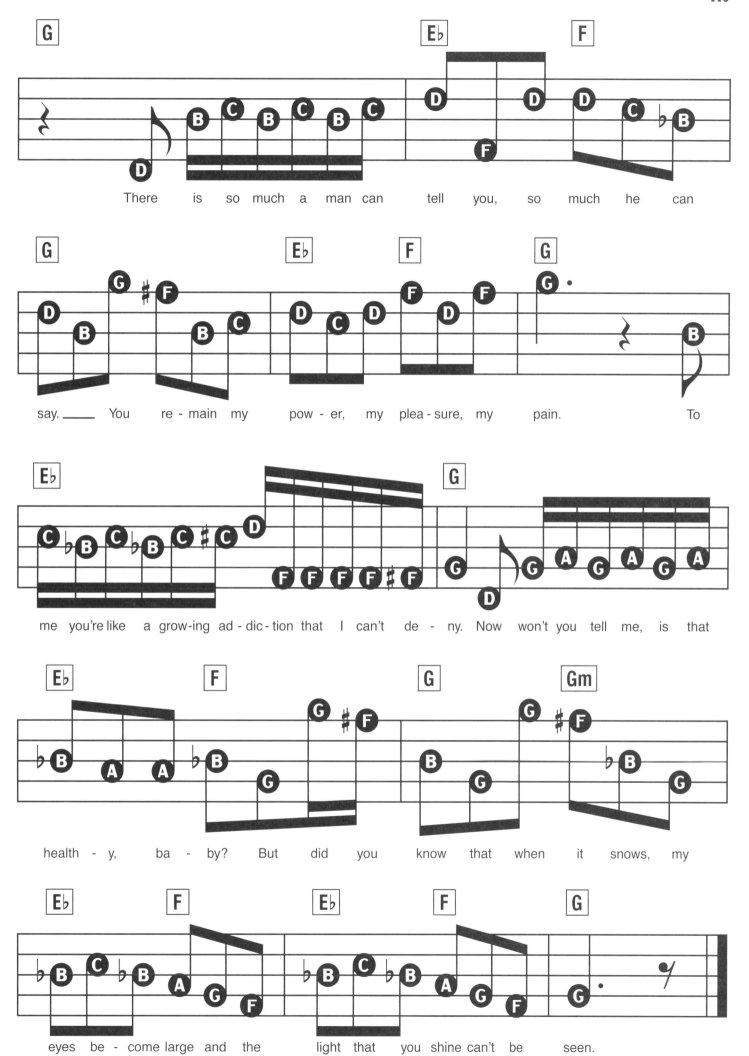

Love Will Keep Us Together

Registration 8
Rhythm: Rock

Words and Music by Neil Sedaka
and Howard Greenfield

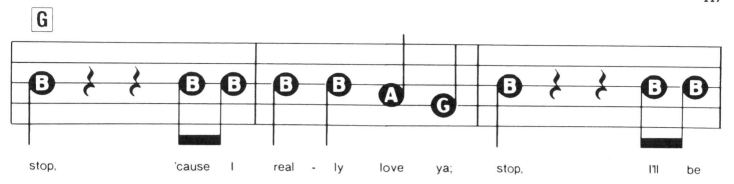

stop,   'cause I real - ly love ya; stop,   I'll be

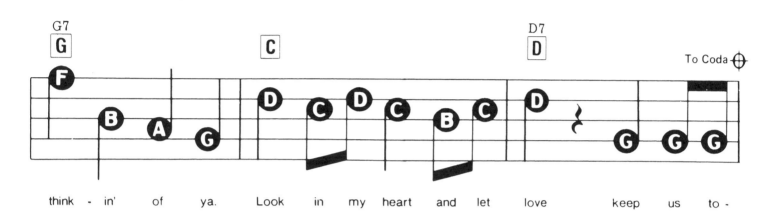

think - in' of ya. Look in my heart and let love keep us to -

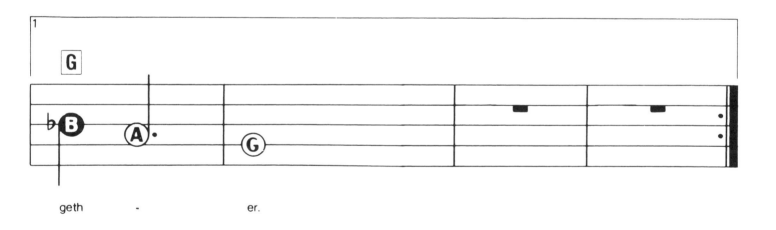

geth - er.

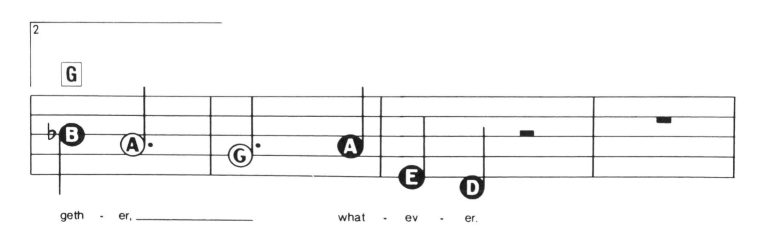

geth - er, _____ what - ev - er.

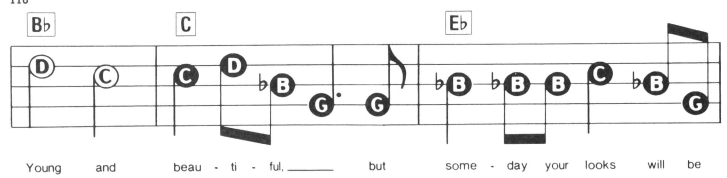

Young and beau - ti - ful, _____ but some - day your looks will be

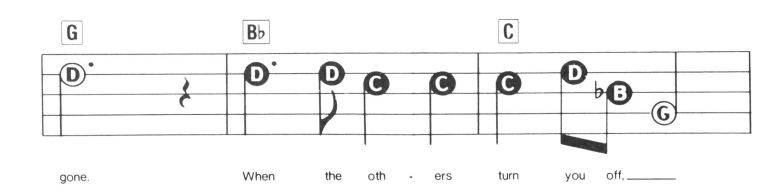

gone. When the oth - ers turn you off, _____

D.C. al Coda
(Return to beginning
Play to ⊕ and skip to Coda)

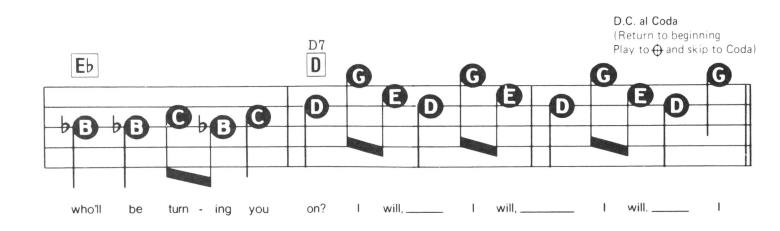

who'll be turn - ing you on? I will, _____ I will, _____ I will. _____ I

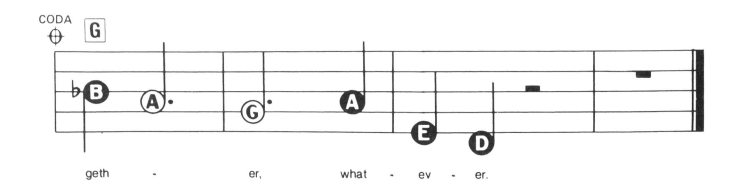

geth - er, what - ev - er.

Mrs. Robinson
from THE GRADUATE

Registration 5
Rhythm: Swing

Words and Music by
Paul Simon

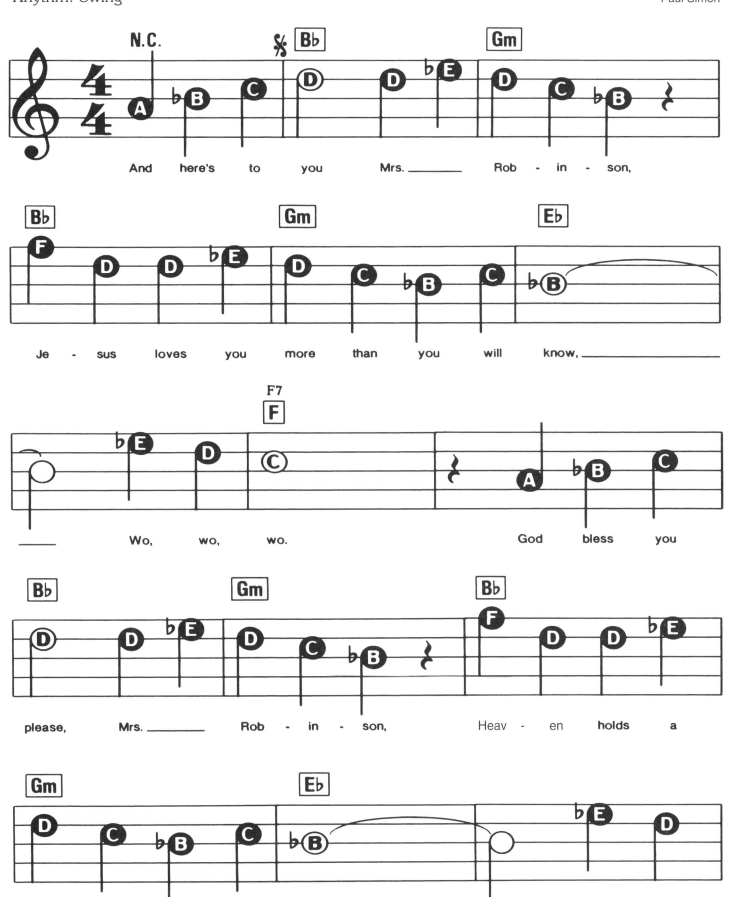

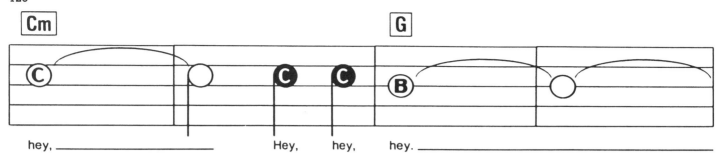

hey, _____ Hey, hey, hey. _____

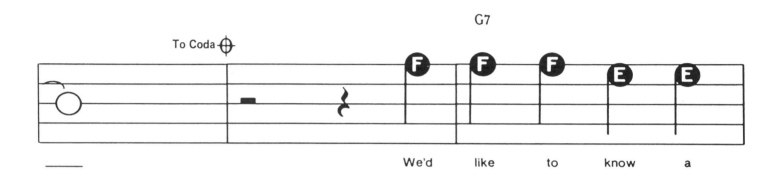

_____ We'd like to know a

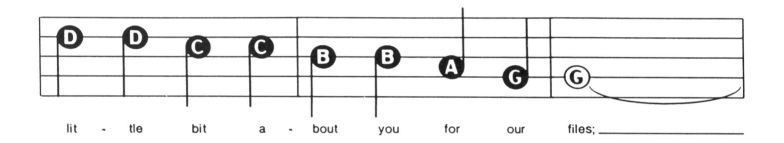

lit - tle bit a - bout you for our files; _____

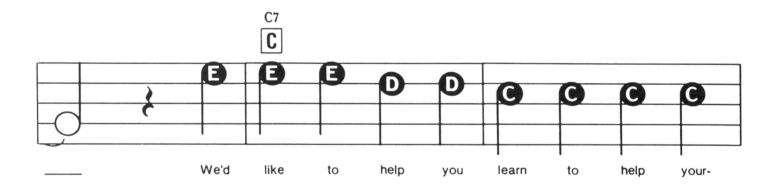

_____ We'd like to help you learn to help your-

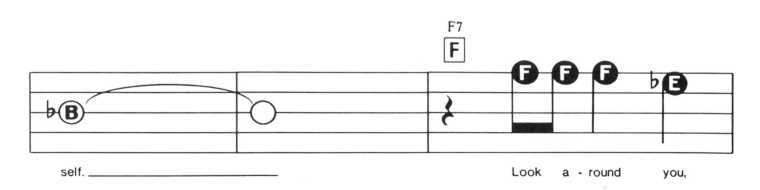

self. _____ Look a - round you,

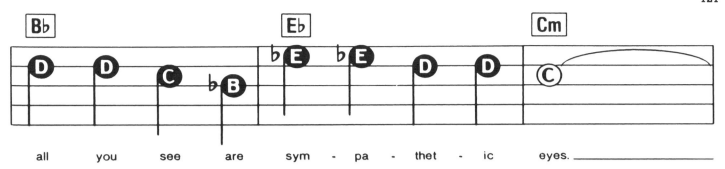

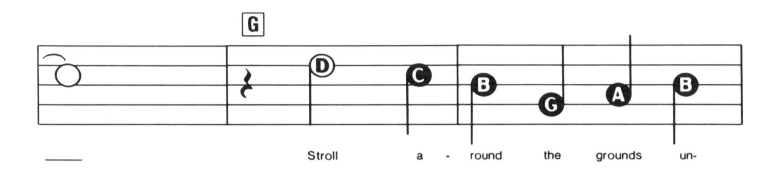

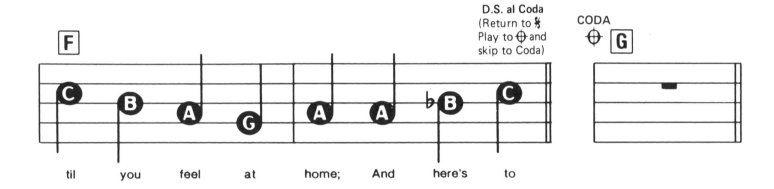

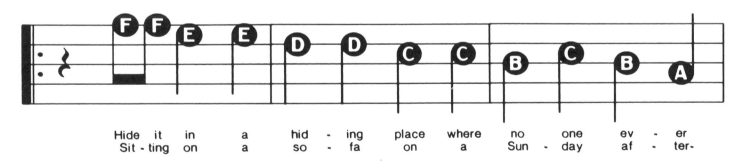

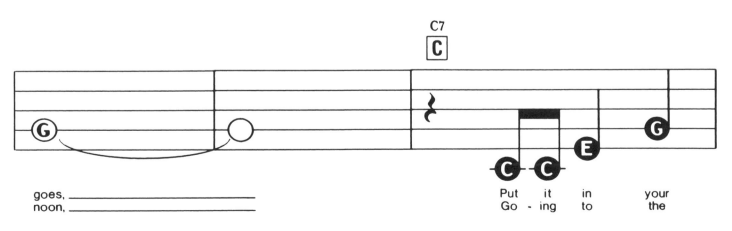

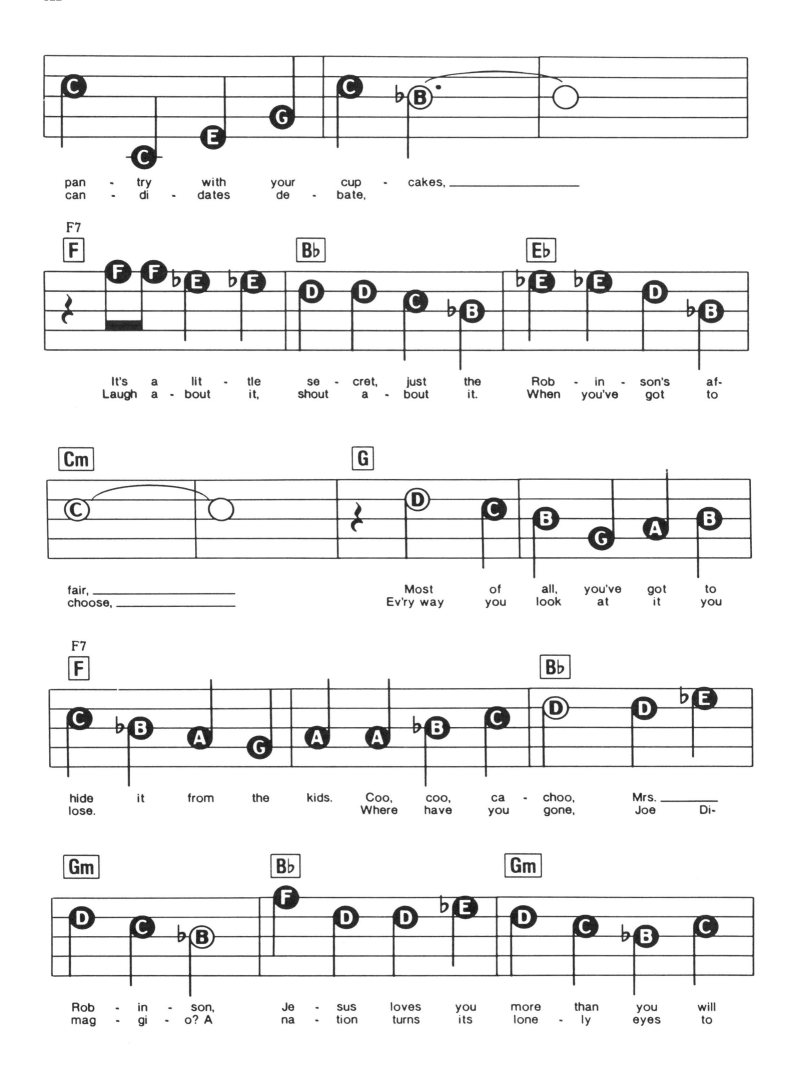

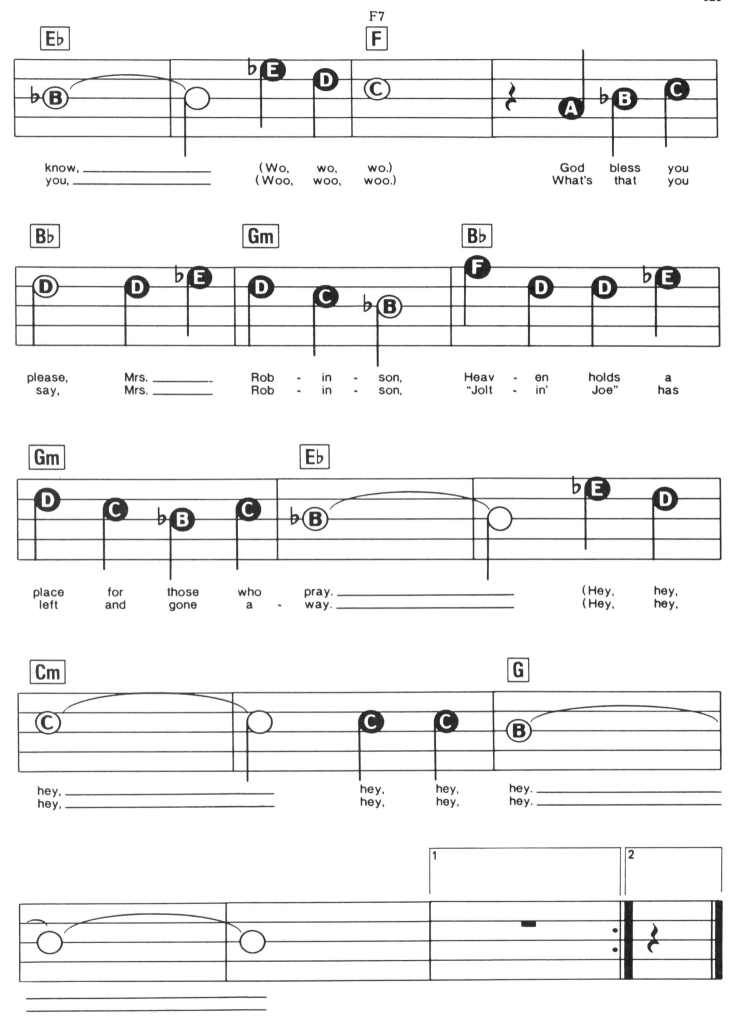

Mack the Knife
from THE THREEPENNY OPERA

English Words by Marc Blitzstein
Original German Words by Bert Brecht
Music by Kurt Weill

Registration 8
Rhythm: Swing

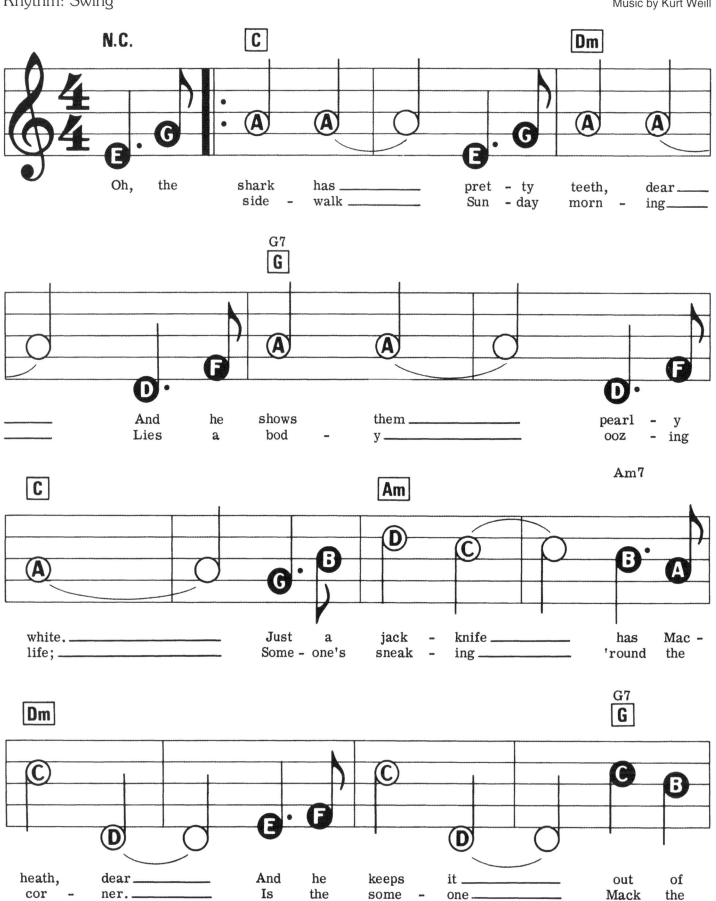

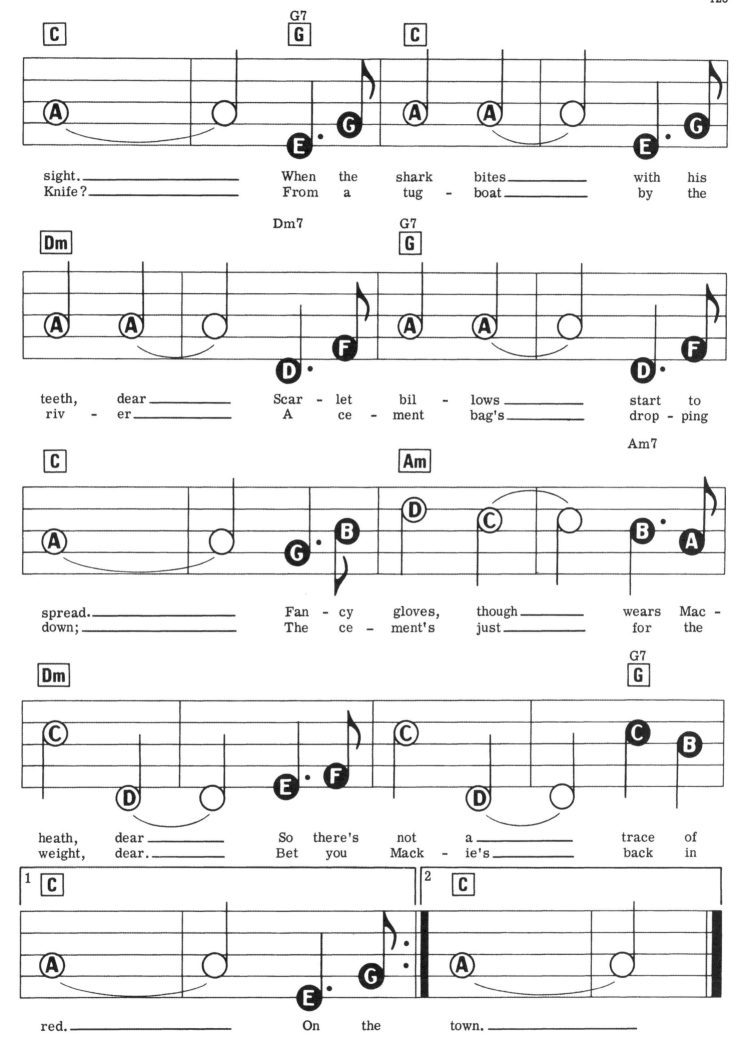

Moon River
from the Paramount Picture BREAKFAST AT TIFFANY'S

Registration 7
Rhythm: Waltz

Words by Johnny Mercer
Music by Henry Mancini

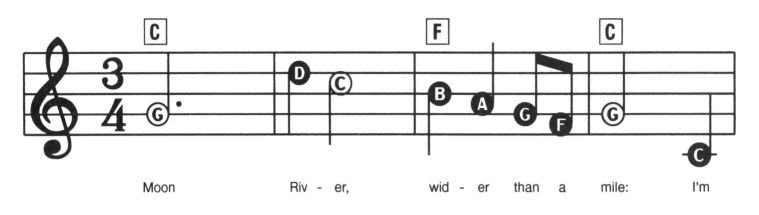

Moon River, wid-er than a mile: I'm

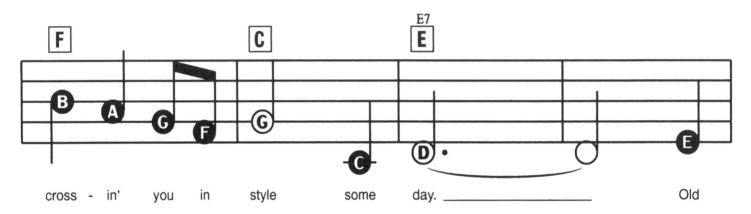

cross-in' you in style some day. _____ Old

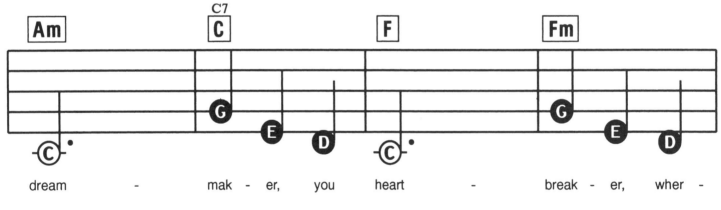

dream - mak-er, you heart - break-er, wher-

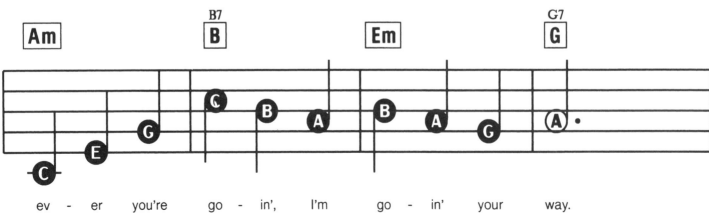

ev-er you're go-in', I'm go-in' your way.

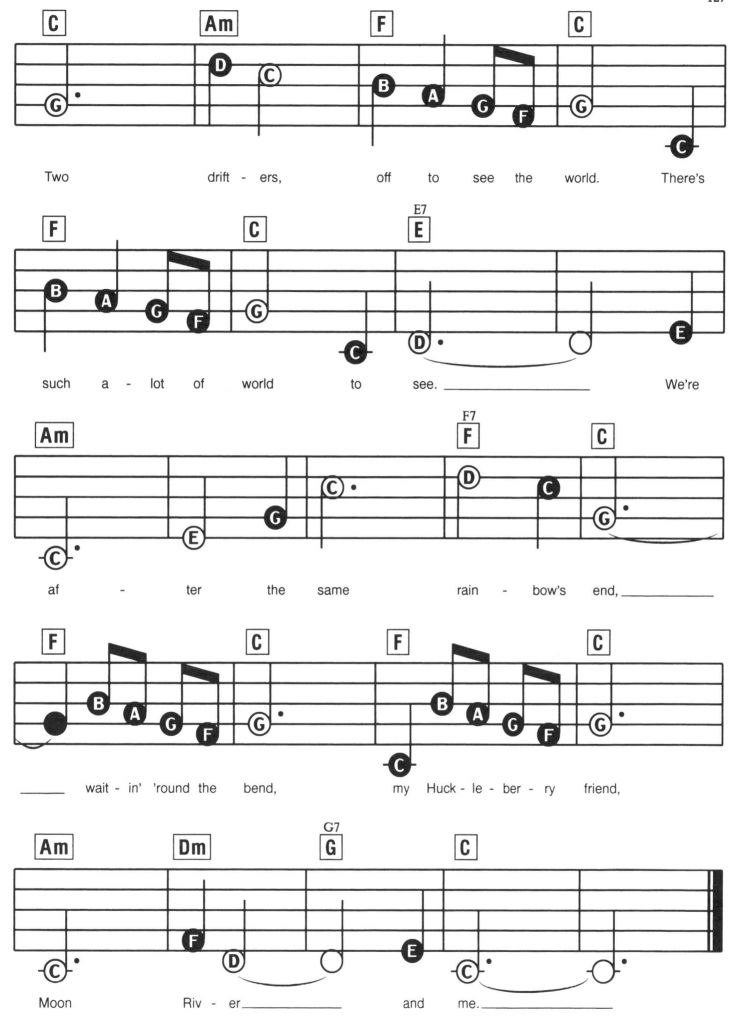

My Heart Will Go On
(Love Theme from 'Titanic')
from the Paramount and Twentieth Century Fox Motion Picture TITANIC

Registration 8
Rhythm: Ballad

Lyric by Will Jennings
Music by James Horner

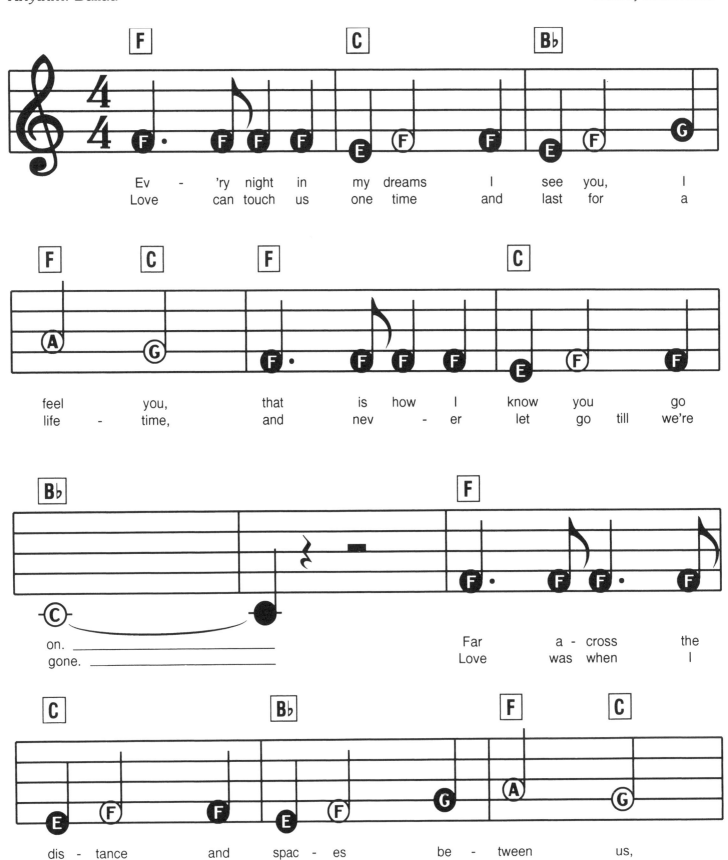

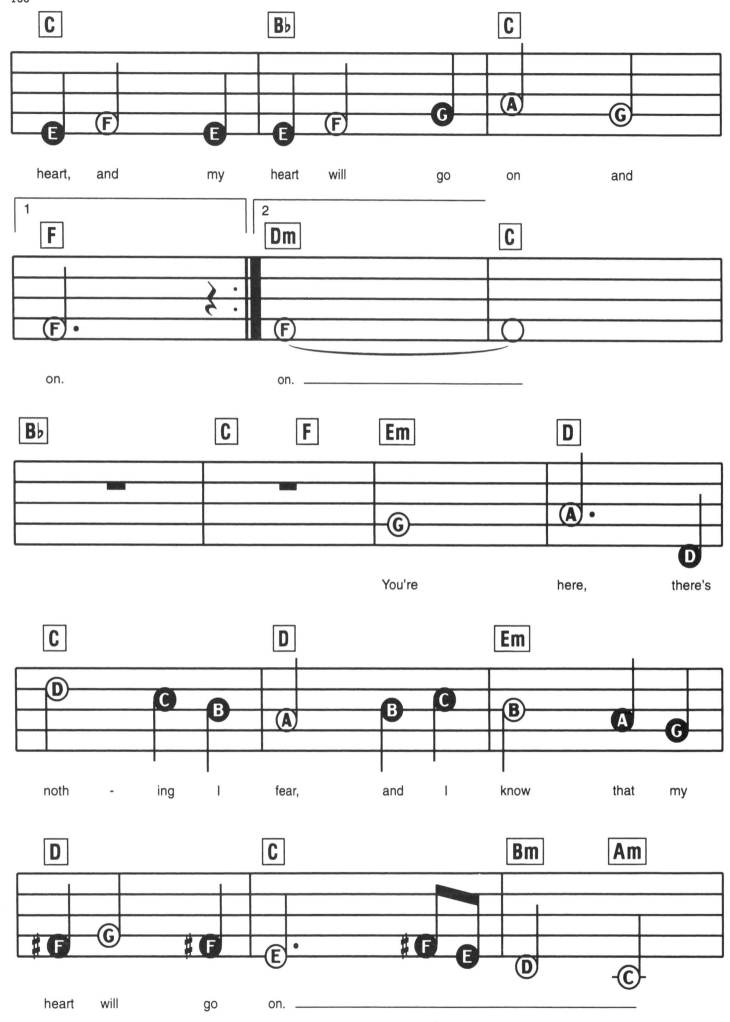

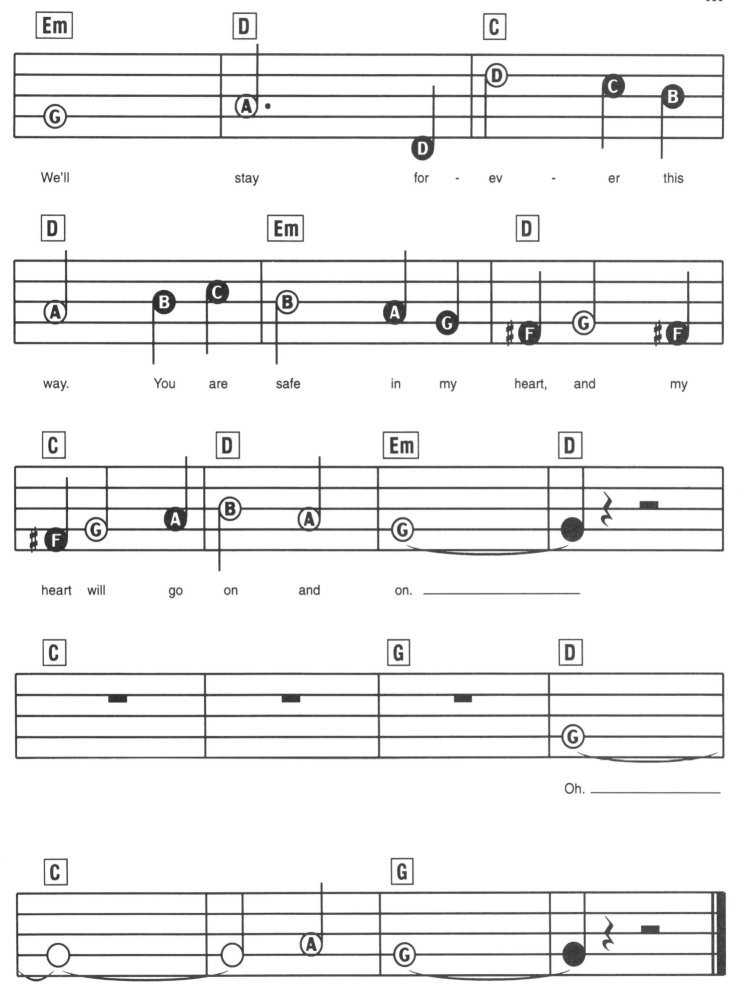

Need You Now

Registration 4
Rhythm: 8-Beat or Rock

Words and Music by Hillary Scott,
Charles Kelley, Dave Haywood
and Josh Kear

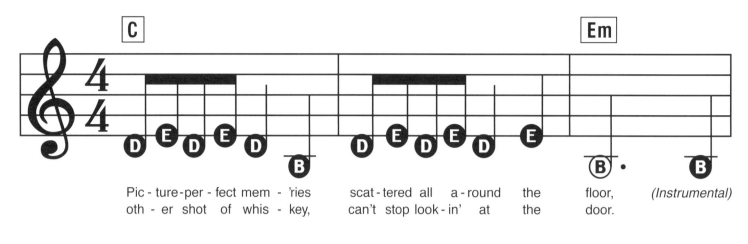

Pic - ture-per - fect mem - 'ries
oth - er shot of whis - key,

scat - tered all a-round the
can't stop look-in' at the

floor,   (Instrumental)
door.

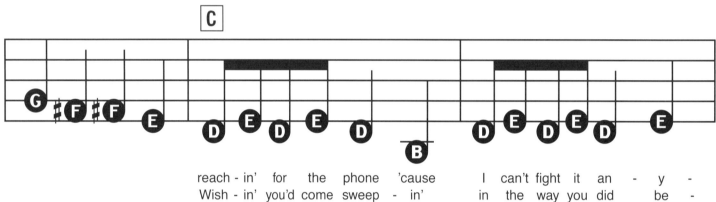

reach - in' for the phone 'cause
Wish - in' you'd come sweep - in'

I can't fight it an - y -
in the way you did be -

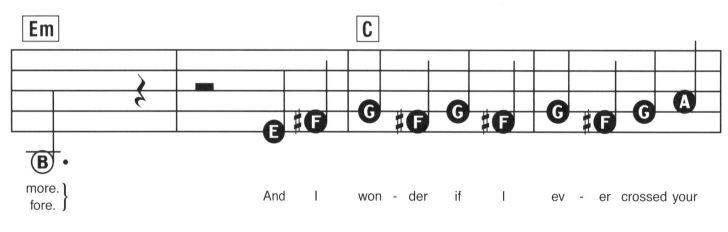

more.
fore.

And I won - der if I ev - er crossed your

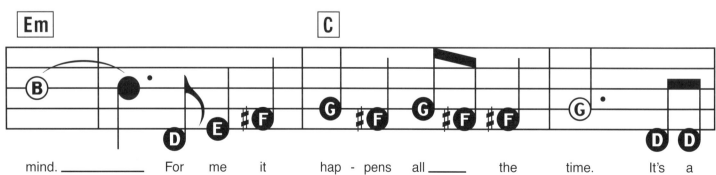

mind. _____ For me it hap - pens all ____ the time. It's a

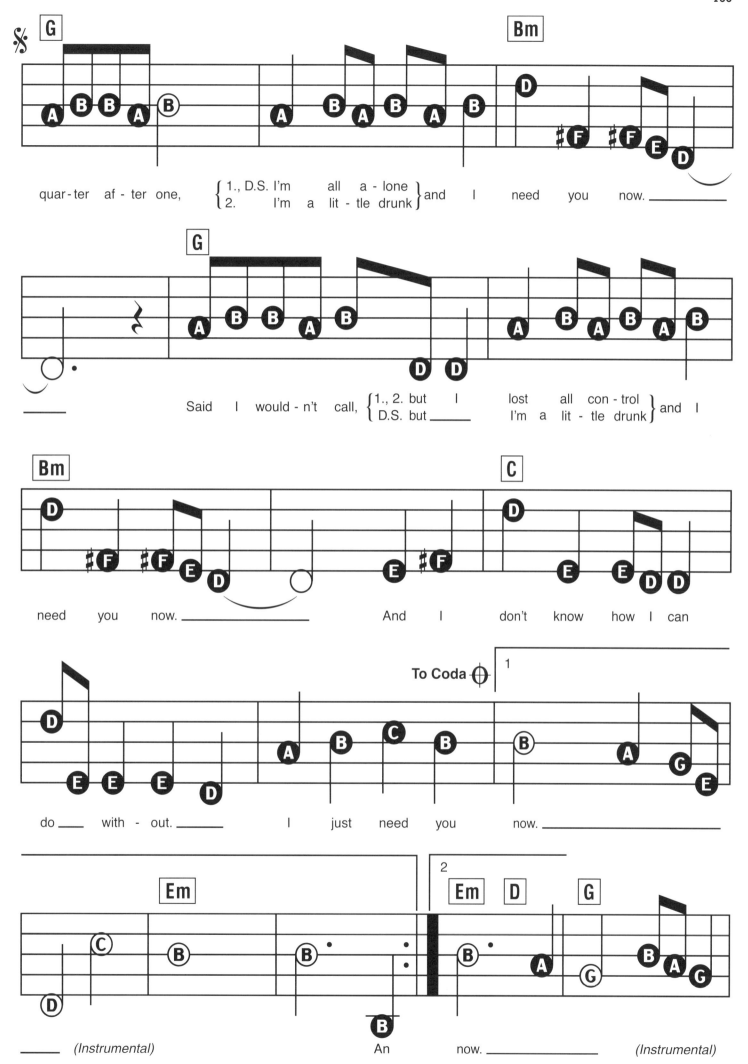

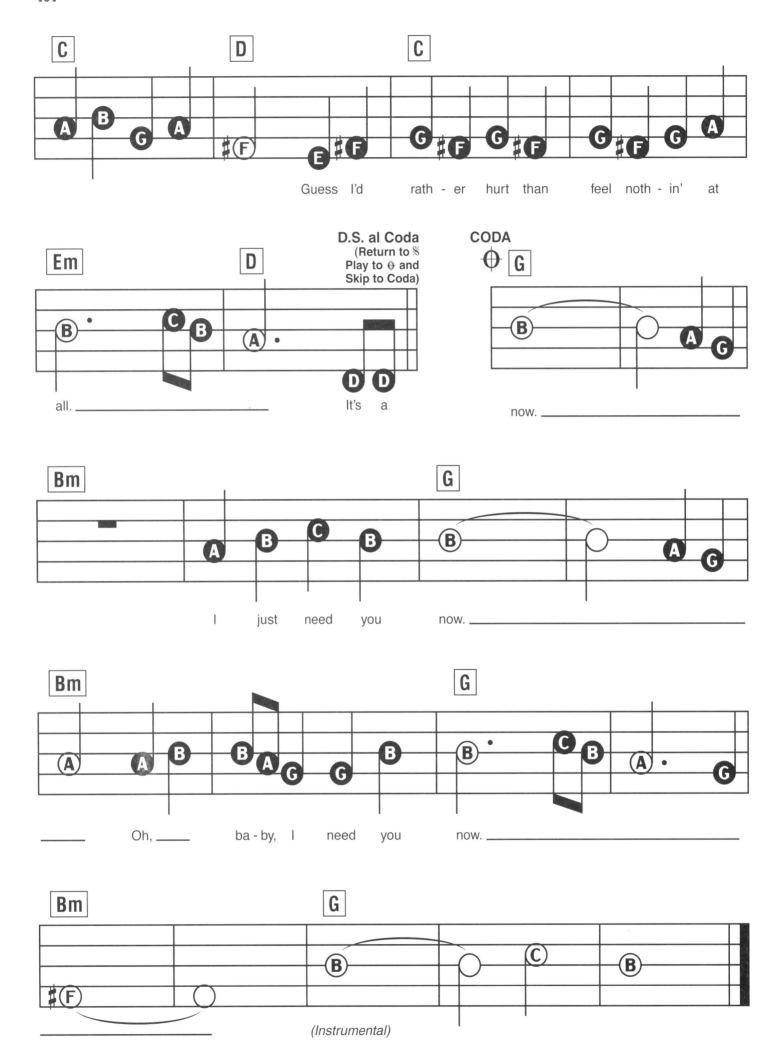

Sailing

Registration 2
Rhythm: Pops or 8-Beat

Words and Music by
Christopher Cross

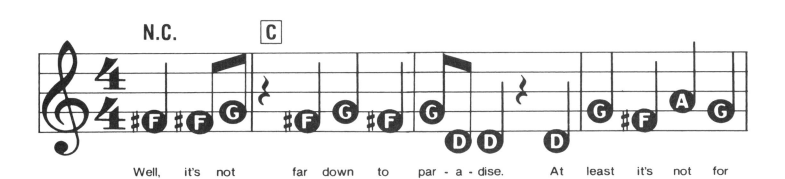

Well, it's not far down to par - a - dise. At least it's not for

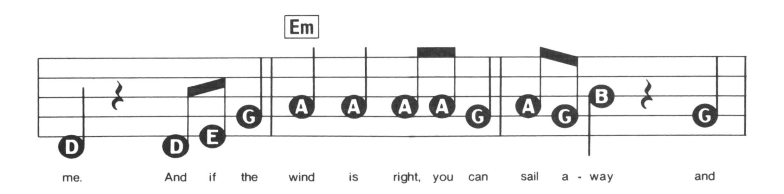

me. And if the wind is right, you can sail a - way and

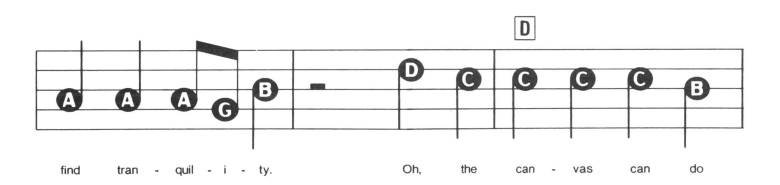

find tran - quil - i - ty. Oh, the can - vas can do

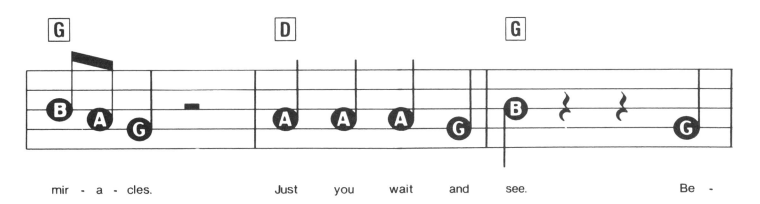

mir - a - cles. Just you wait and see. Be -

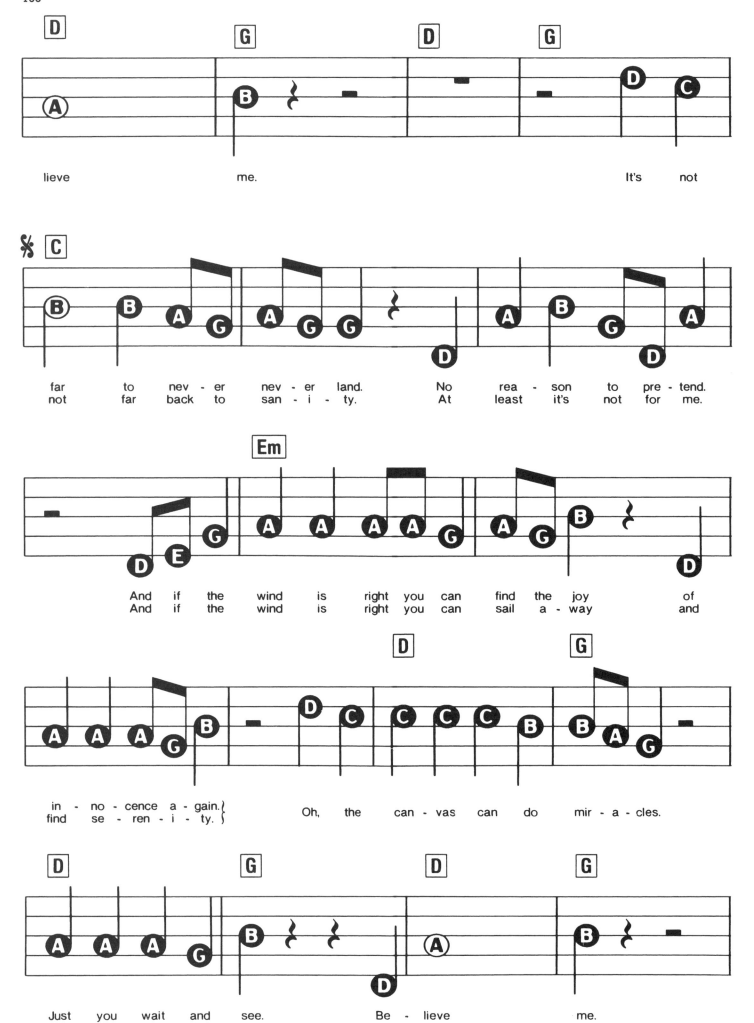

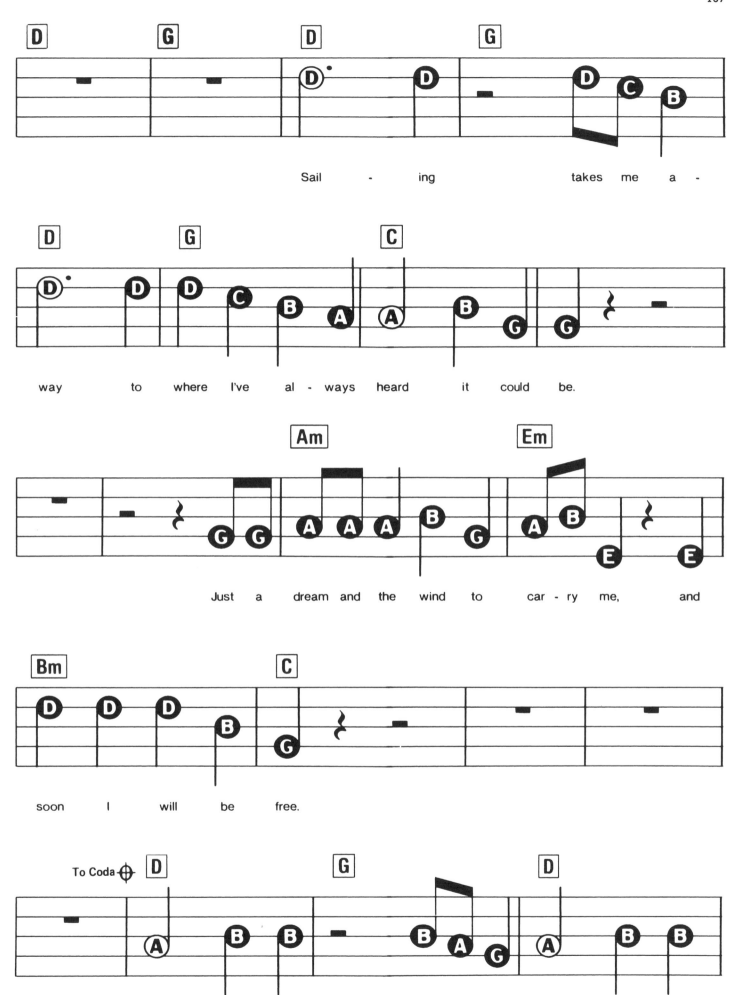

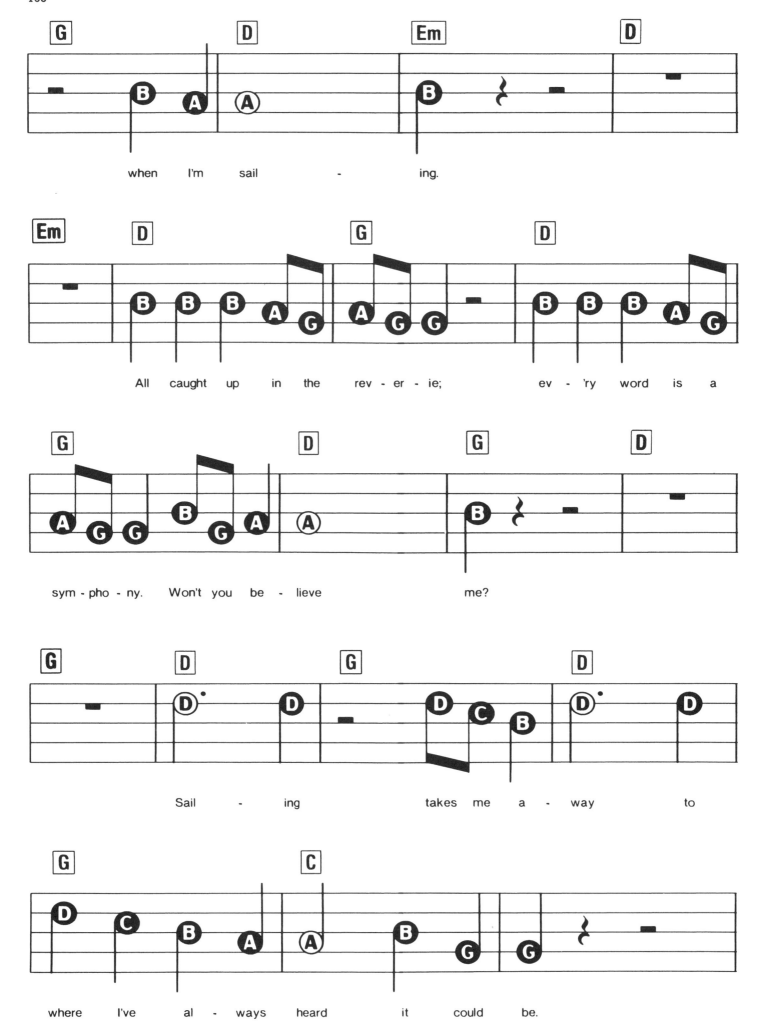

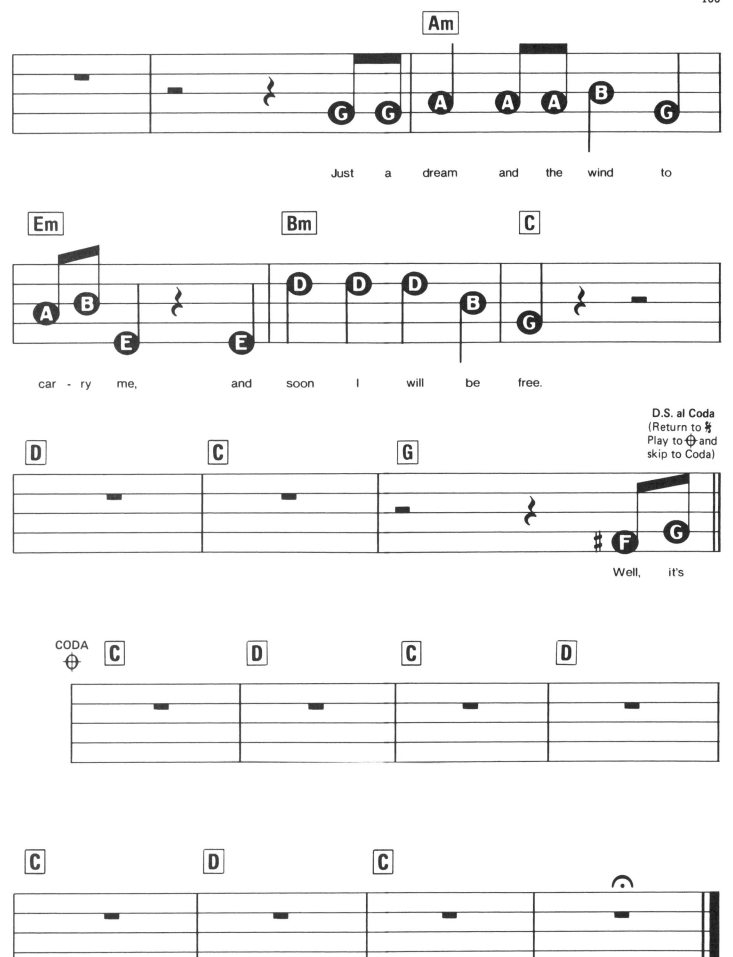

Not Ready to Make Nice

Registration 2
Rhythm: 8-Beat or Rock

Words and Music by Dan Wilson, Emily Robison,
Martie Maguire and Natalie Maines

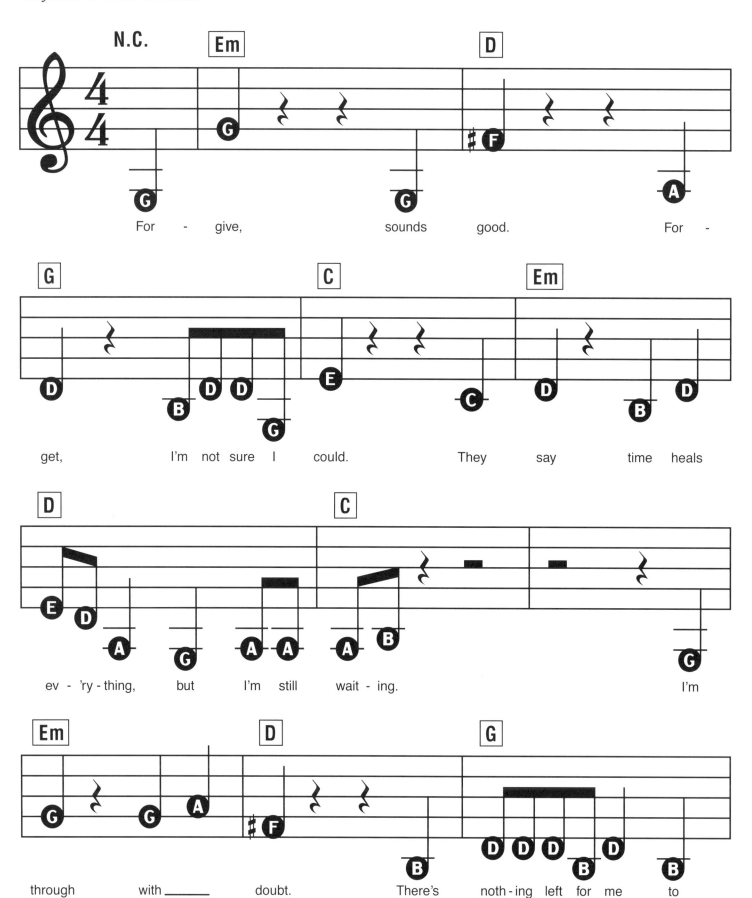

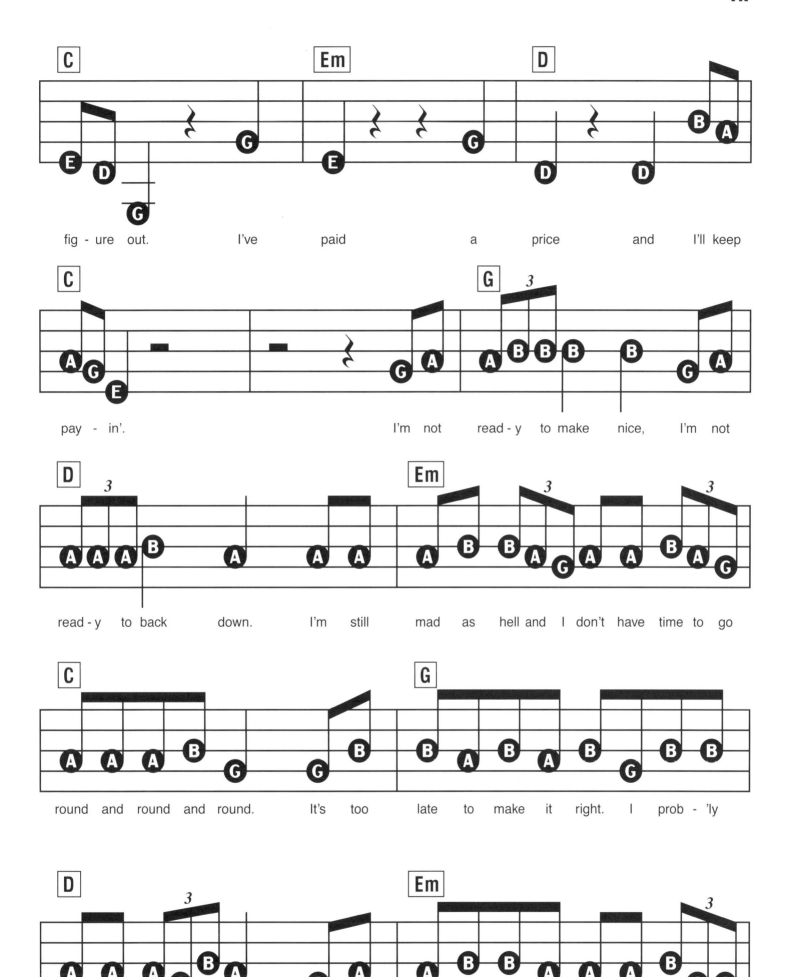

142

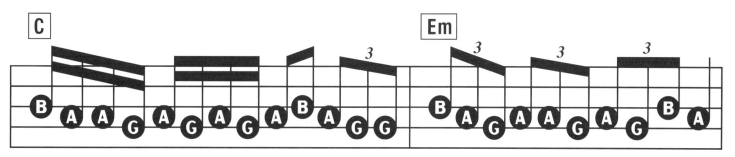

daugh - ter that she ought to hate a per - fect stran - ger. And how in the world can the words that I said

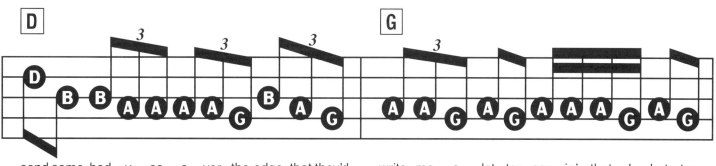

send some - bod - y so o - ver the edge that they'd write me a let - ter, say - in' that I bet - ter

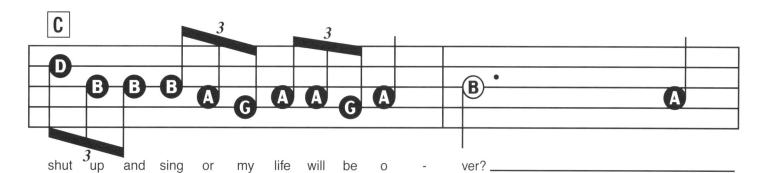

shut up and sing or my life will be o - ver?

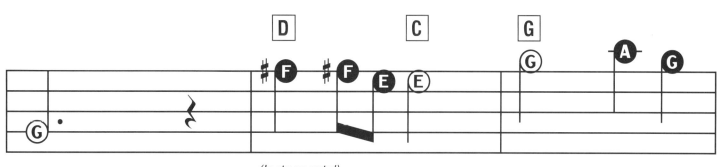

(Instrumental)

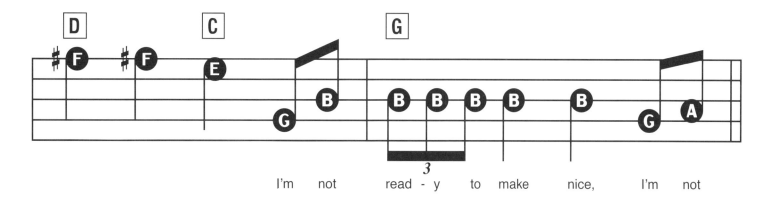

I'm not read - y to make nice, I'm not

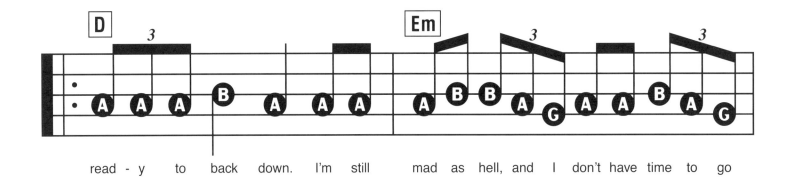

read - y   to   back   down.   I'm   still   mad   as   hell, and   I   don't have time   to   go

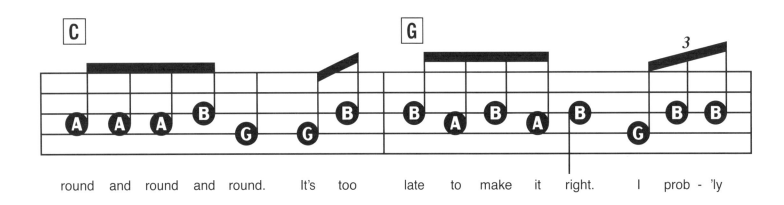

round   and   round   and   round.   It's   too   late   to   make   it   right.   I   prob - 'ly

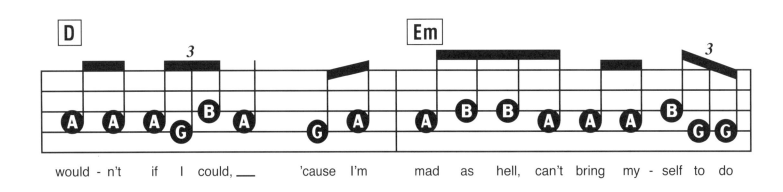

would - n't   if   I   could, __   'cause I'm   mad   as   hell, can't   bring   my - self   to   do

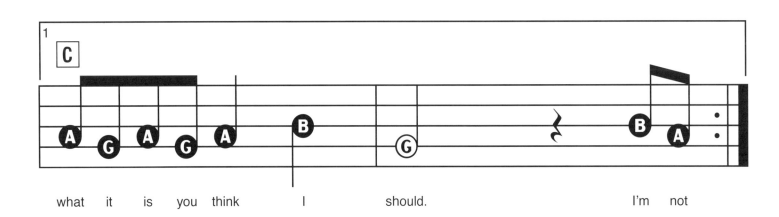

what   it   is   you   think   I   should.   I'm   not

145

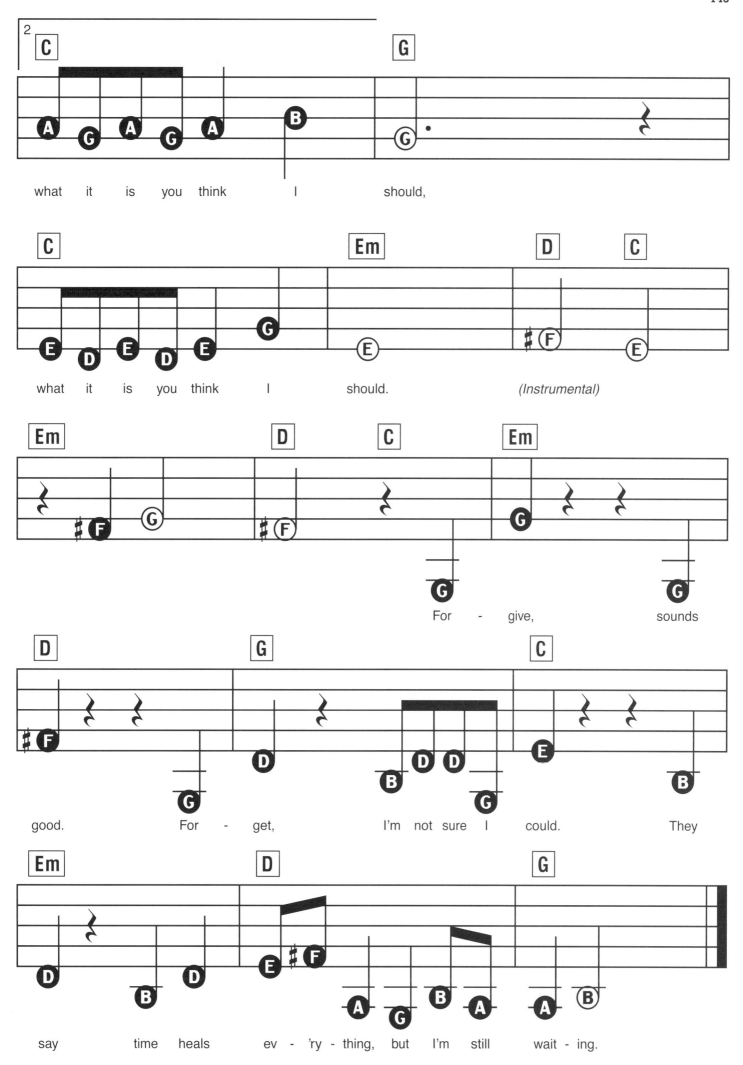

Please Read the Letter

Registration 4
Rhythm: 8-Beat or Rock

Words and Music by Robert Plant, Jimmy Page,
Michael Pearson and Stephen Jones

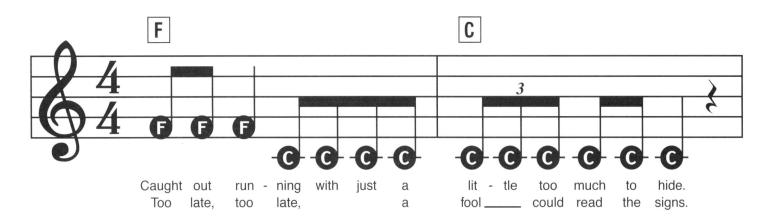

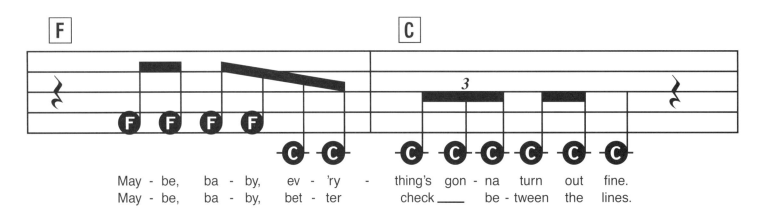

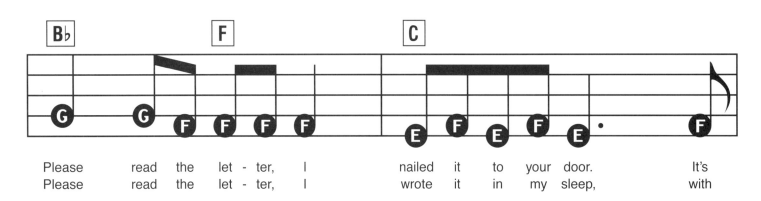

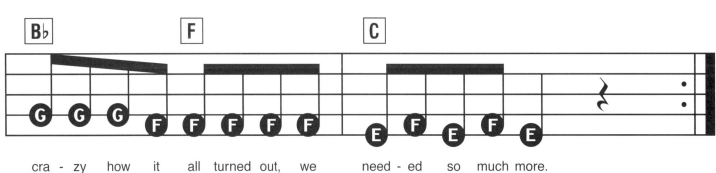

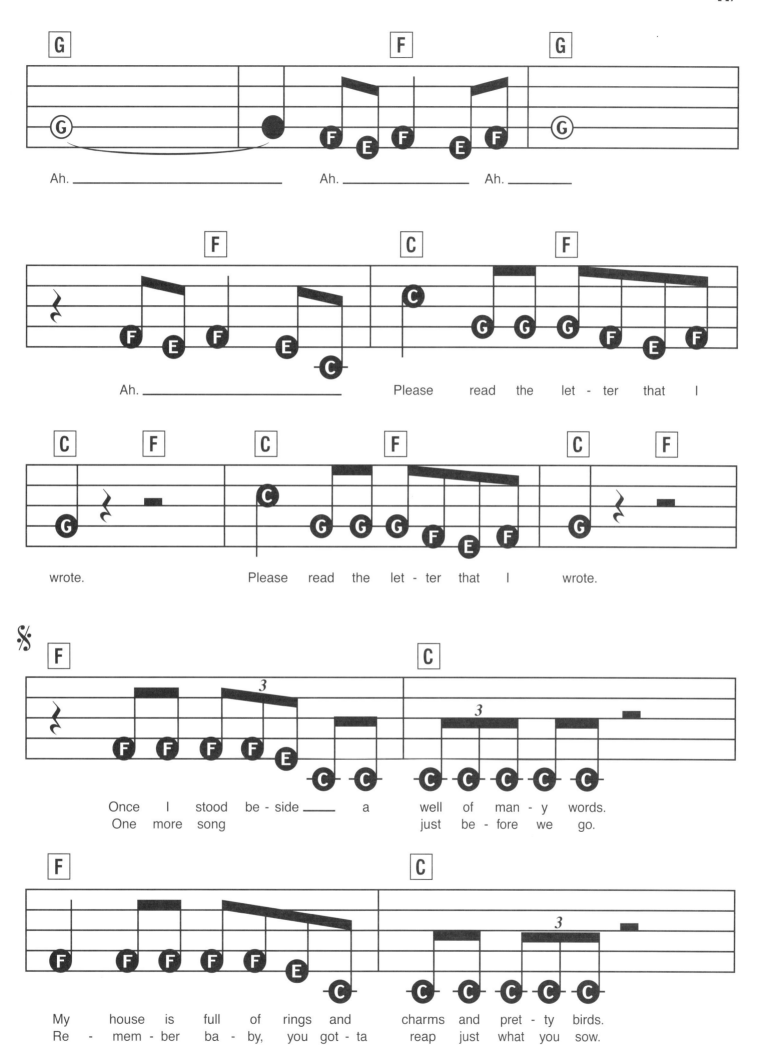

149

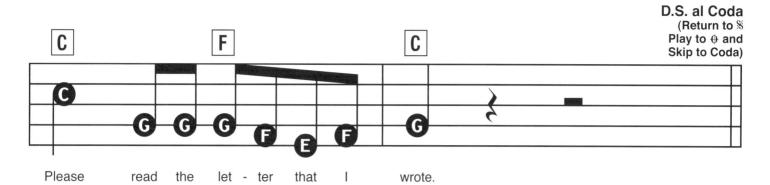

Please read the let-ter that I wrote.

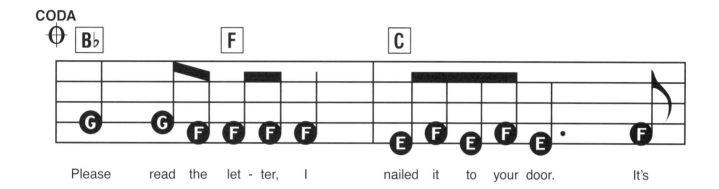

Please read the let-ter, I nailed it to your door. It's

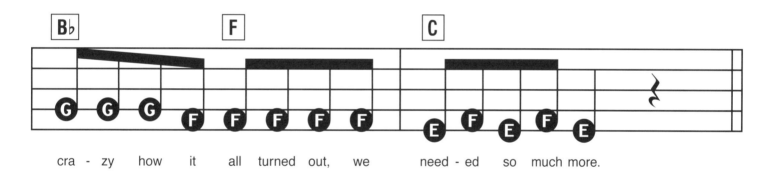

cra-zy how it all turned out, we need-ed so much more.

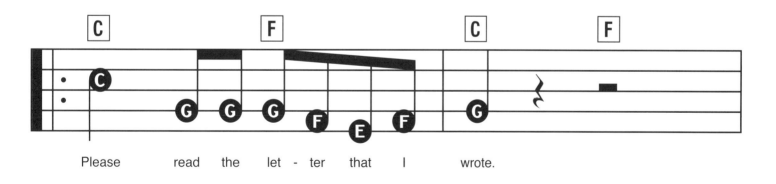

Please read the let-ter that I wrote.

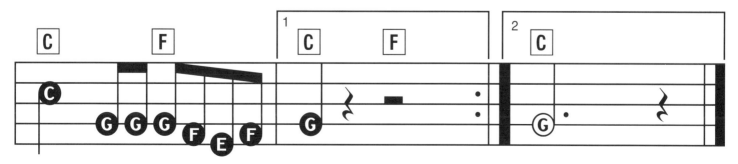

Please read the let-ter that I wrote. wrote.

Rehab

Registration 4
Rhythm: Rock

Words and Music by
Amy Winehouse

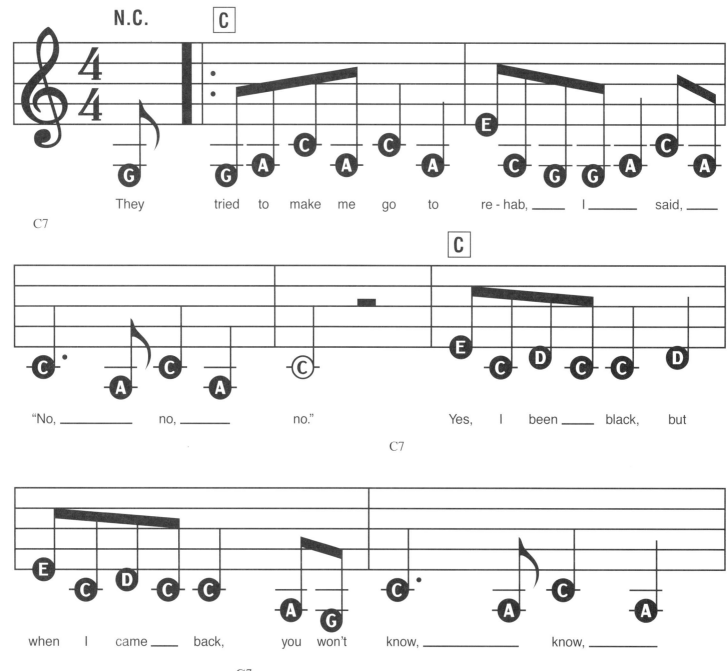

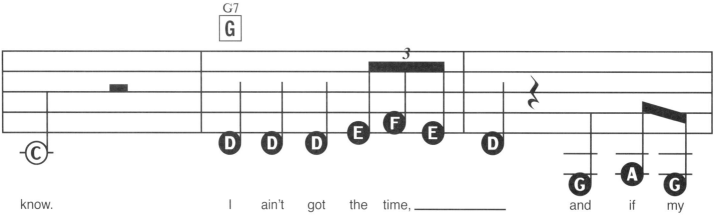

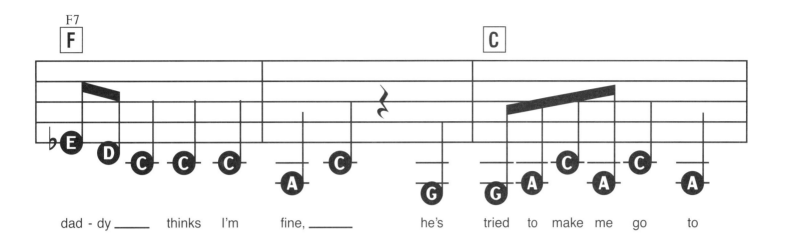

dad - dy _____ thinks I'm fine, _____ he's tried to make me go to

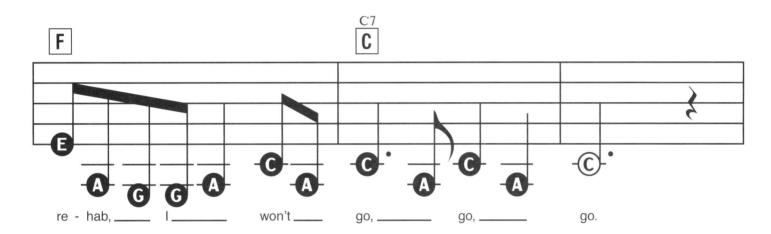

re - hab, _____ I _____ won't _____ go, _____ go, _____ go.

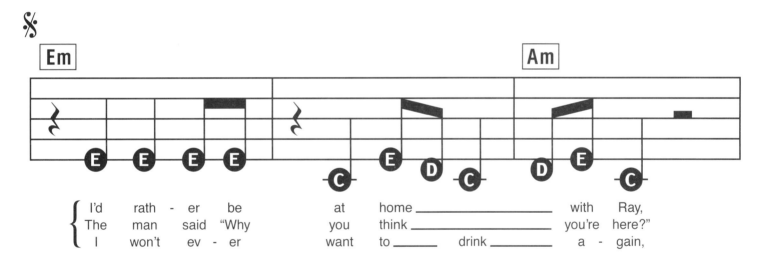

I'd rath - er be at home _____ with Ray,
The man said "Why you think _____ you're here?"
I won't ev - er want to _____ drink _____ a - gain,

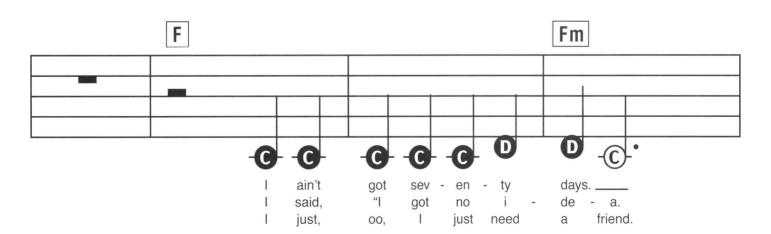

I ain't got sev - en - ty days. _____
I said, "I got no i - de - a.
I just, oo, I just need a friend.

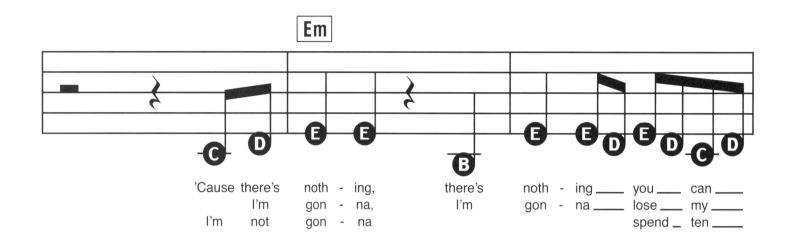

'Cause there's noth - ing, there's noth - ing ___ you ___ can ___
I'm gon - na, I'm gon - na ___ lose ___ my ___
I'm not gon - na spend _ ten ___

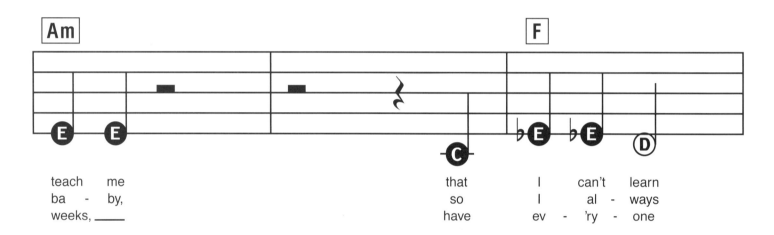

teach me that I can't learn
ba - by, so I al - ways
weeks, ___ have ev - 'ry - one

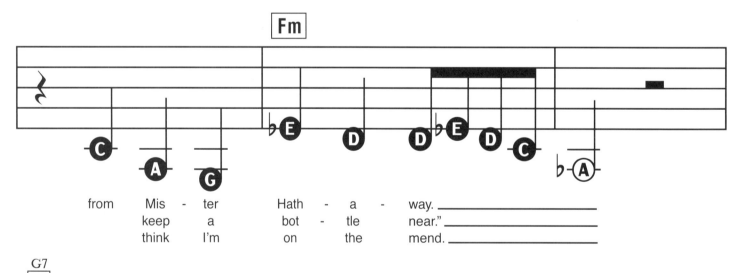

from Mis - ter Hath - a - way. ___
keep a bot - tle near." ___
think I'm on the mend. ___

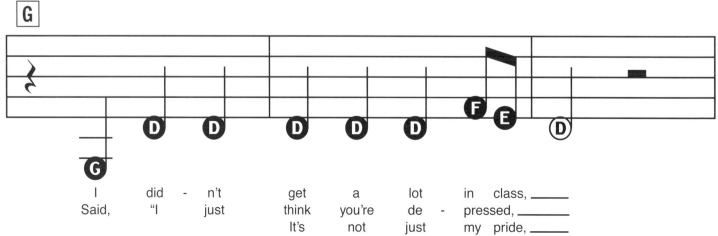

I did - n't get a lot in class, ___
Said, "I just think you're de - pressed, ___
It's not just my pride, ___

153

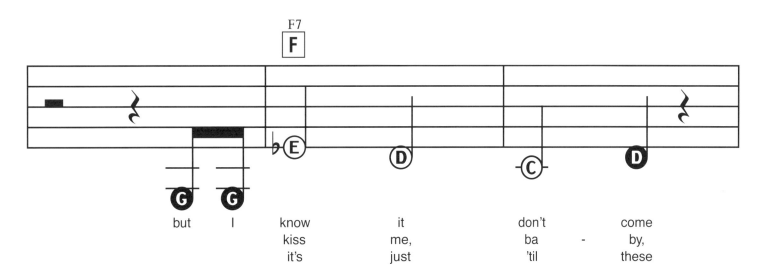

but I know it don't come
kiss me, it don't ba - by,
it's just 'til these

To Coda ⊕

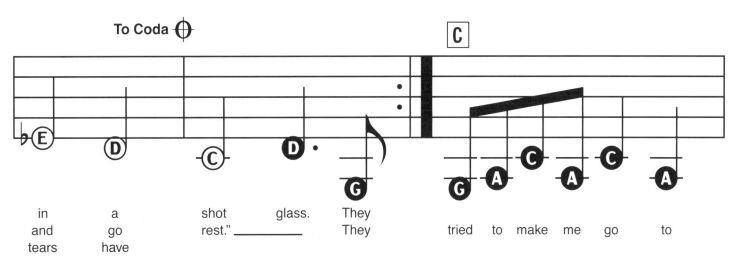

in a shot glass. They
and go rest." They
tears have

C7

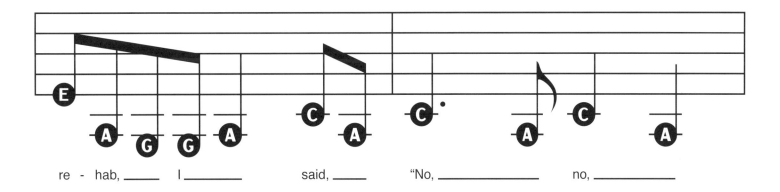

re - hab, I said, "No, no,

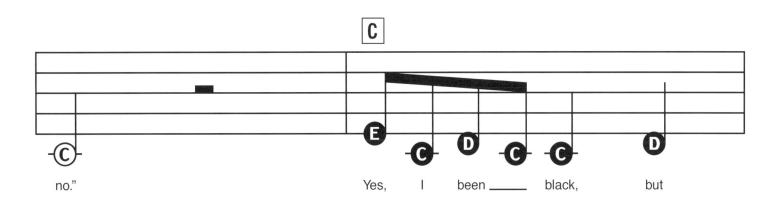

no." Yes, I been black, but

C7

D.S. al Coda
(Return to %
Play to ⊕ and
Skip to Coda)

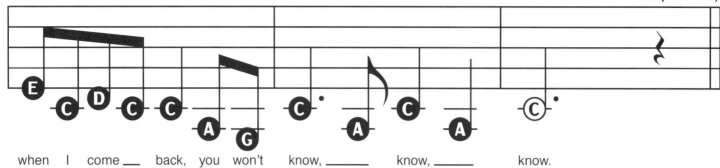

when I come ___ back, you won't know, _____ know, _____ know.

CODA
⊕

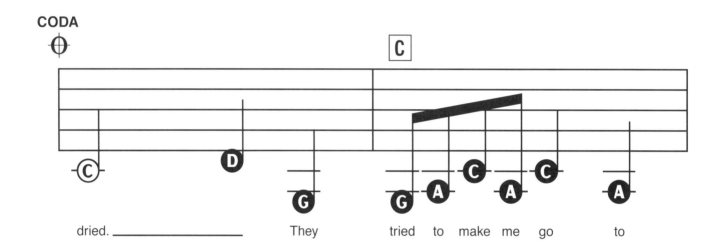

dried. _____ They tried to make me go to

C7

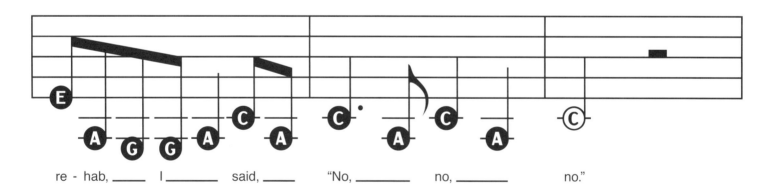

re - hab, ___ I _____ said, _____ "No, _____ no, _____ no."

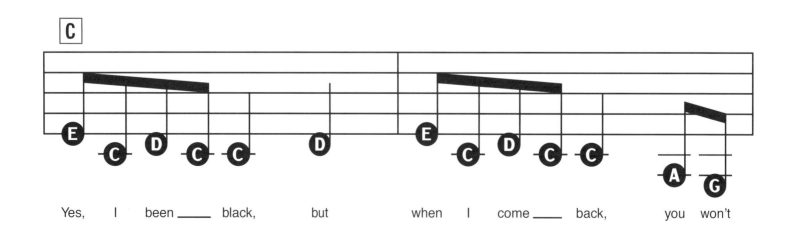

Yes, I been ___ black, but when I come ___ back, you won't

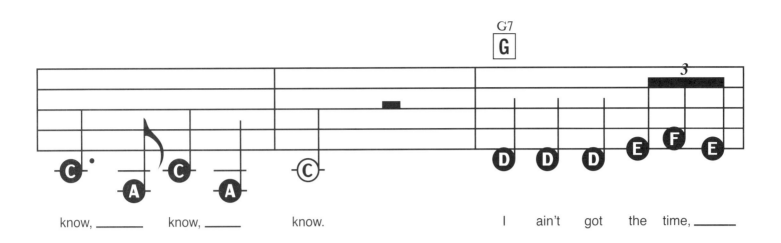

know, _____ know, _____ know. I ain't got the time, _____

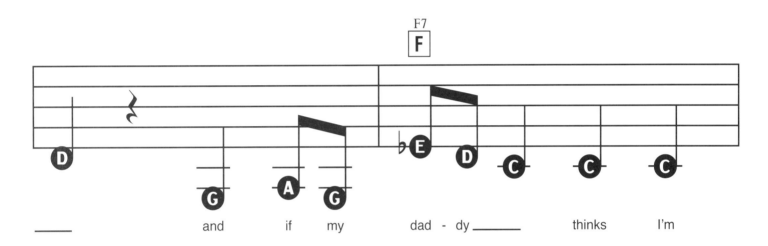

_____ and if my dad - dy _____ thinks I'm

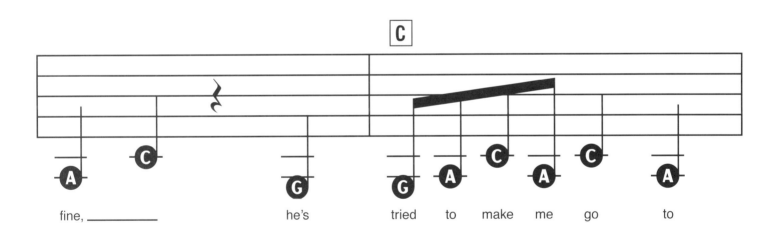

fine, _____ he's tried to make me go to

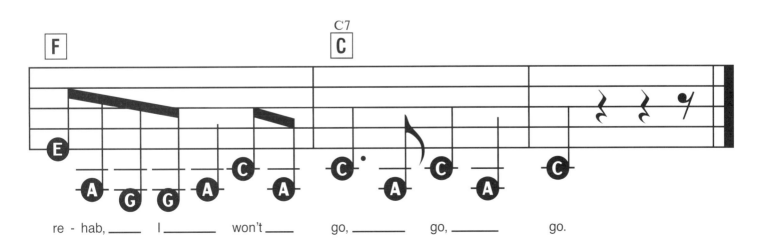

re - hab, _____ I _____ won't _____ go, _____ go, _____ go.

Rolling in the Deep

Registration 4
Rhythm: Rock or Pop

Words and Music by Adele Adkins
and Paul Epworth

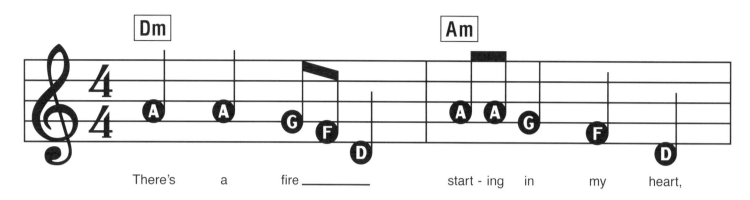

There's a fire _____ start-ing in my heart,

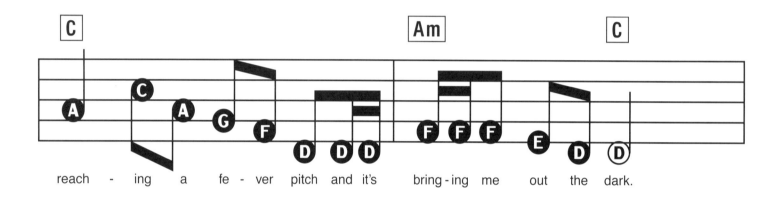

reach - ing a fe - ver pitch and it's bring-ing me out the dark.

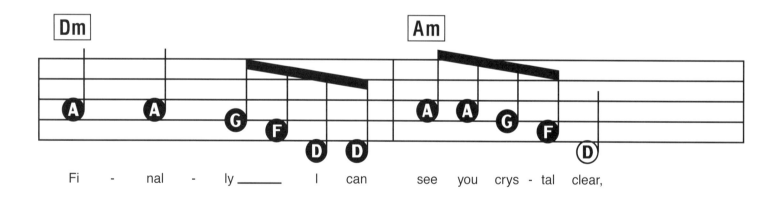

Fi - nal - ly _____ I can see you crys - tal clear,

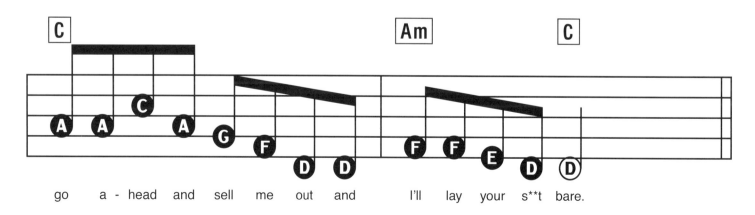

go a - head and sell me out and I'll lay your s**t bare.

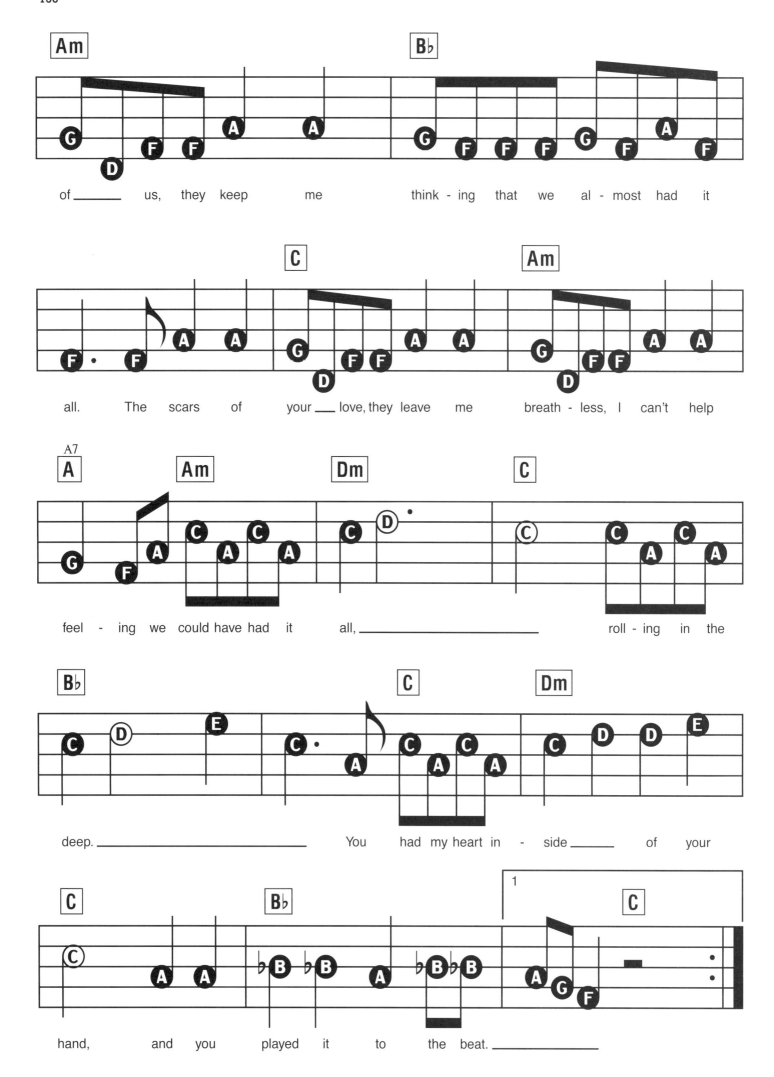

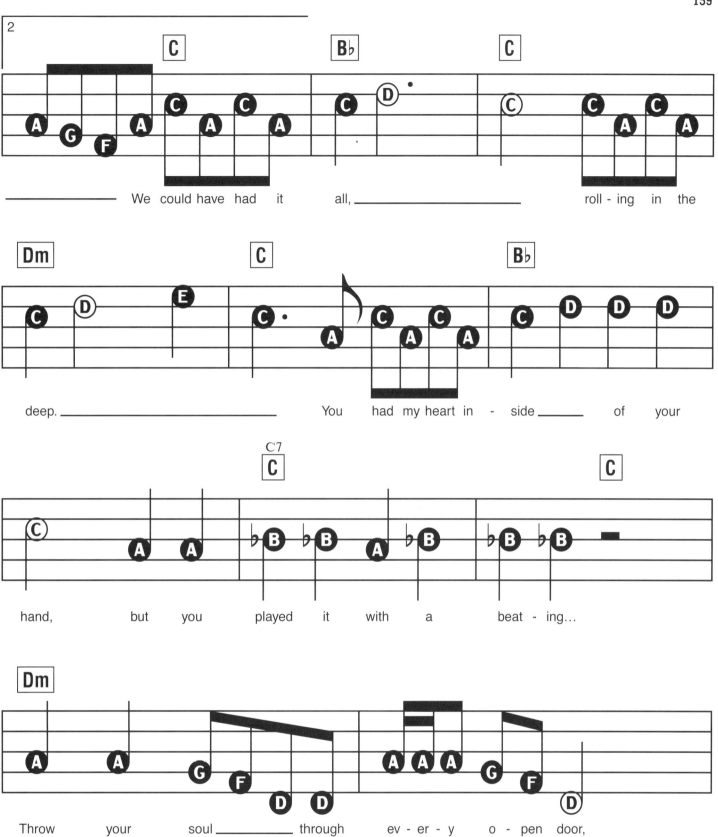

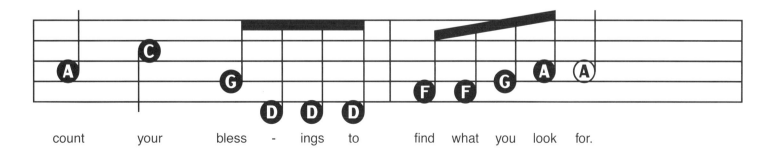

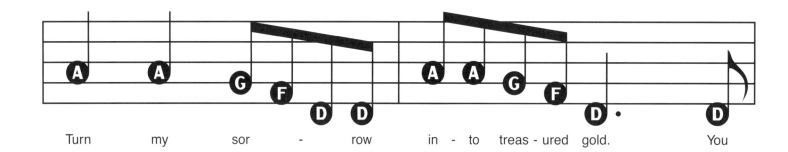

Turn my sor - row in - to treas - ured gold. You

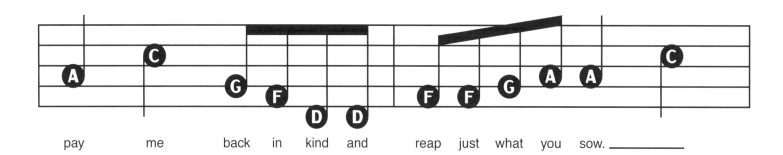

pay me back in kind and reap just what you sow. _____

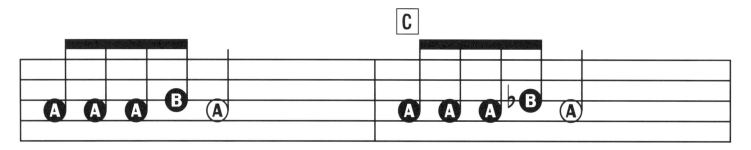

You're gon - na wish you nev - er had met me,

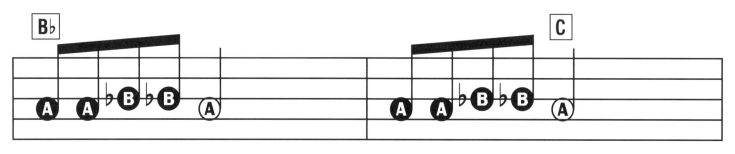

tears are gon - na fall, roll - ing in the deep.

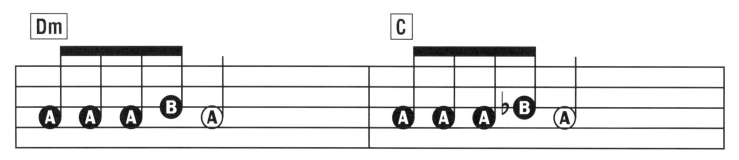

You're gon - na wish you nev - er had met me,

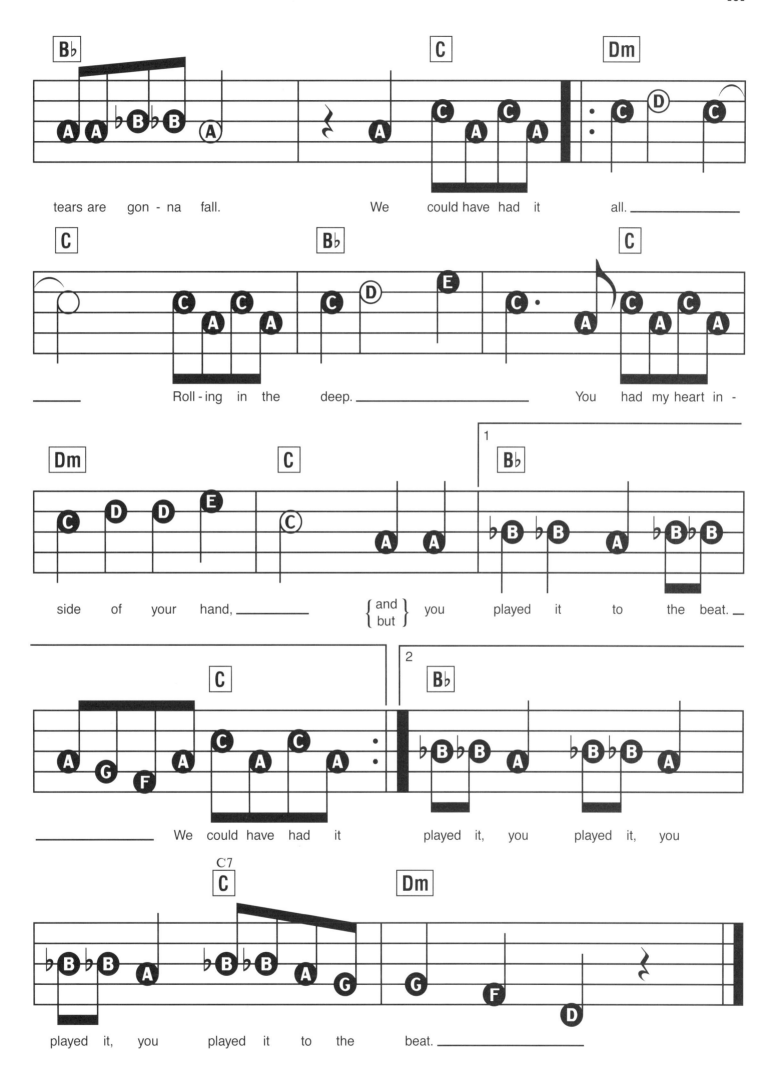

Rosanna

Registration 4
Rhythm: Rock

Words and Music by
David Paich

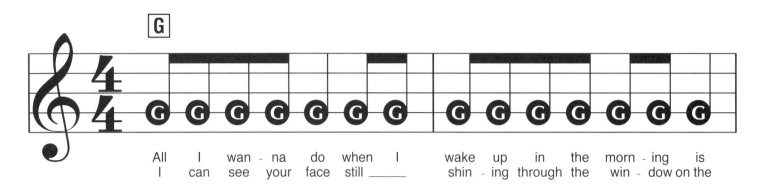

All I wan - na do when I   wake up in the morn - ing is
I can see your face still _____   shin - ing through the win - dow on the

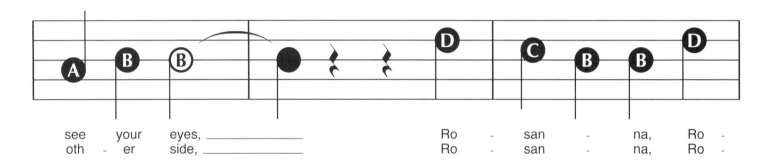

see your eyes, _____   Ro - san - na, Ro -
oth - er side, _____   Ro - san - na, Ro -

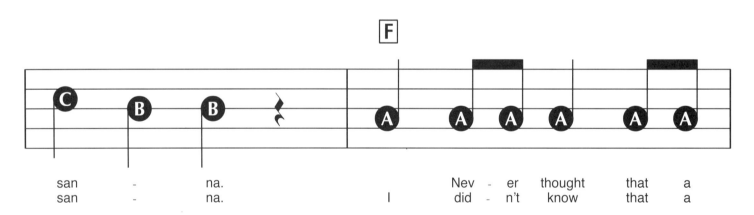

san - na.   Nev - er thought that a
san - na.   I   did - n't know that a

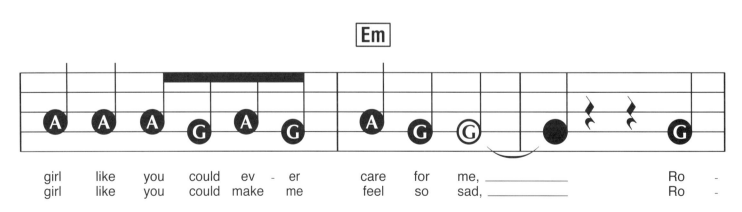

girl like you could ev - er   care for me, _____   Ro -
girl like you could make me   feel so sad, _____   Ro

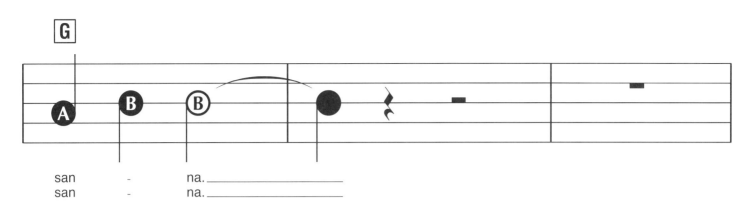

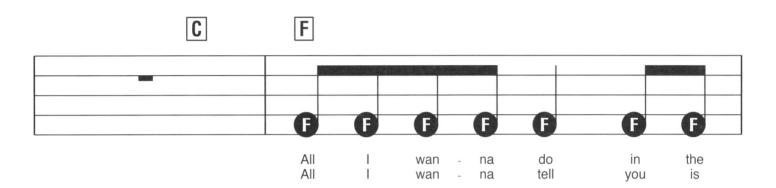

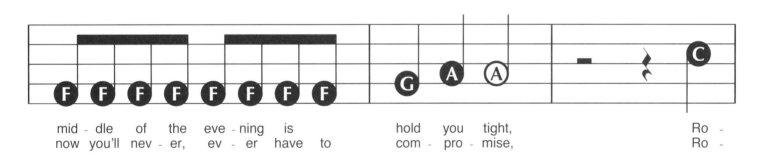

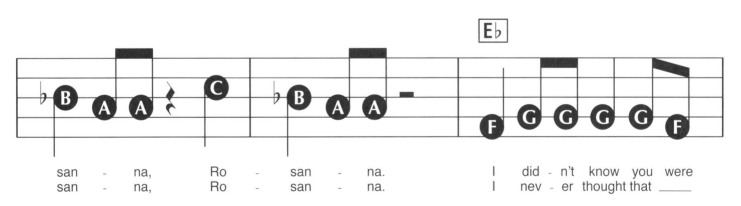

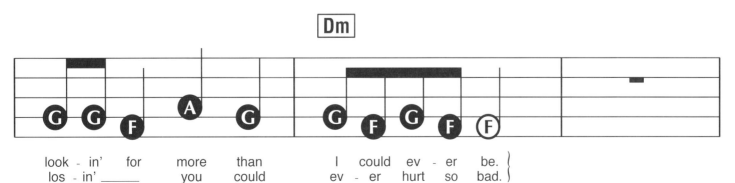

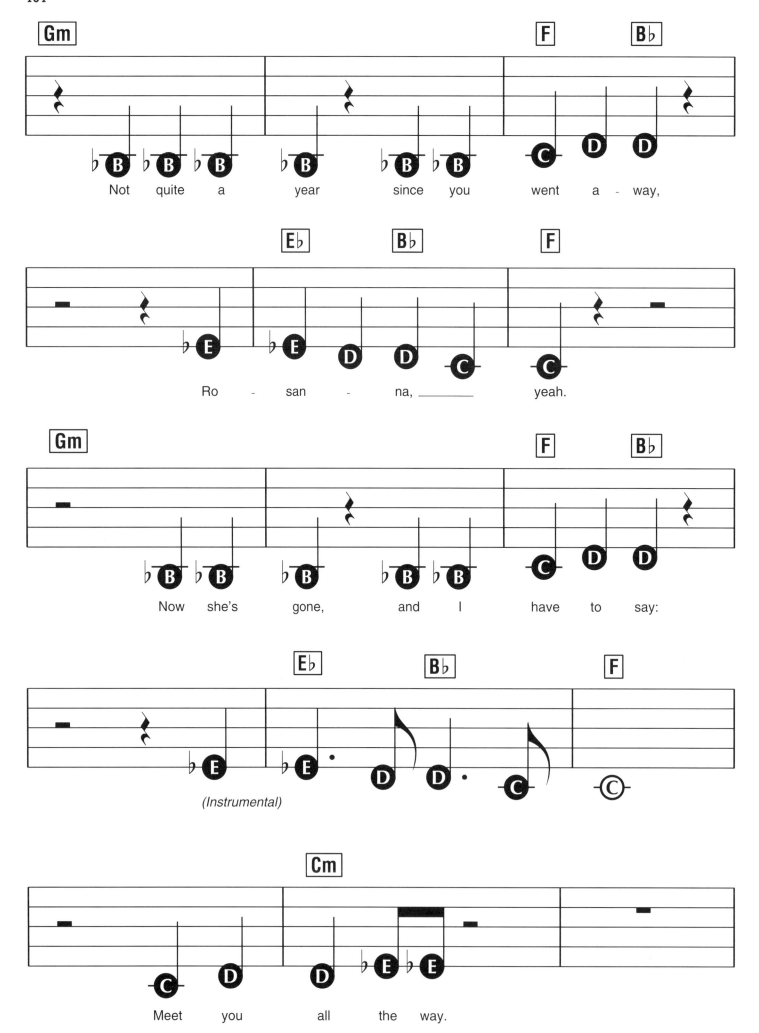

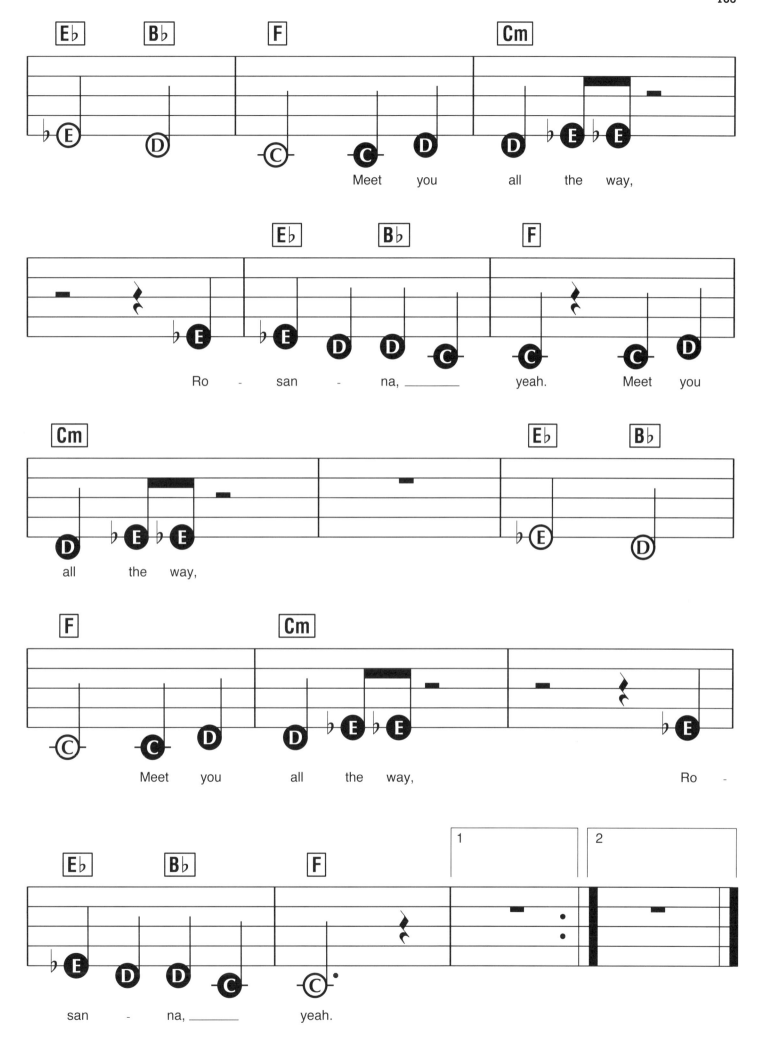

Smooth

Registration 8
Rhythm: Latin or Rock

Words by Rob Thomas
Music by Rob Thomas and Itaal Shur

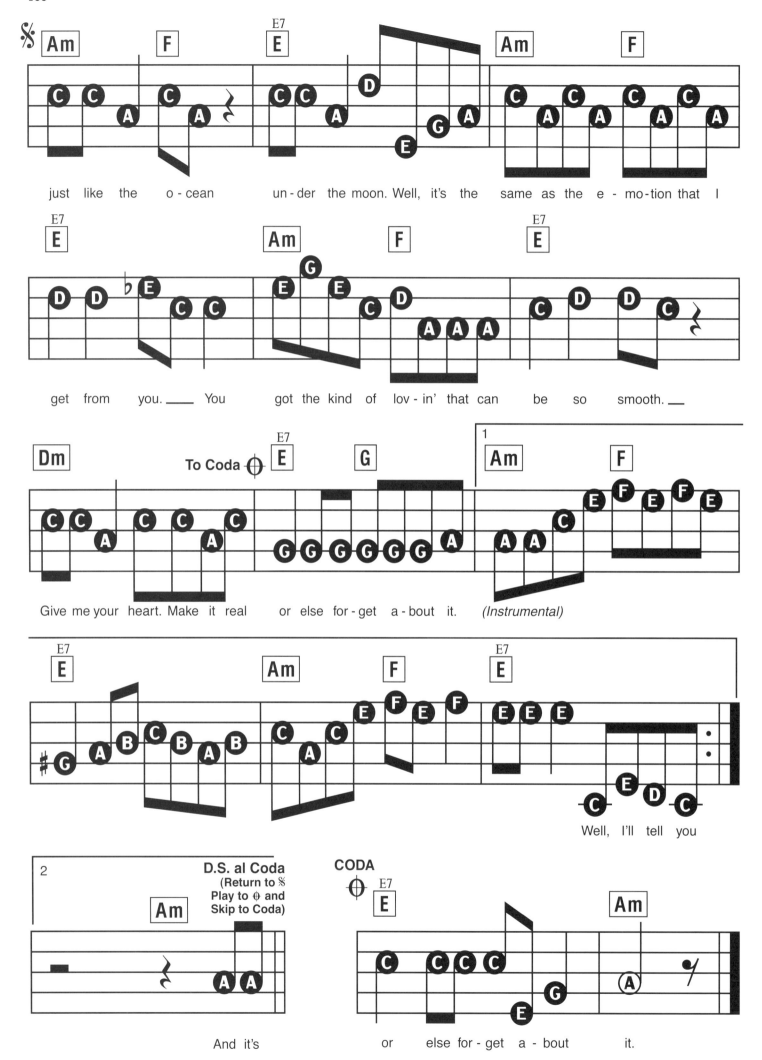

Sunny Came Home

Registration 8
Rhythm: 8-Beat or Rock

Words and Music by Shawn Colvin
and John Leventhal

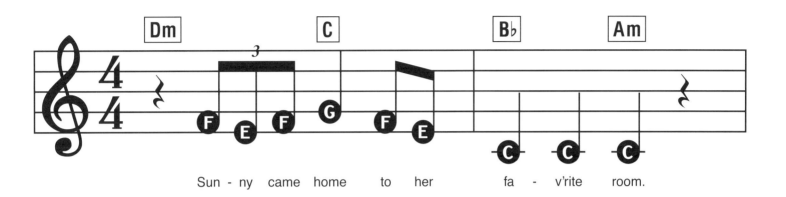

Sun - ny came home to her fa - v'rite room.

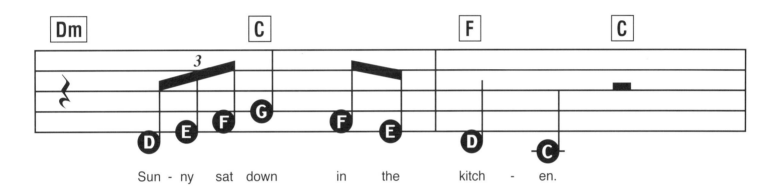

Sun - ny sat down in the kitch - en.

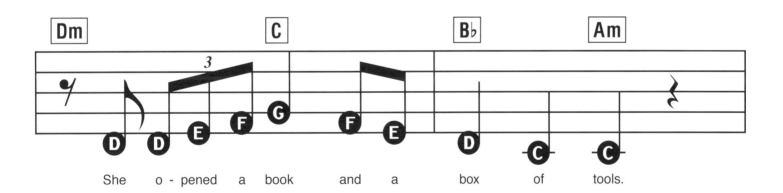

She o - pened a book and a box of tools.

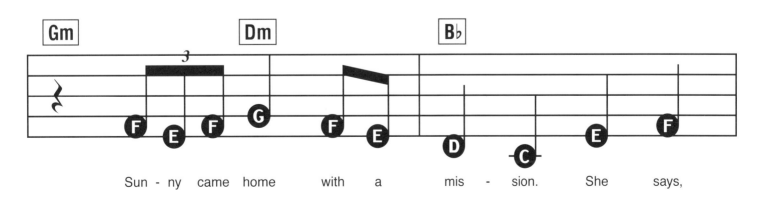

Sun - ny came home with a mis - sion. She says,

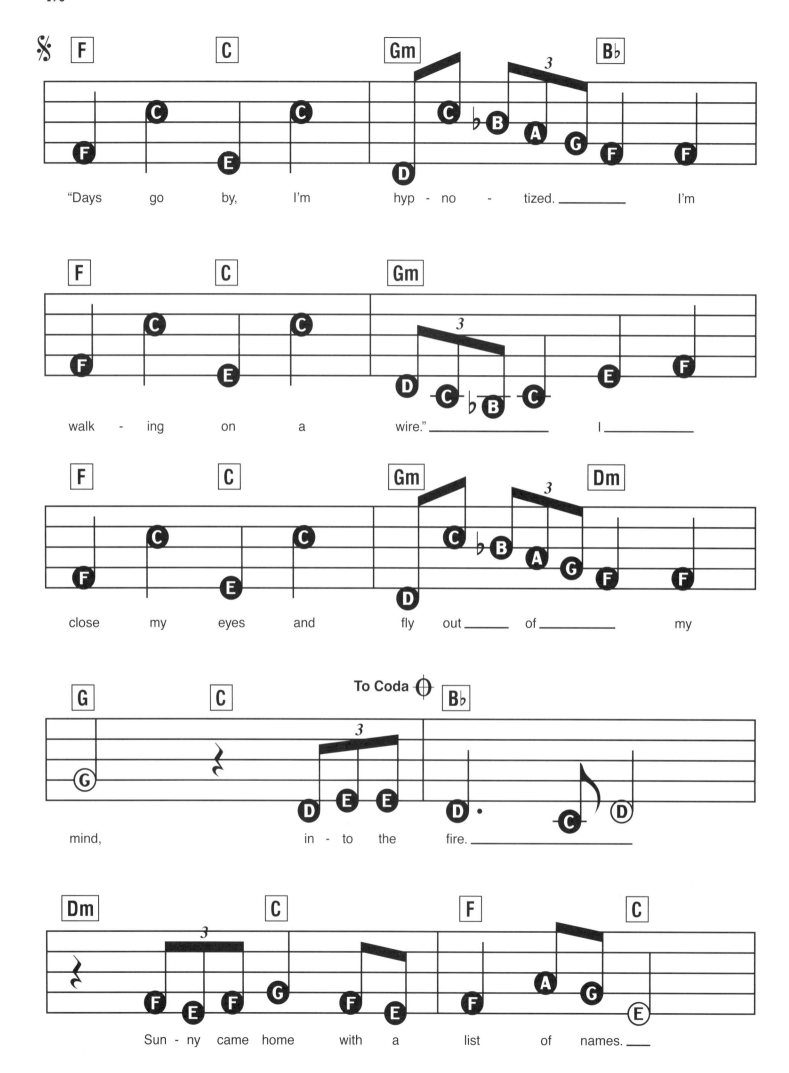

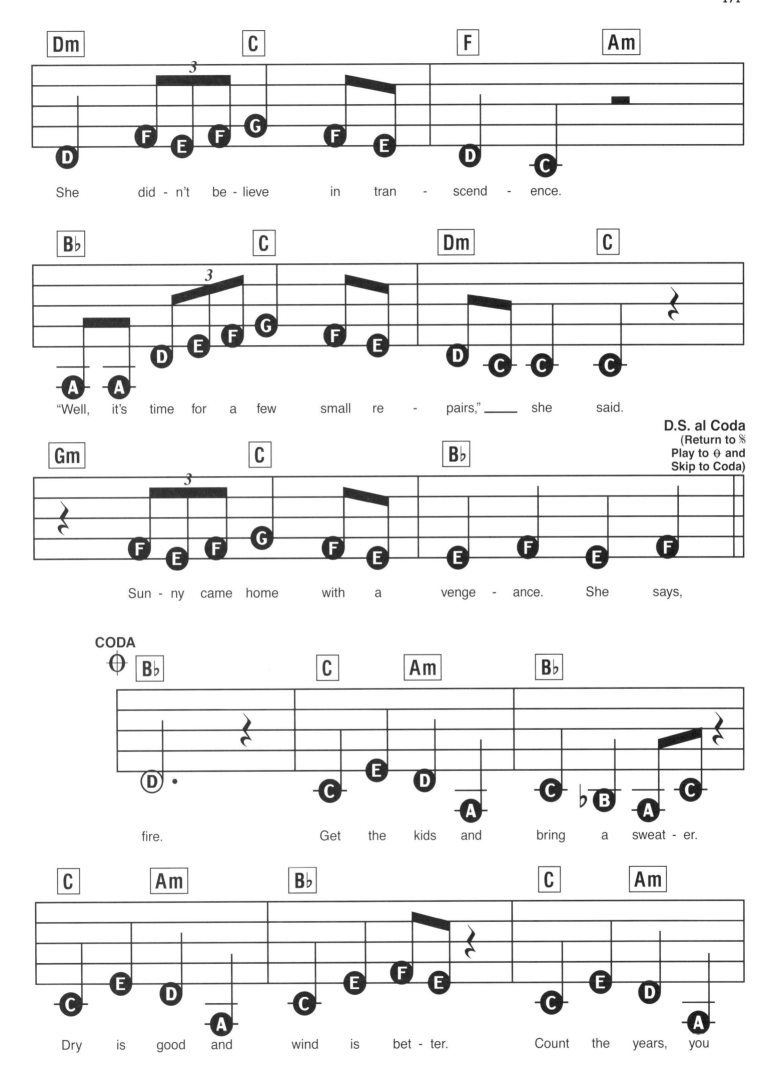

She did - n't be - lieve in tran - scend - ence.

"Well, it's time for a few small re - pairs," ____ she said.

D.S. al Coda
(Return to 𝄋
Play to ⊕ and
Skip to Coda)

Sun - ny came home with a venge - ance. She says,

CODA

fire. Get the kids and bring a sweat - er.

Dry is good and wind is bet - ter. Count the years, you

172

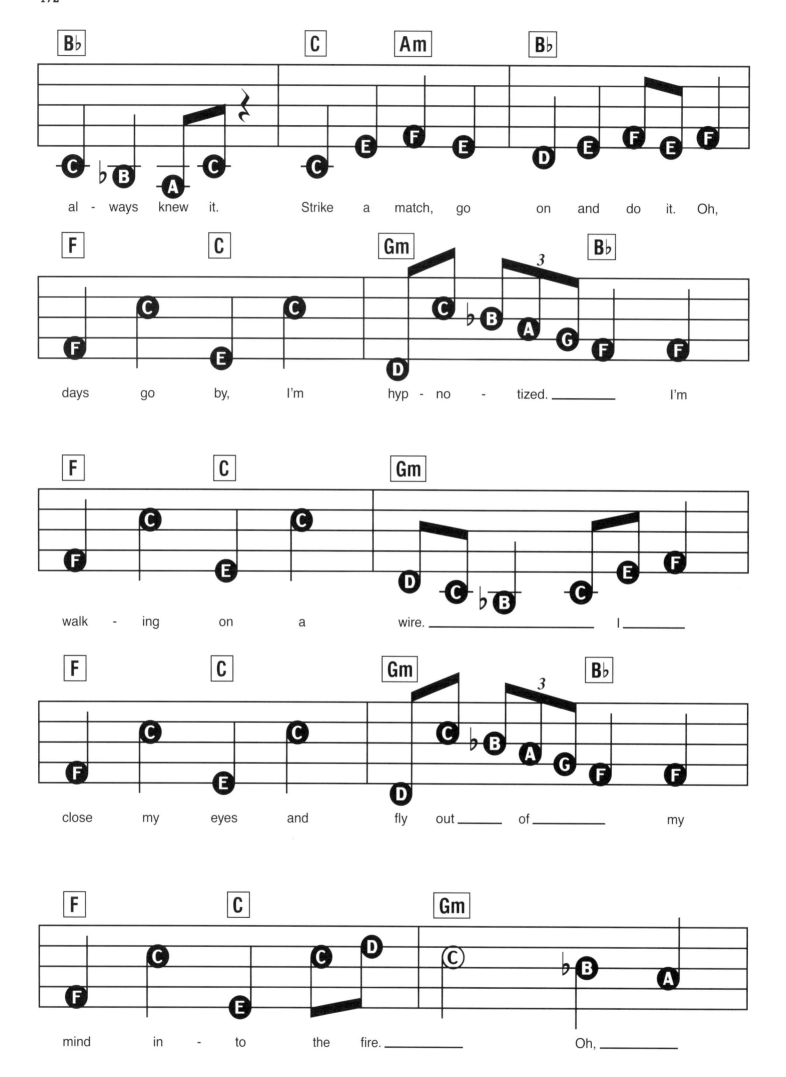

Strangers in the Night
adapted from A MAN COULD GET KILLED

Registration 5
Rhythm: Ballad or Slow Rock

Words by Charles Singleton and Eddie Snyder
Music by Bert Kaempfert

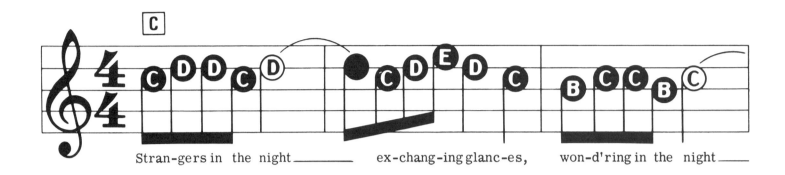

Stran-gers in the night _____ ex-chang-ing glanc-es, won-d'ring in the night _____

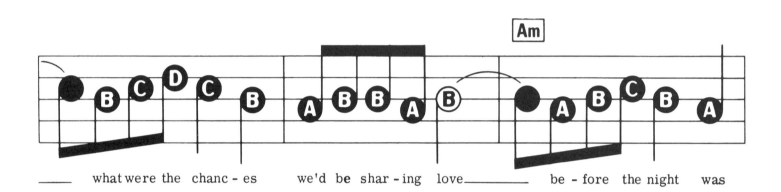

_____ what were the chanc-es we'd be shar-ing love _____ be - fore the night was

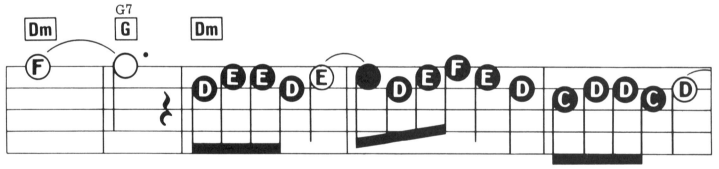

through. _____ Some-thing in your eyes _____ was so in - vit - ing, Some-thing in your smile _____

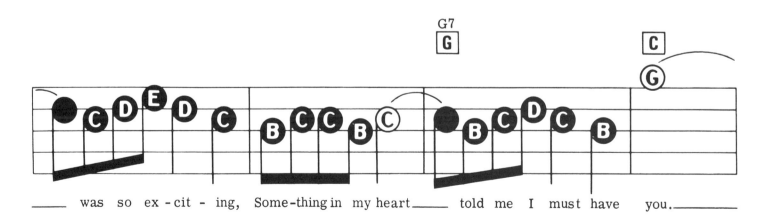

_____ was so ex-cit - ing, Some-thing in my heart _____ told me I must have you. _____

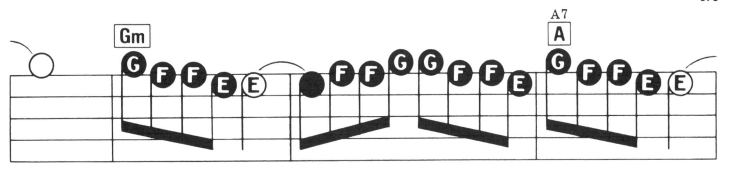

Stran-gers in the night____ two lone-ly peo-ple, we were stran-gers in the night____

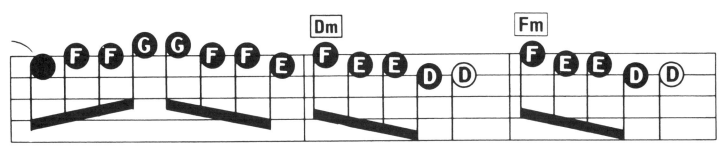

____ up to the mo-ment when we said our first hel - lo, Lit - tle did we know

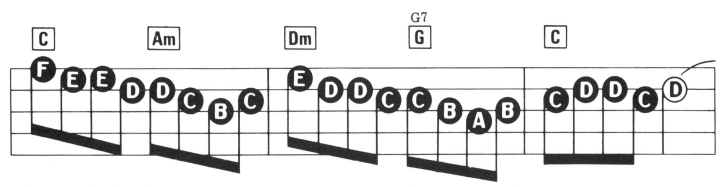

love was just a glance a-way, a warm em-brac-ing dance a-way and ev - er since that night____

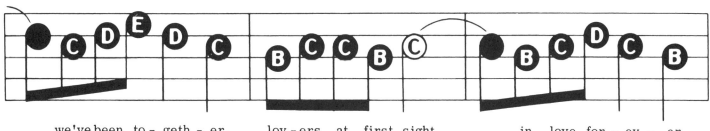

____ we've been to-geth - er, lov-ers at first sight____ in love for - ev - er.

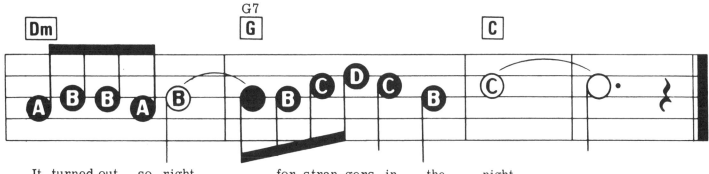

It turned out so right____ for stran-gers in the night.____

(Theme from)
A Summer Place

Registration 8
Rhythm: Slow Rock or Rock

Words by Mack Discant
Music by Max Steiner

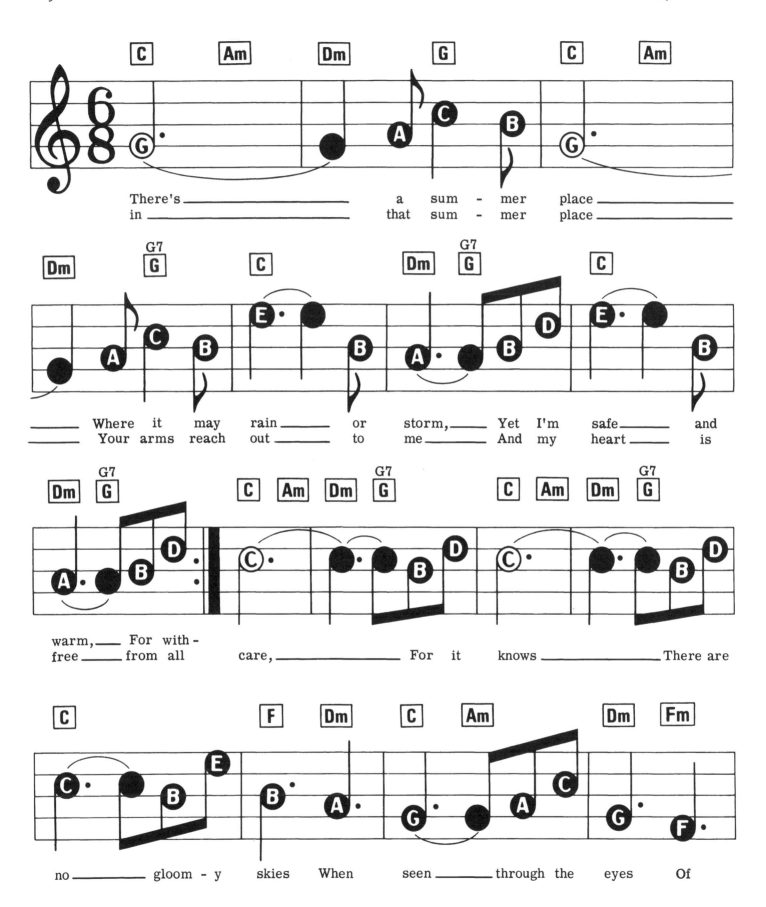

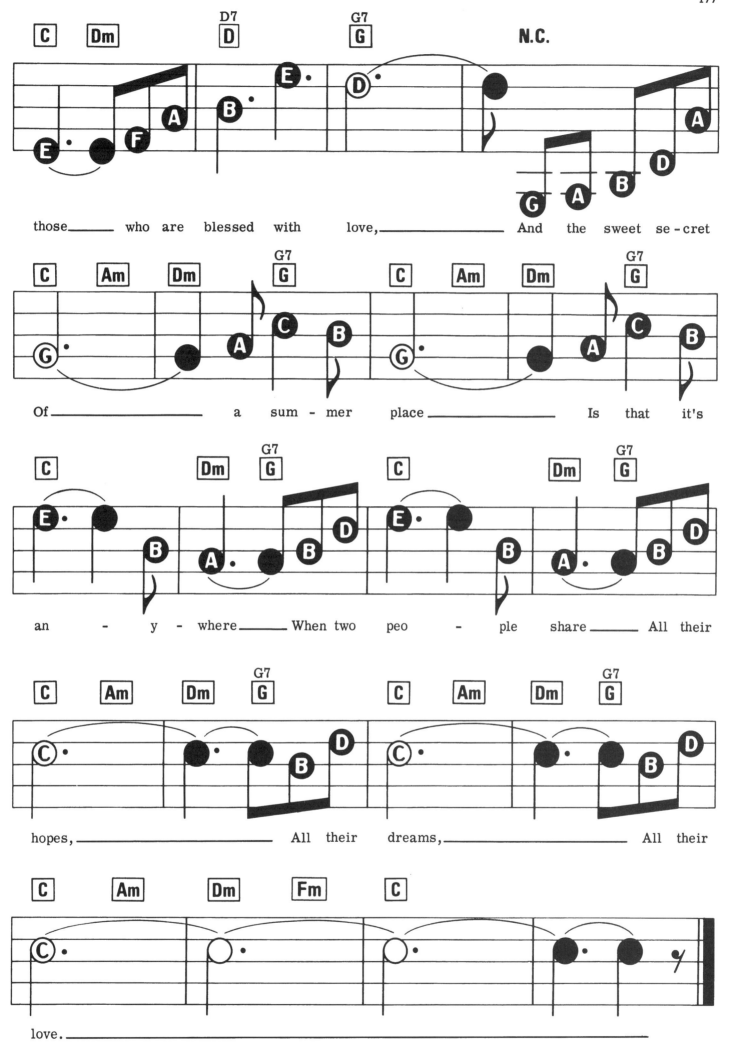

A Taste of Honey

Registration 9
Rhythm: Waltz

Words by Ric Marlow
Music by Bobby Scott

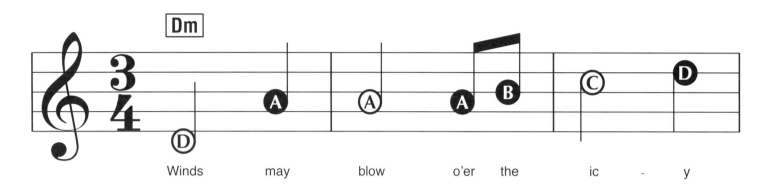

Winds may blow o'er the ic - y

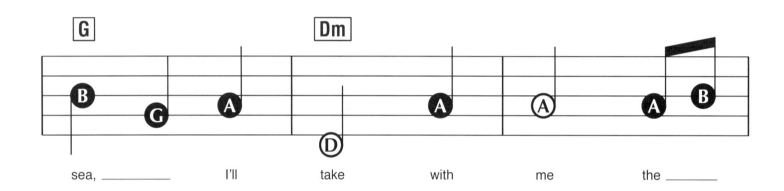

sea, _____ I'll take with me the _____

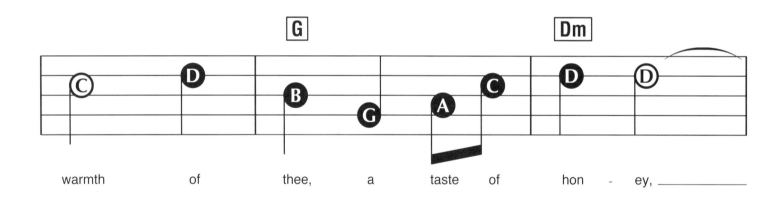

warmth of thee, a taste of hon - ey, _____

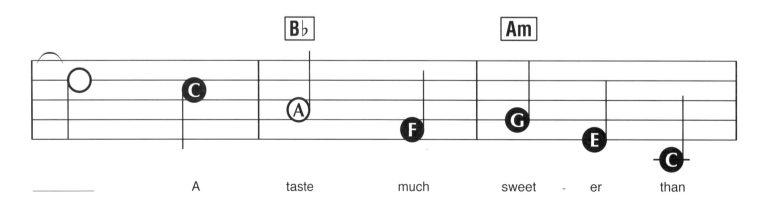

_____ A taste much sweet - er than

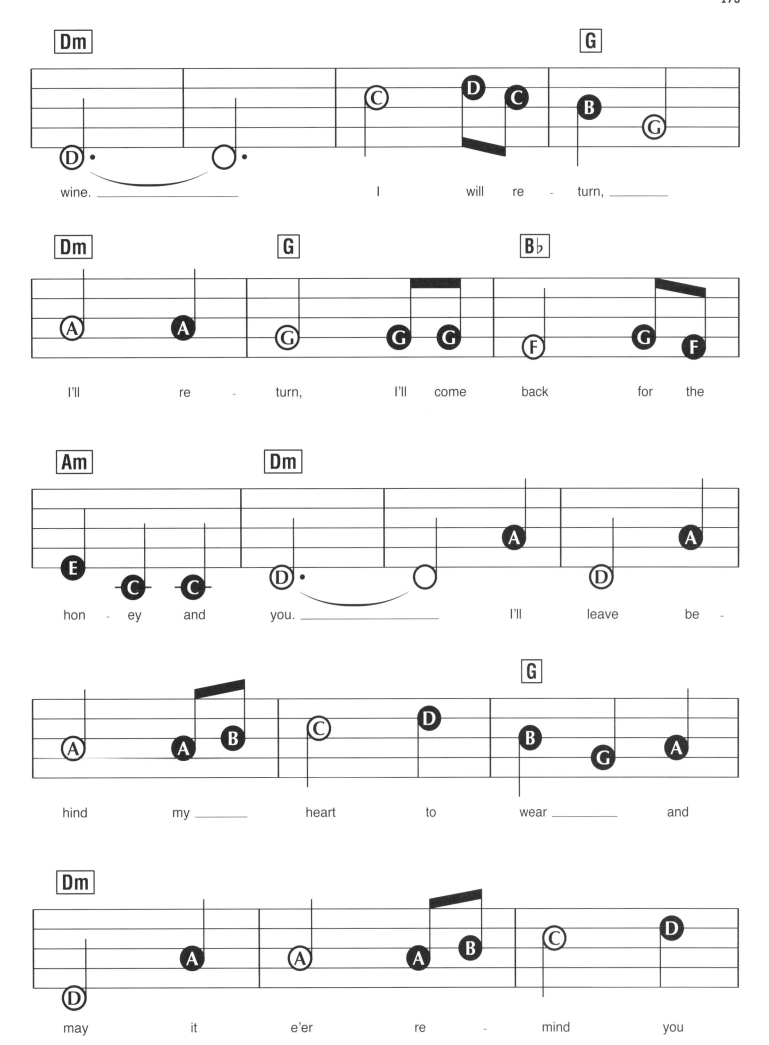

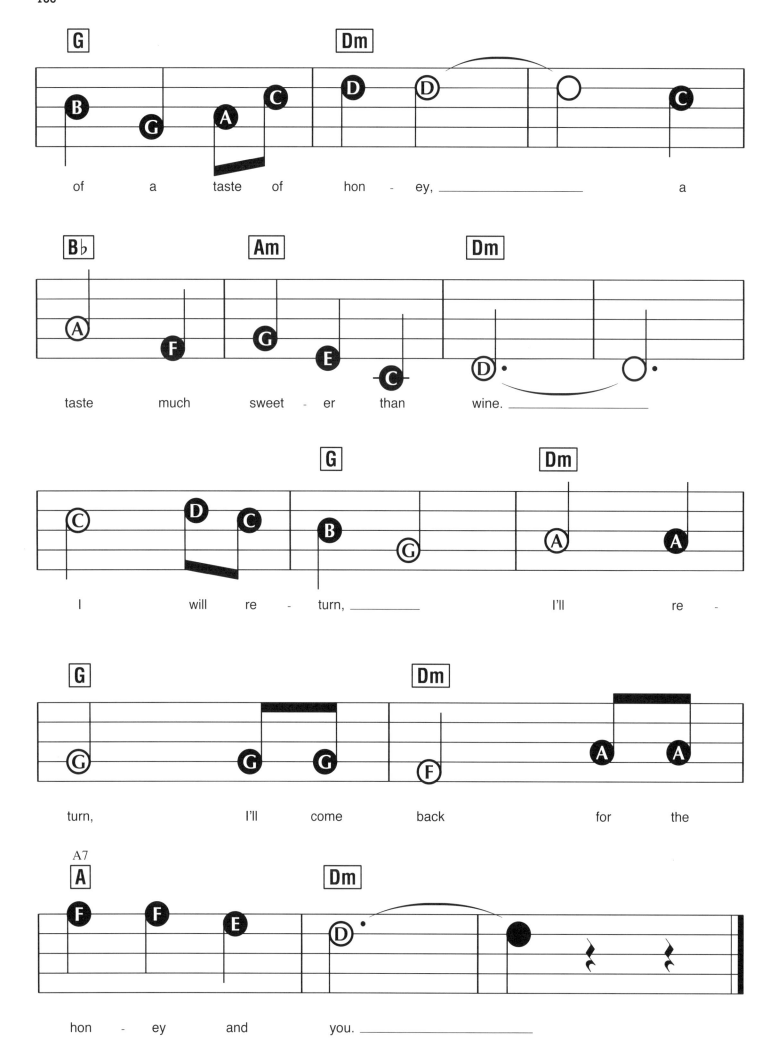

Tears in Heaven

Registration 8
Rhythm: 8-Beat or Ballad

Words and Music by Eric Clapton
and Will Jennings

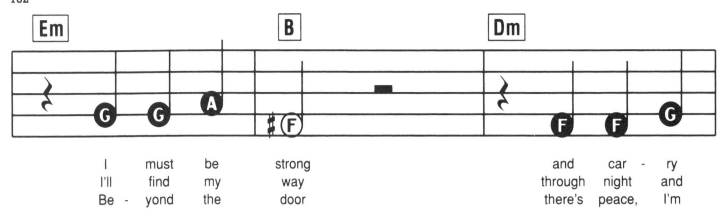

I must be strong
I'll find my way
Be - yond the door

and car - ry
through night and
there's peace, I'm

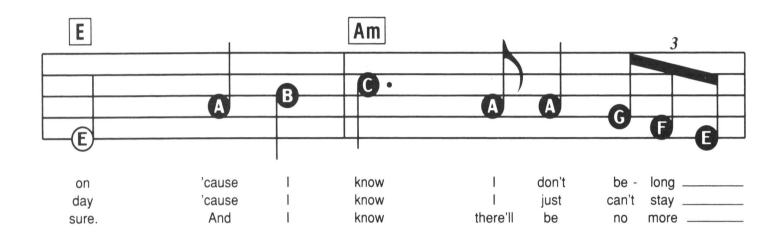

on 'cause I know I don't be - long _____
day 'cause I know I just can't stay _____
sure. And I know there'll be no more _____

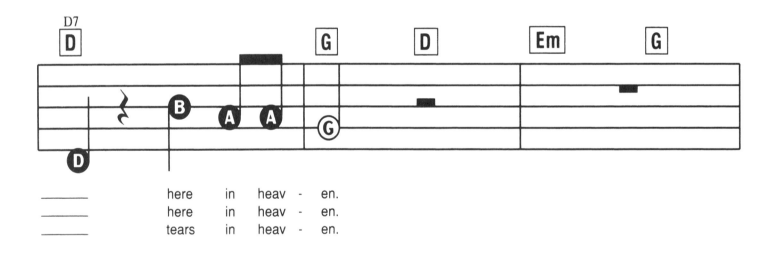

_____ here in heav - en.
_____ here in heav - en.
_____ tears in heav - en.

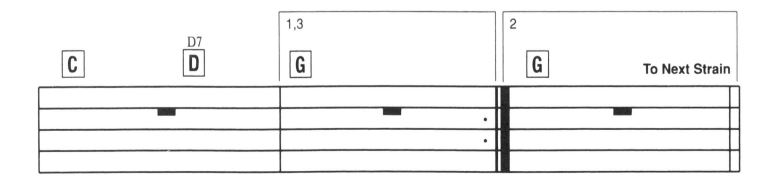

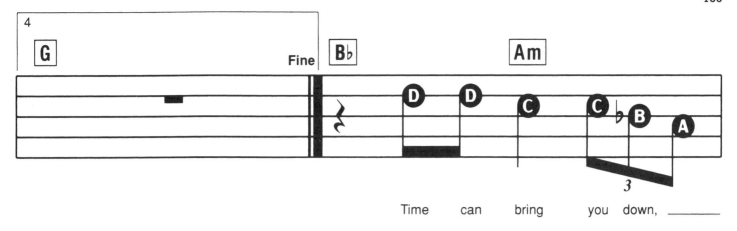

Time can bring you down, _____

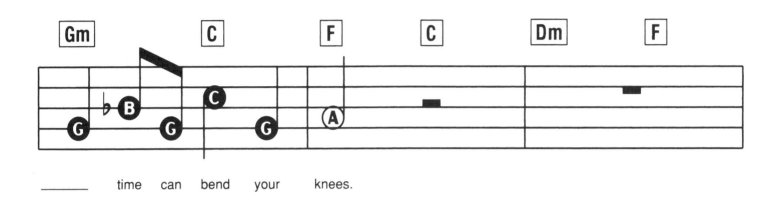

_____ time can bend your knees.

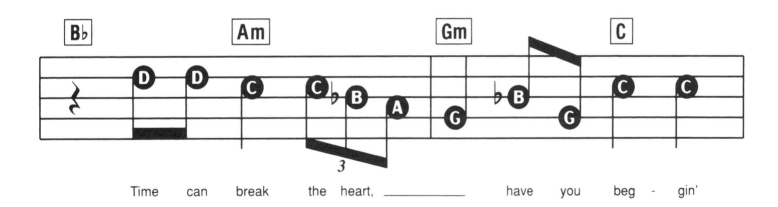

Time can break the heart, _____ have you beg - gin'

D.C. and Fade
(Return to beginning
and Fade)

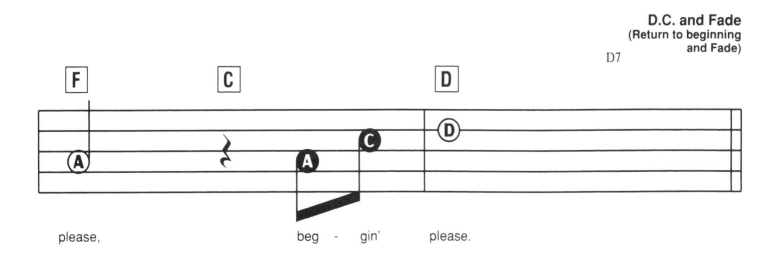

please, beg - gin' please.

This Masquerade

Registration 4
Rhythm: Bossa Nova or Latin

Words and Music by
Leon Russell

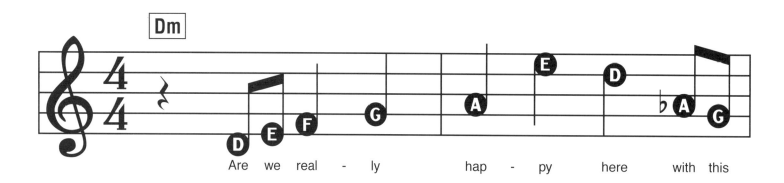

Are we real - ly hap - py here with this

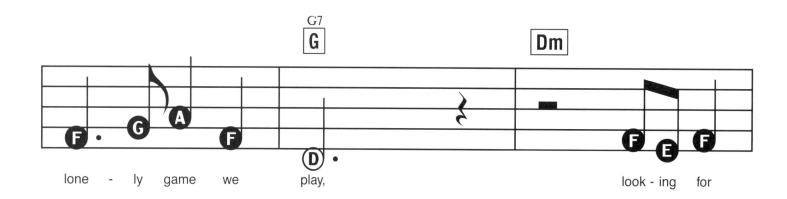

lone - ly game we play, look - ing for

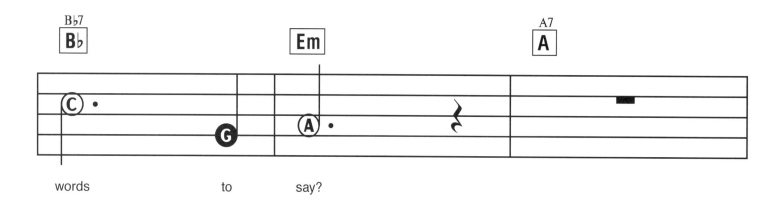

words to say?

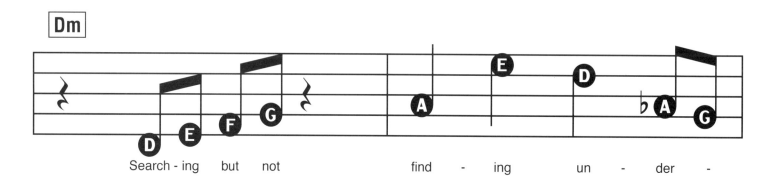

Search - ing but not find - ing un - der-

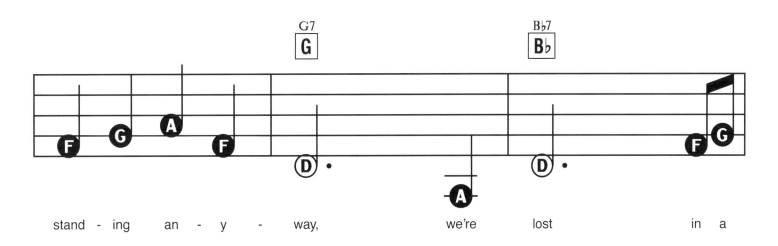

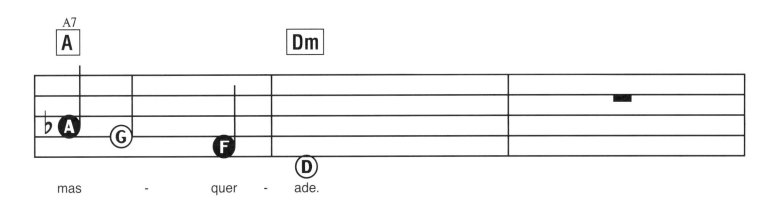

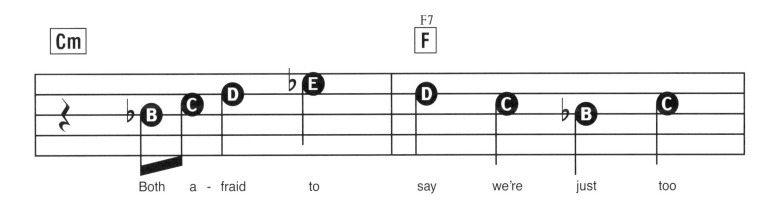

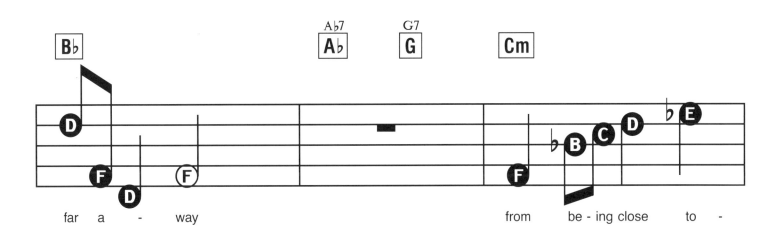

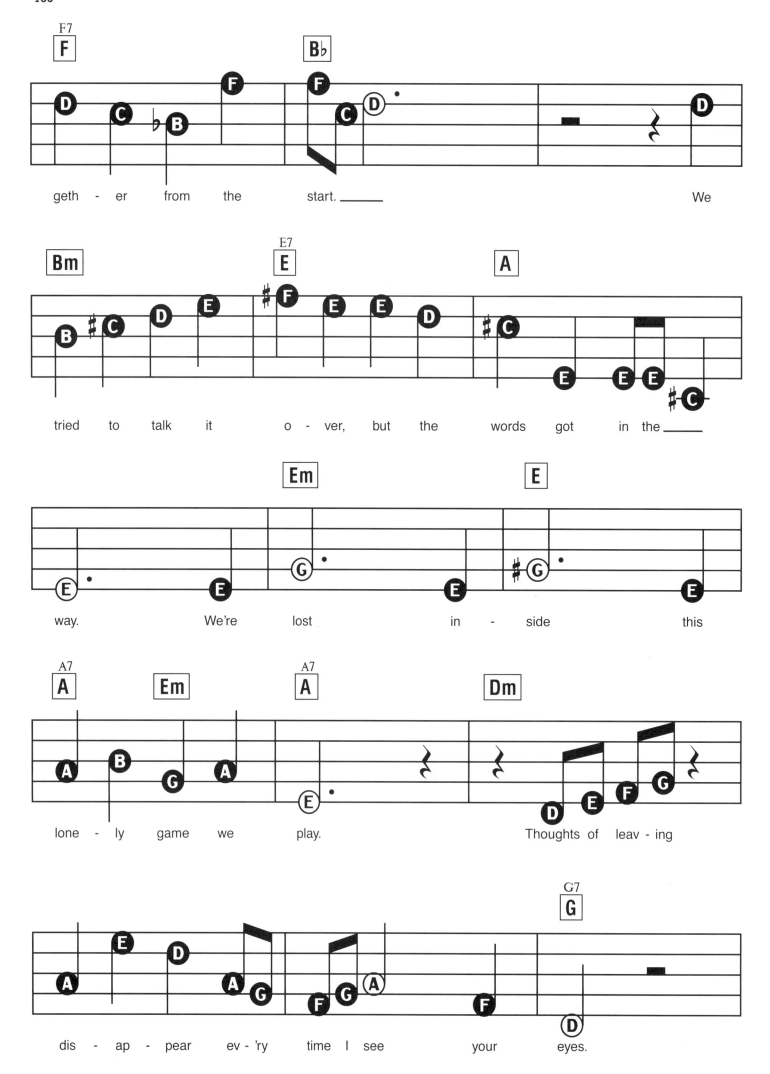

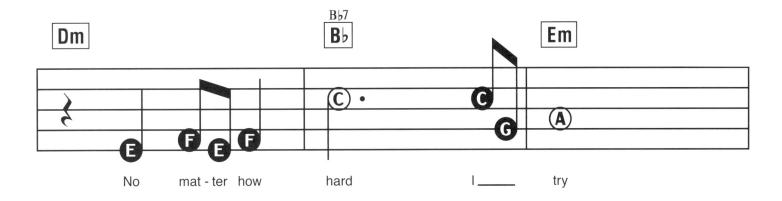

No mat - ter how hard I _____ try

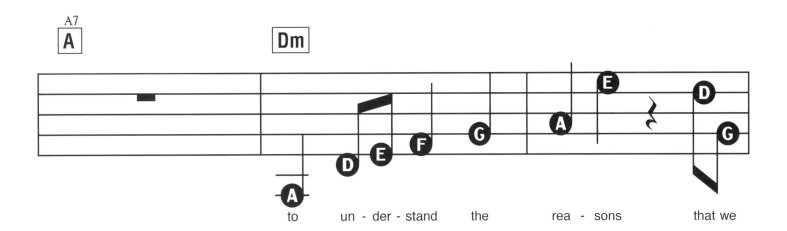

to un - der - stand the rea - sons that we

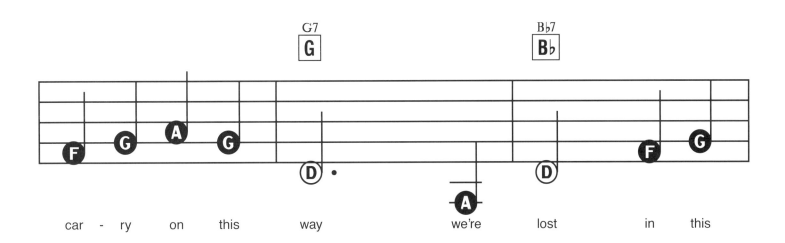

car - ry on this way we're lost in this

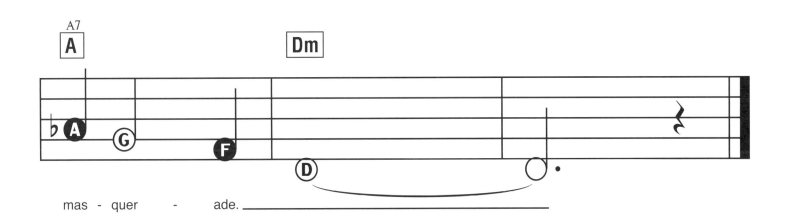

mas - quer - ade. _____

Unforgettable

Registration 3
Rhythm: Fox Trot or Swing

Words and Music by
Irving Gordon

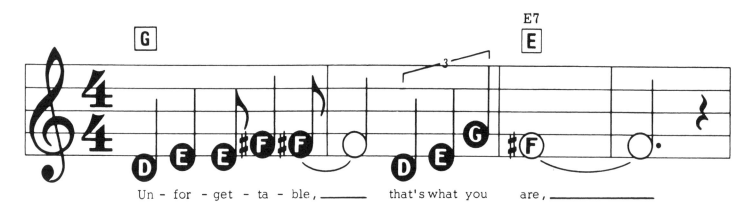

Un - for - get - ta - ble, _____ that's what you are, _____

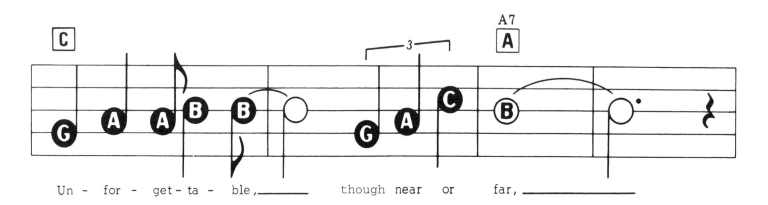

Un - for - get - ta - ble, _____ though near or far, _____

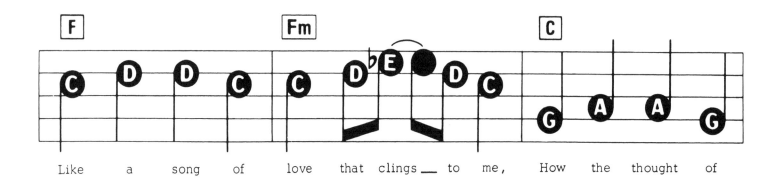

Like a song of love that clings __ to me, How the thought of

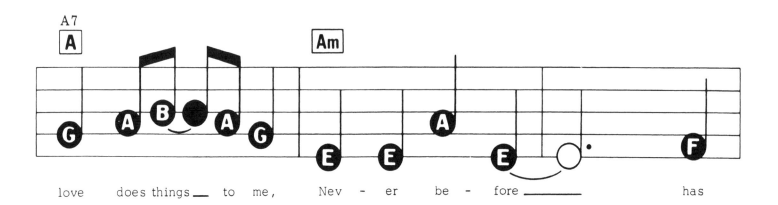

love does things __ to me, Nev - er be - fore _____ has

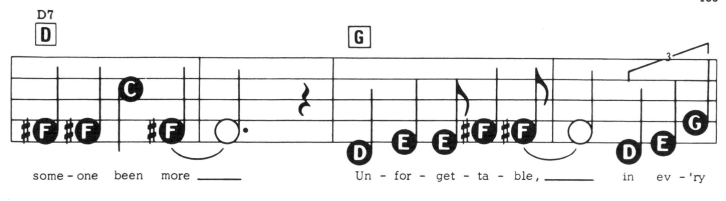

some - one been more _____ Un - for - get - ta - ble, _____ in ev - 'ry

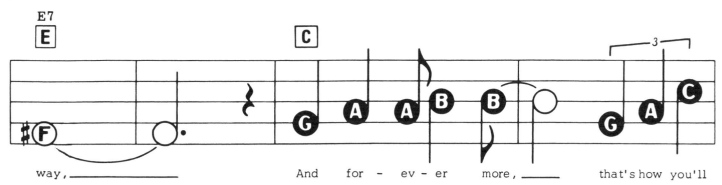

way, _____ And for - ev - er more, _____ that's how you'll

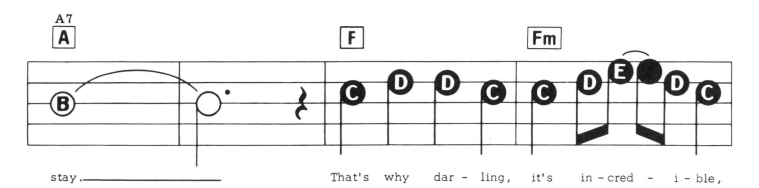

stay. _____ That's why dar - ling, it's in - cred - i - ble,

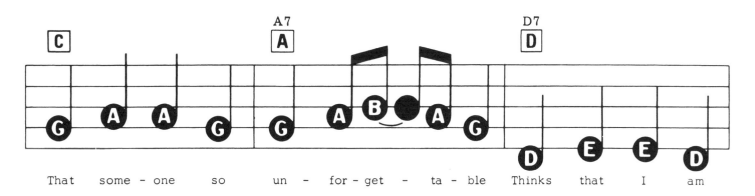

That some - one so un - for - get - ta - ble Thinks that I am

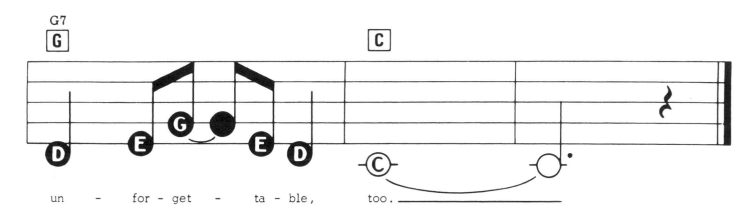

un - for - get - ta - ble, too. _____

Up, Up and Away

Registration 2
Rhythm: Rock or Jazz Rock

Words and Music by
Jimmy Webb

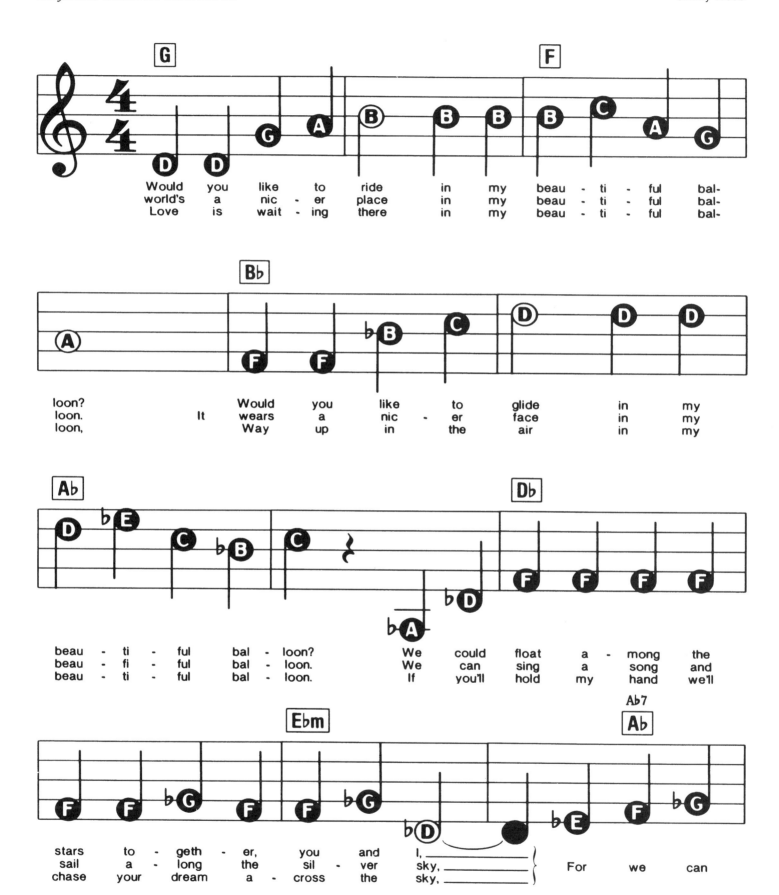

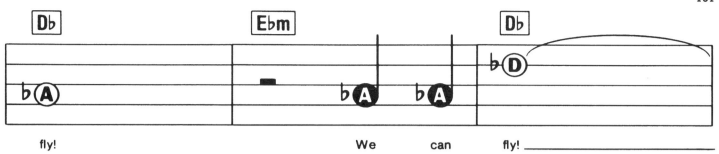

fly!   We   can   fly! _____

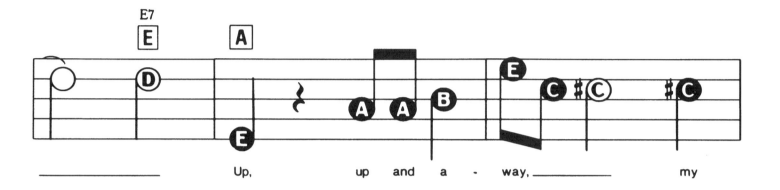

_____   Up,   up   and   a - way, _____   my

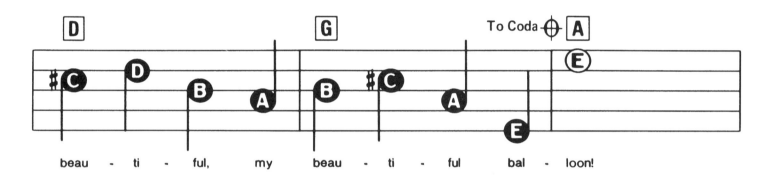

beau - ti - ful,   my   beau - ti - ful   bal - loon!

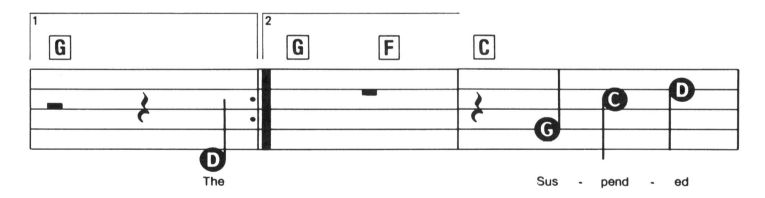

The   Sus - pend - ed

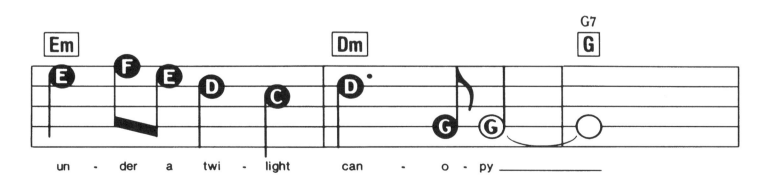

un - der a twi - light   can - o - py _____

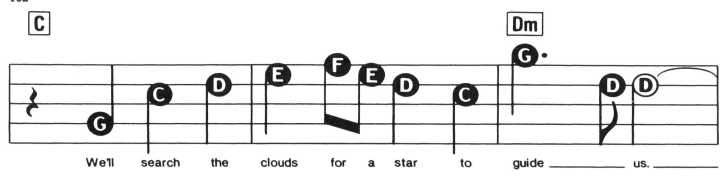

We'll search the clouds for a star to guide _____ us. _____

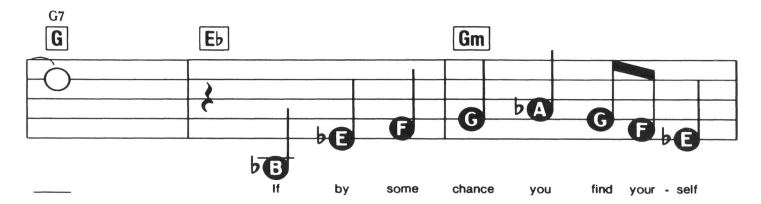

_____ If by some chance you find your - self

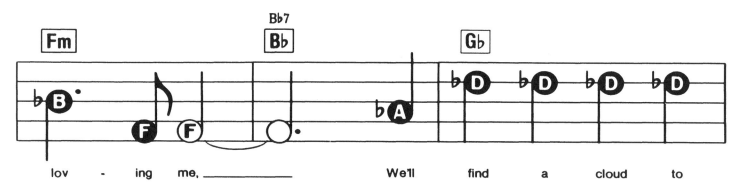

lov - ing me, _____ We'll find a cloud to

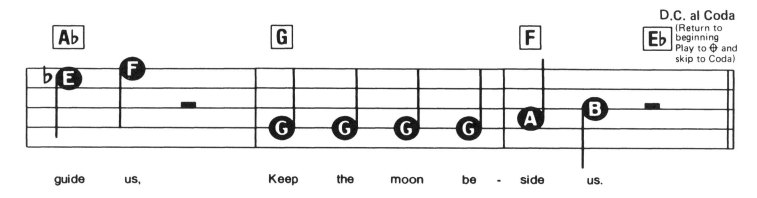

guide us, Keep the moon be - side us.

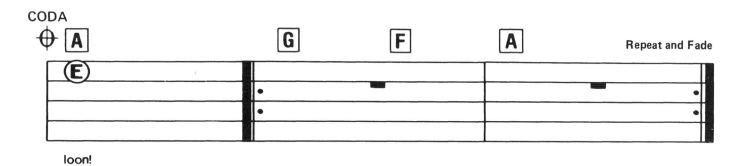

loon!

Use Somebody

Registration 4
Rhythm: Rock

Words and Music by Caleb Followill,
Nathan Followill, Jared Followill
and Matthew Followill

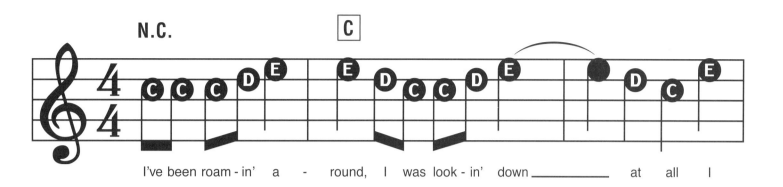

I've been roam-in' a - round, I was look-in' down _____ at all I

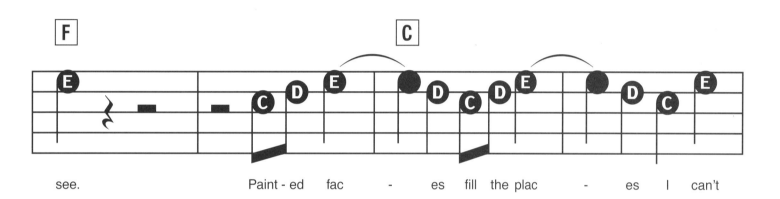

see. Paint - ed fac - es fill the plac - es I can't

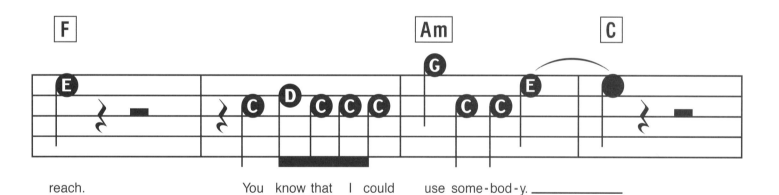

reach. You know that I could use some-bod-y. _____

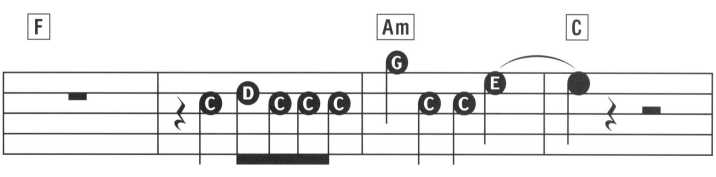

You know that I could use some-bod-y. _____

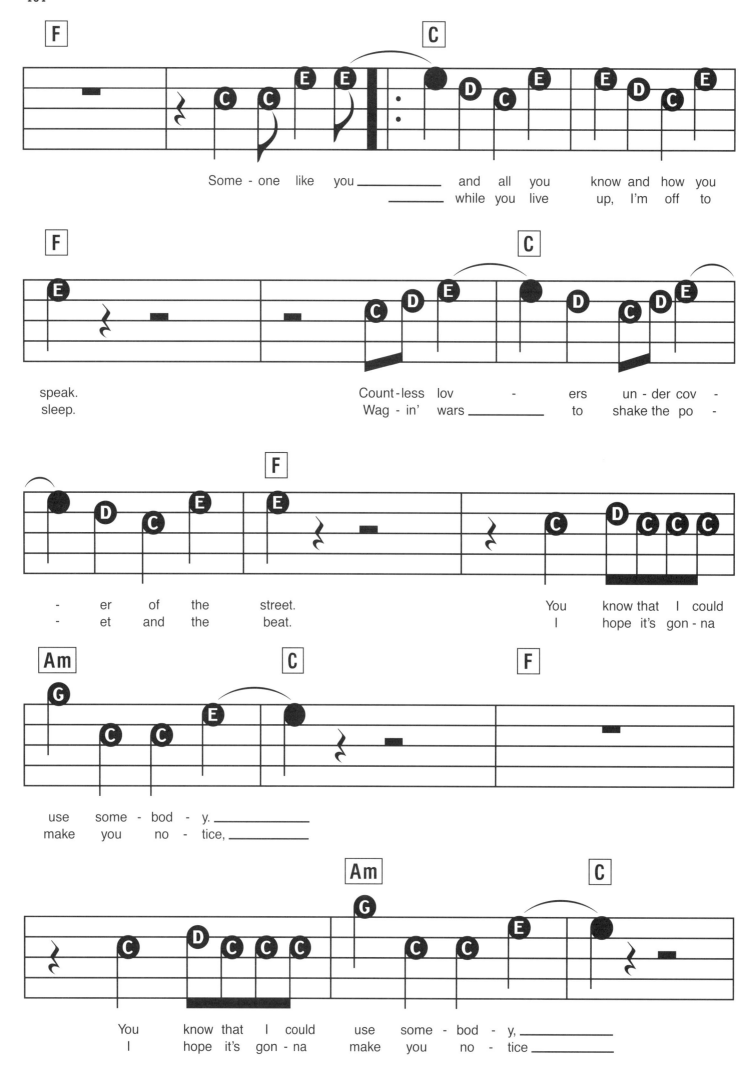

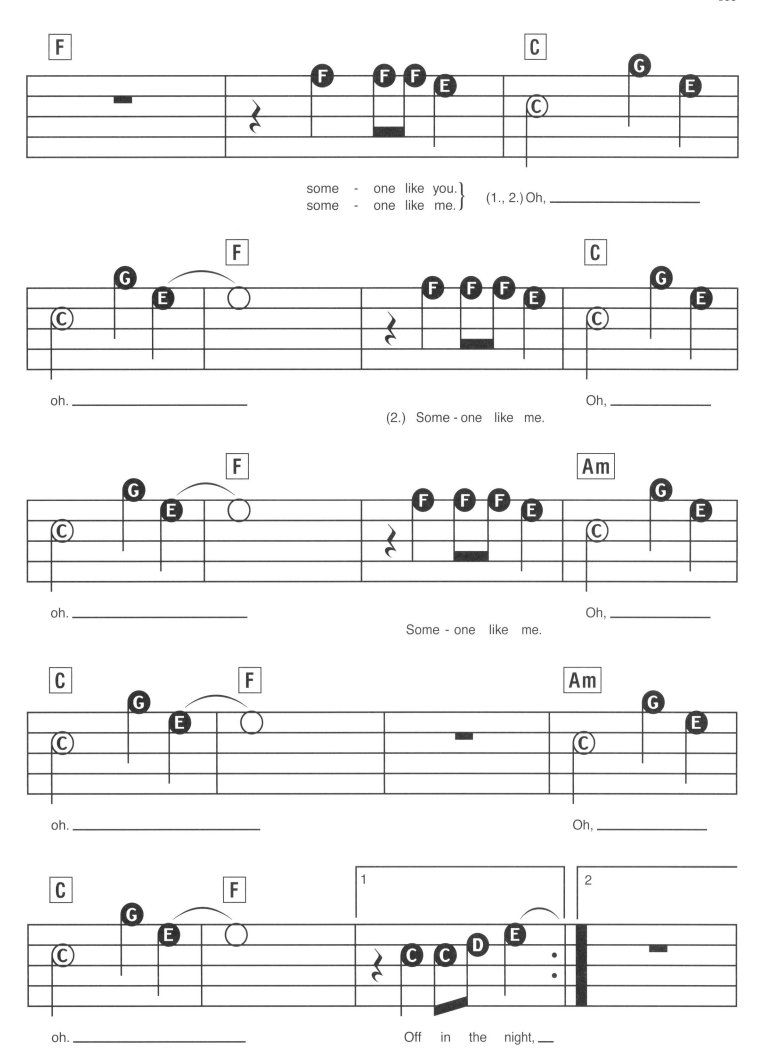

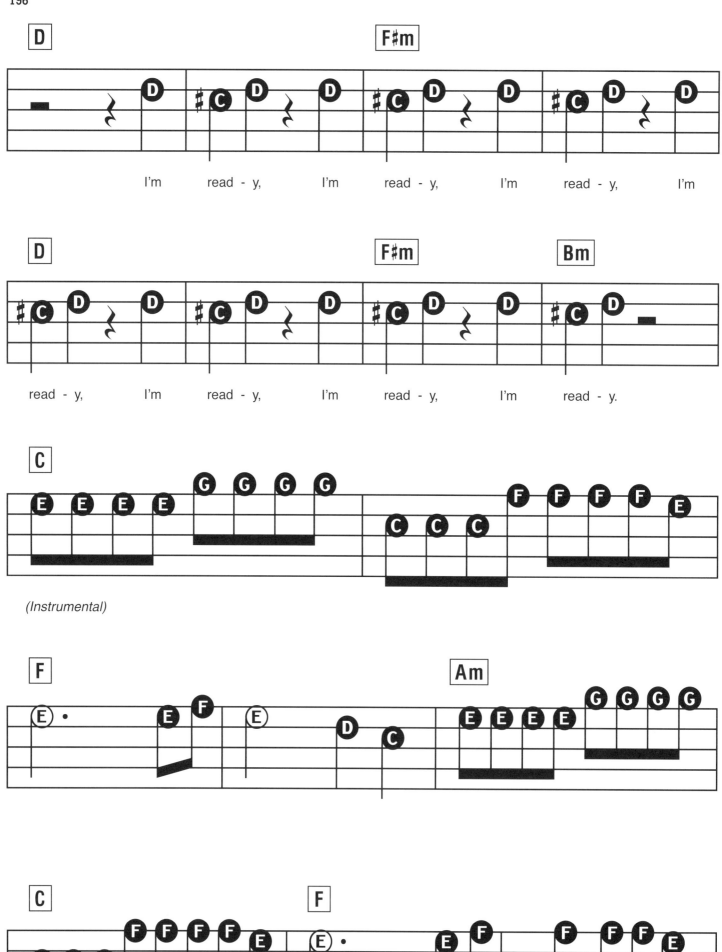

(Instrumental)

Some - one like you,

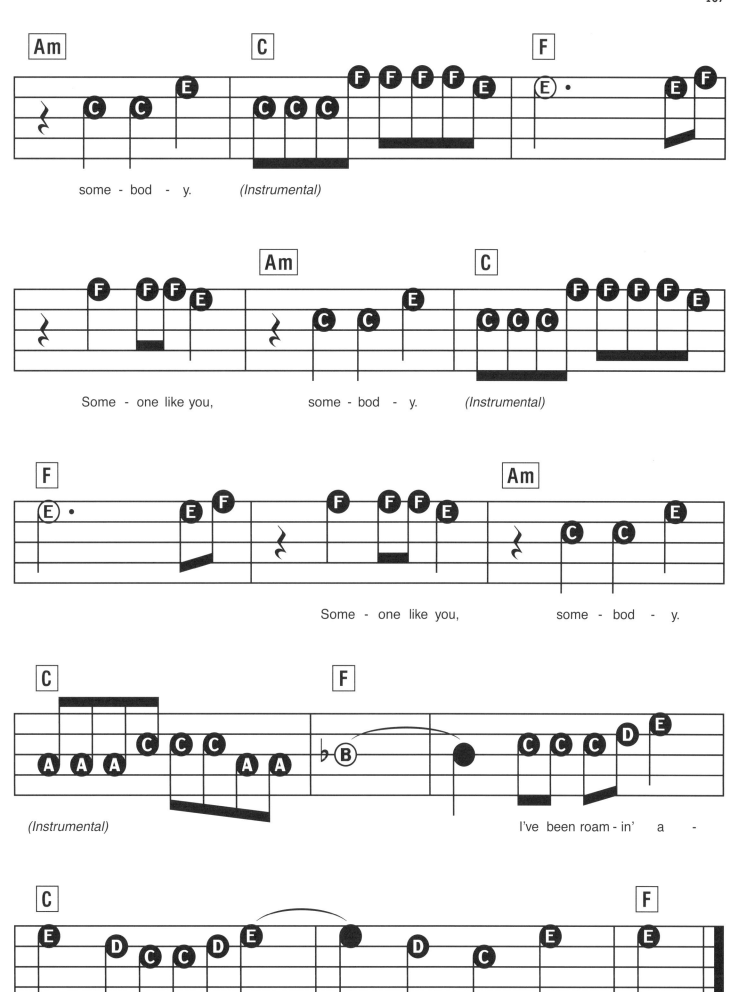

Walk On
Dedicated to Aung San Suu Kyi

Registration 4
Rhythm: 8-Beat or Rock

Words by Bono
Music by U2

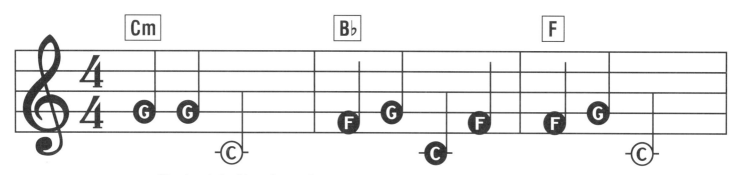

(Spoken:) And love is not the easy thing, the only baggage that you can bring. Love, not the easy

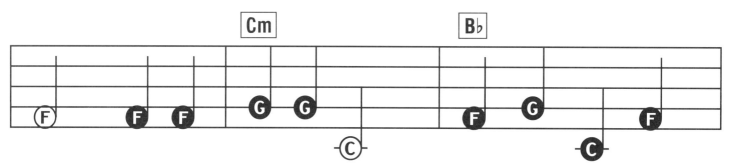

thing. The only baggage you can bring is all that you can't leave behind.   (Instrumental)

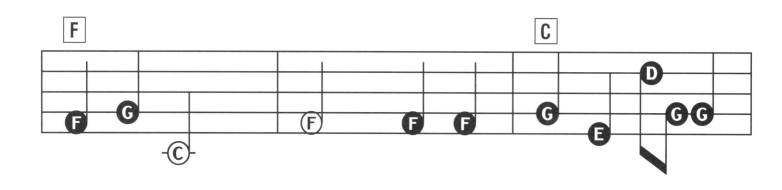

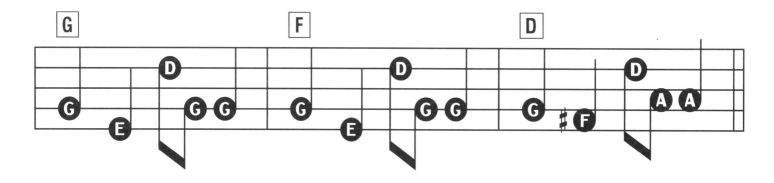

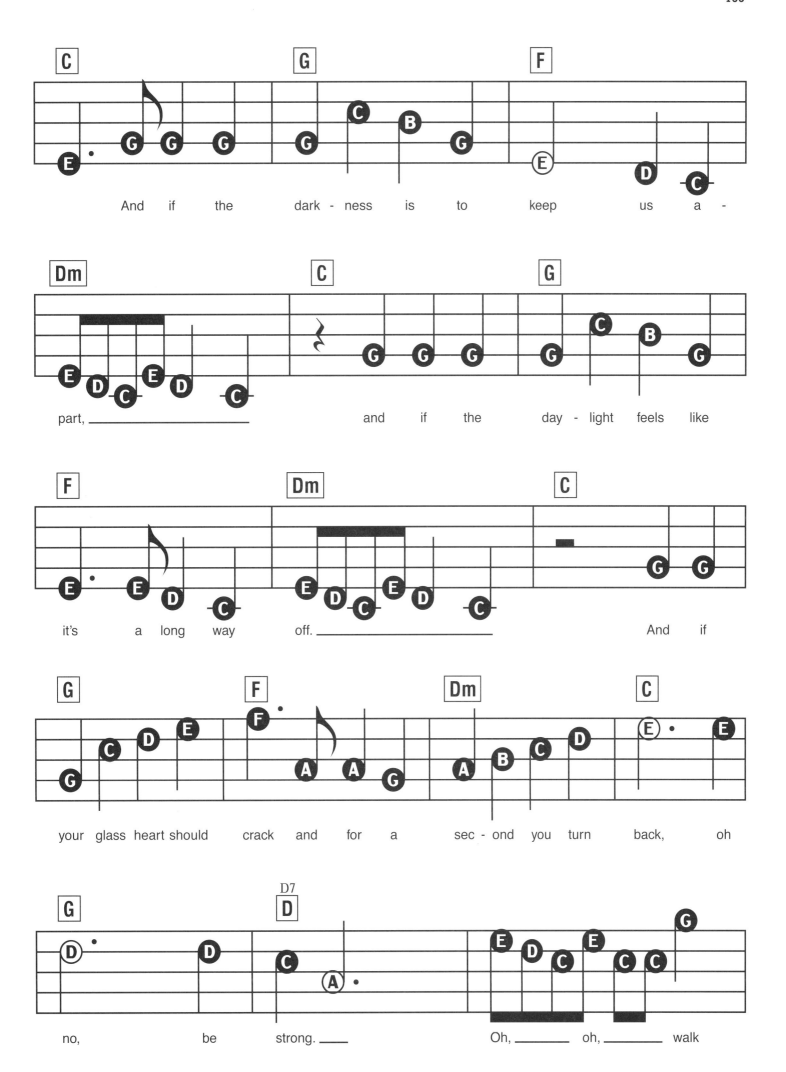

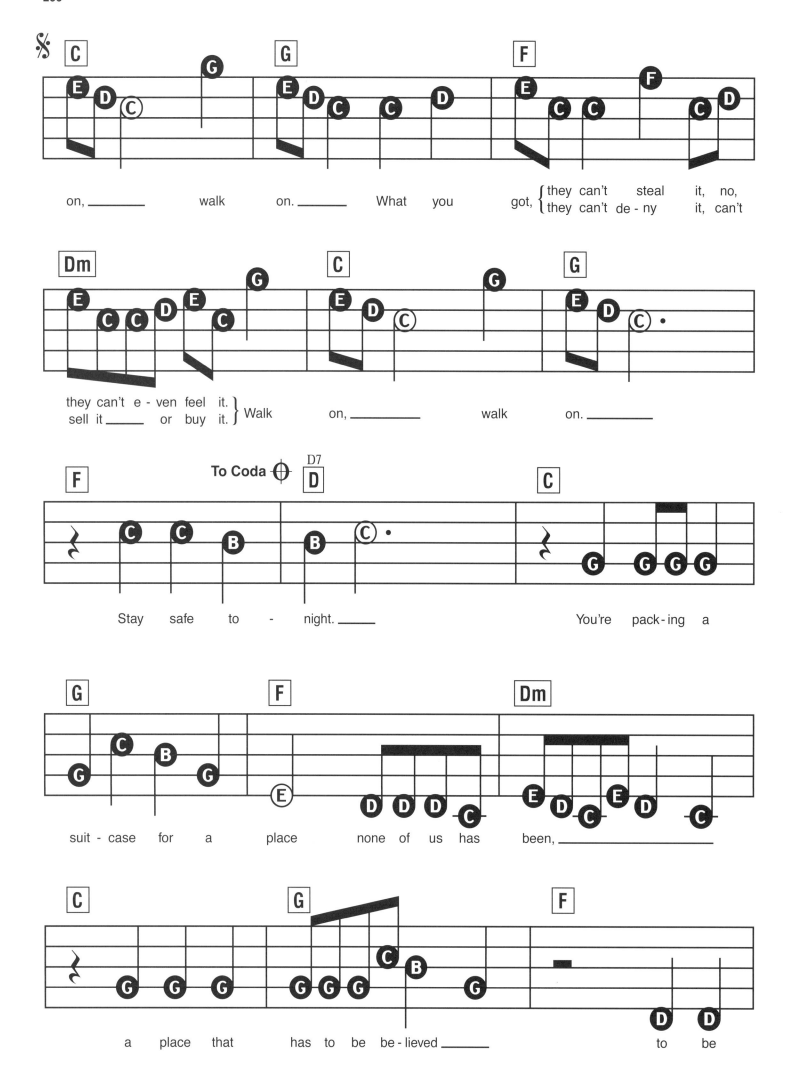

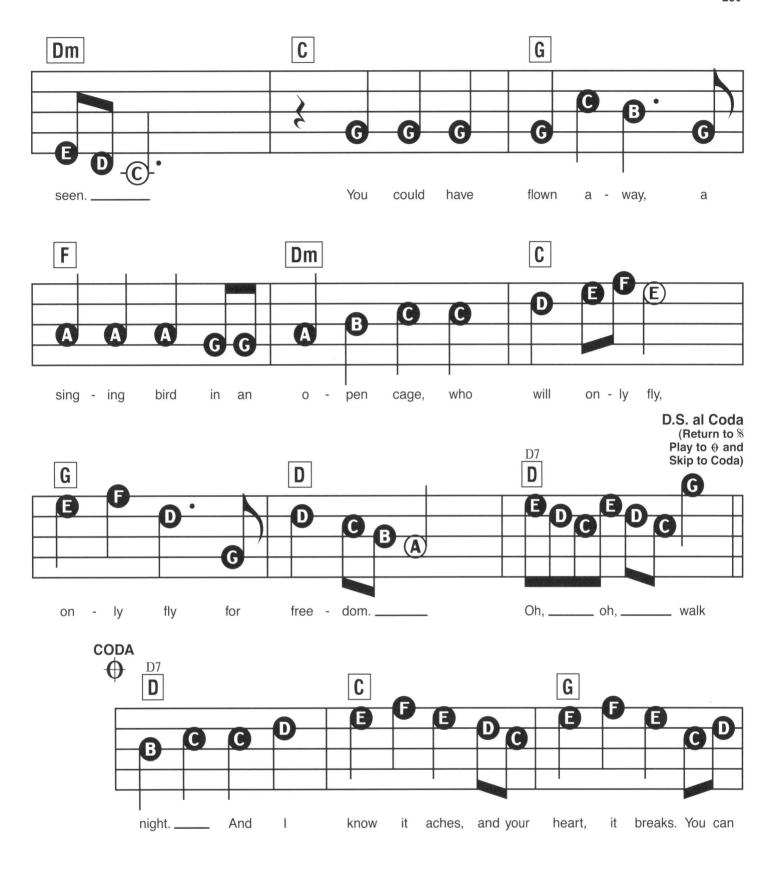

D.S. al Coda
(Return to ※
Play to ⊕ and
Skip to Coda)

CODA

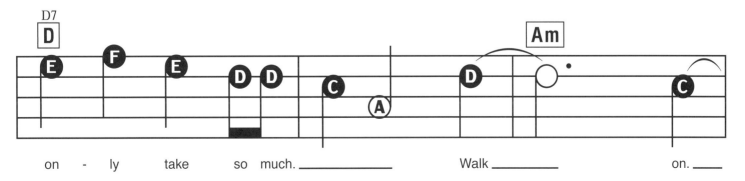

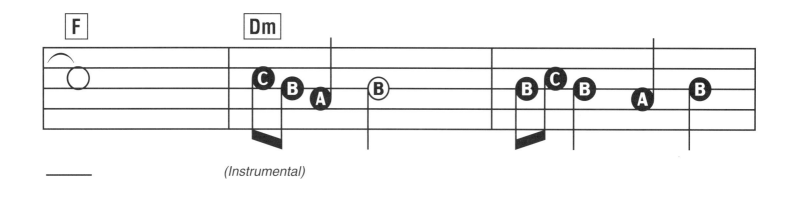

_____ *(Instrumental)*

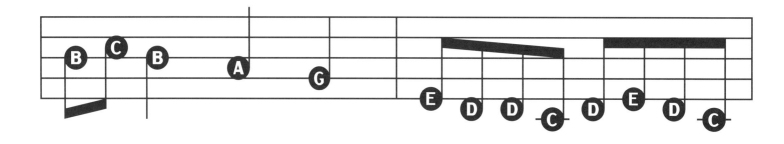

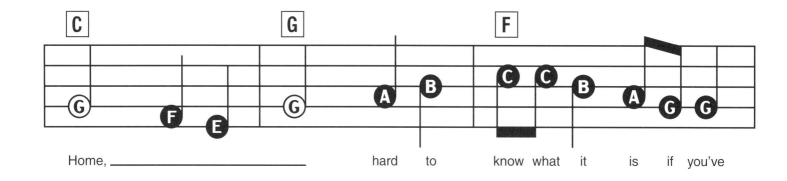

Home, _____ hard to know what it is if you've

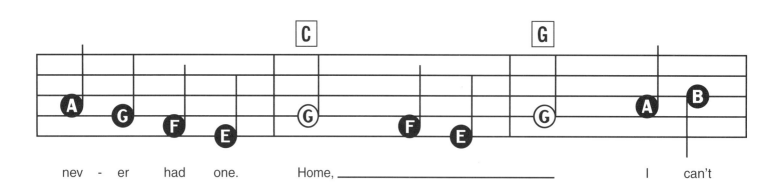

nev - er had one. Home, _____ I can't

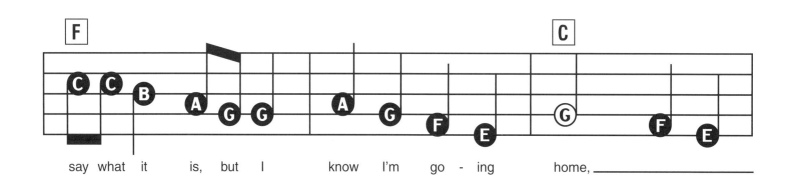

say what it is, but I know I'm go - ing home, _____

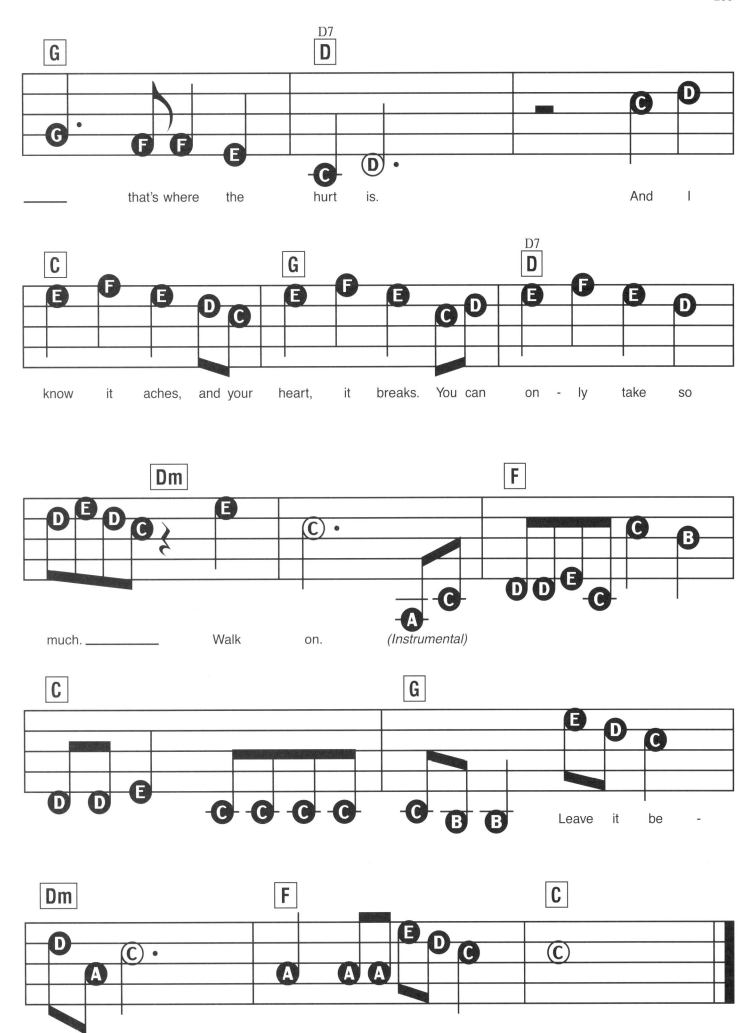

We Are the World

Registration 3
Rhythm: Pops or 8-Beat

Words and Music by Lionel Richie
and Michael Jackson

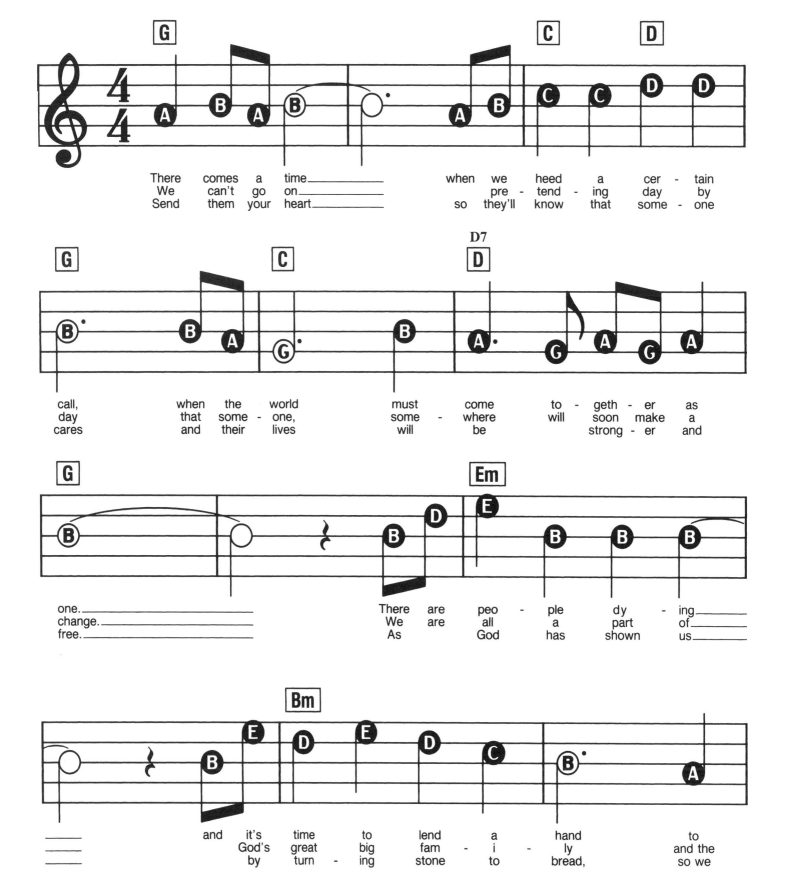

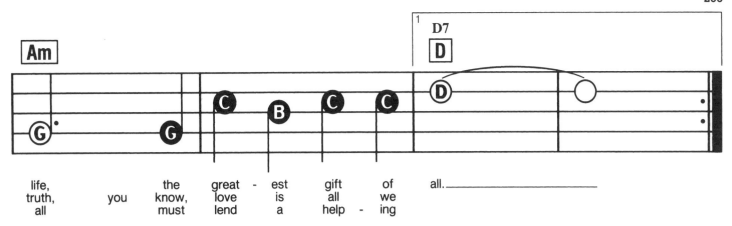

life, you the great - est gift of all. _____
truth, you know, love is all we
all must lend a help - ing

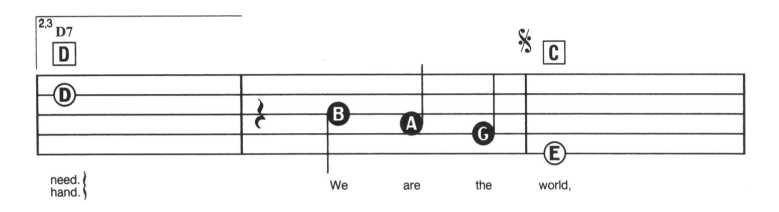

need. }
hand. } We are the world,

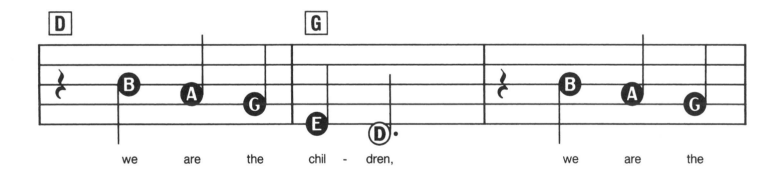

we are the chil - dren, we are the

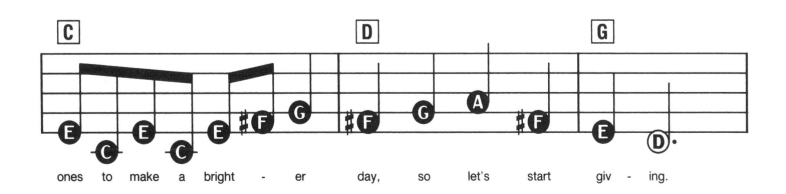

ones to make a bright - er day, so let's start giv - ing.

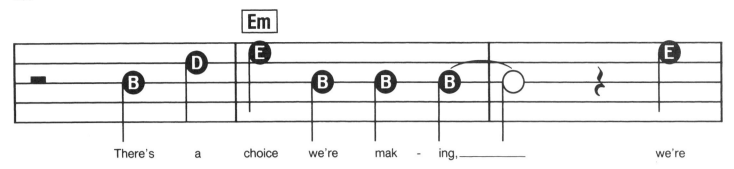

There's a choice we're mak - ing,_____ we're

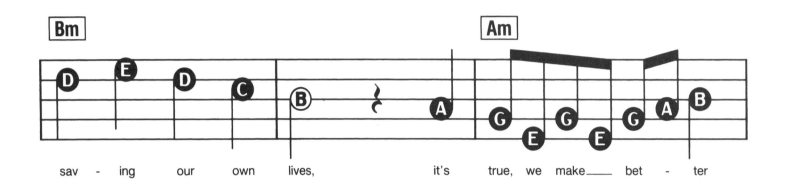

sav - ing our own lives, it's true, we make___ bet - ter

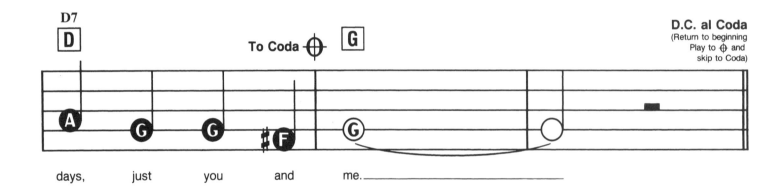

days, just you and me._____

D.C. al Coda
(Return to beginning
Play to ⊕ and
skip to Coda)

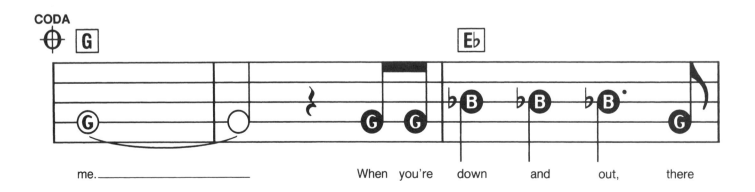

me._____ When you're down and out, there

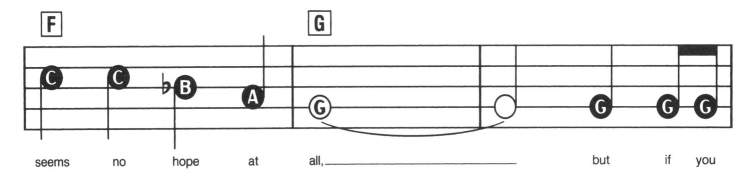

seems no hope at all, _____ but if you

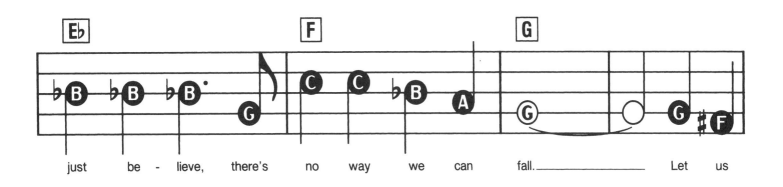

just be - lieve, there's no way we can fall. _____ Let us

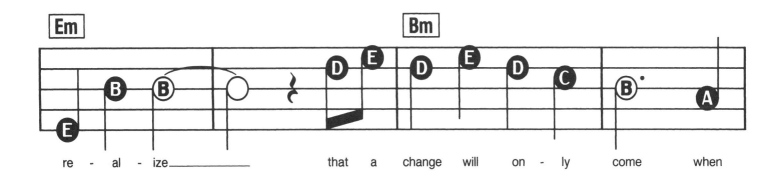

re - al - ize _____ that a change will on - ly come when

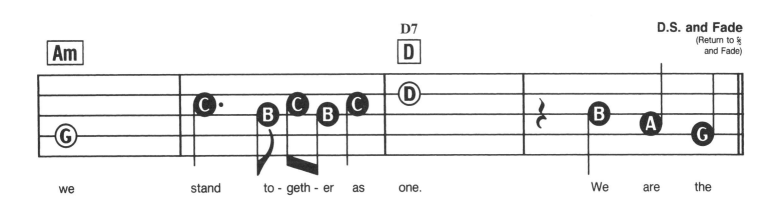

we stand to - geth - er as one. We are the

What a Fool Believes

Registration 5
Rhythm: Rock or Disco

Words and Music by Michael McDonald
and Kenny Loggins

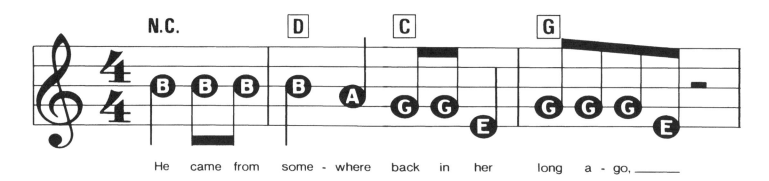

He came from some-where back in her long a-go, _____

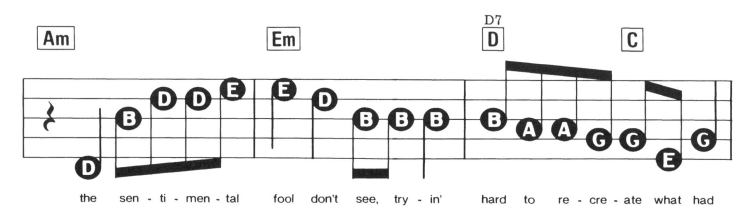

the sen-ti-men-tal fool don't see, try-in' hard to re-cre-ate what had

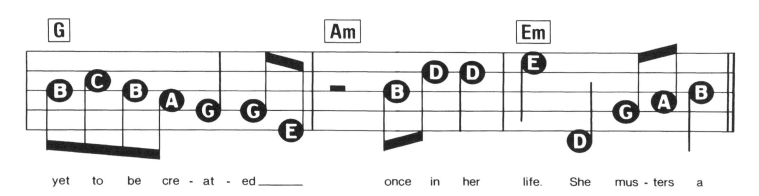

yet to be cre-at-ed _____ once in her life. She mus-ters a

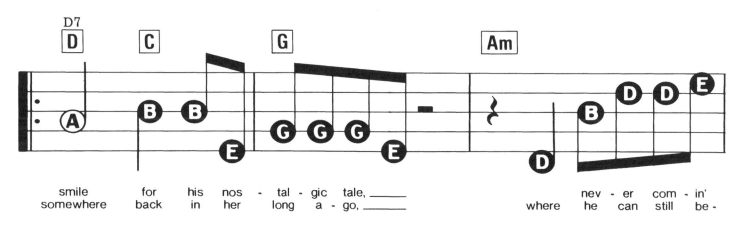

smile for his nos-tal-gic tale, _____ nev-er com-in'
somewhere back in her long a-go, _____ where he can still be-

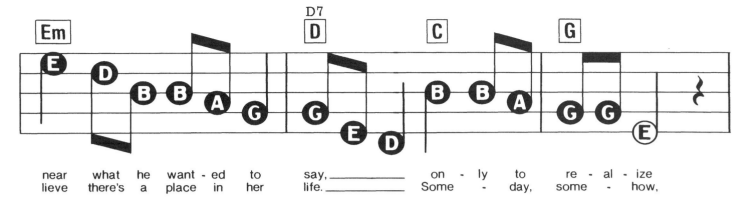

near what he want-ed to say,_____ on - ly to re - al -ize
lieve there's a place in her life._____ Some - day, some - how,

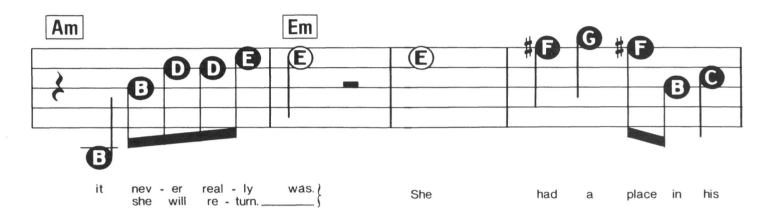

it nev - er real - ly was.
she will re - turn._____ She had a place in his

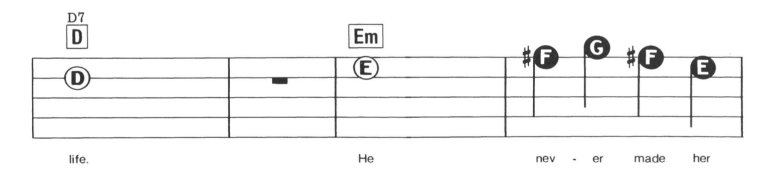

life. He nev - er made her

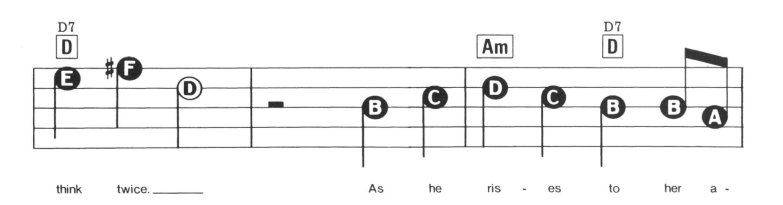

think twice._____ As he ris - es to her a-

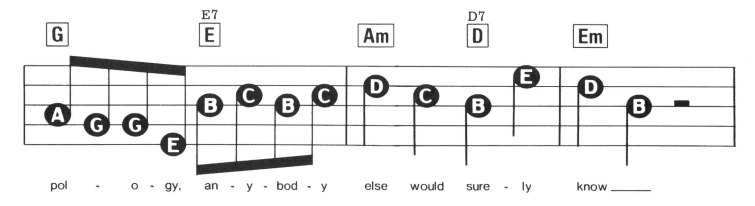

pol - o - gy, an - y - bod - y else would sure - ly know _____

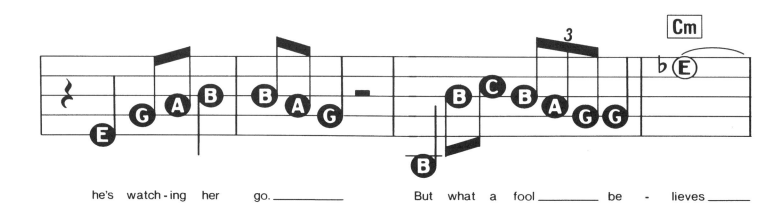

he's watch - ing her go. _____ But what a fool _____ be - lieves _____

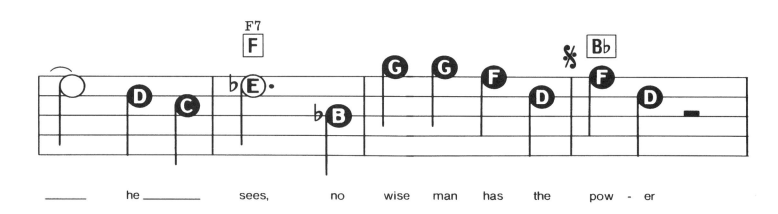

_____ he _____ sees, no wise man has the pow - er

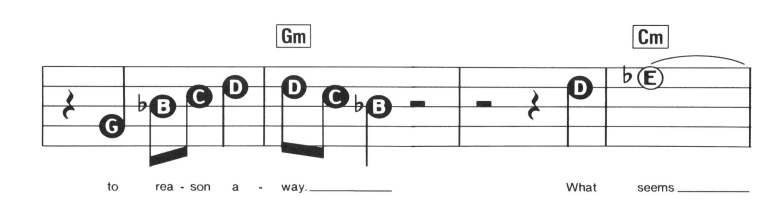

to rea - son a - way. _____ What seems _____

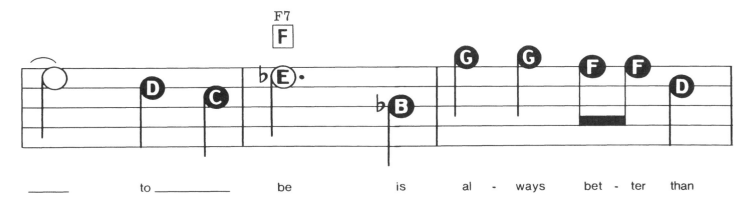

to _____ be   is al - ways bet - ter than

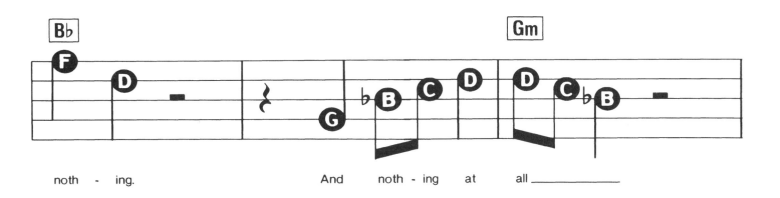

noth - ing.   And noth - ing at all _____

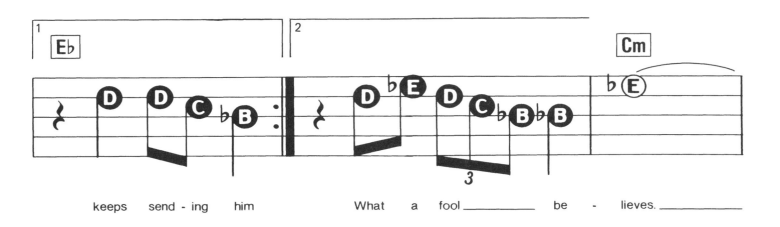

keeps send - ing him   What a fool _____ be - lieves. _____

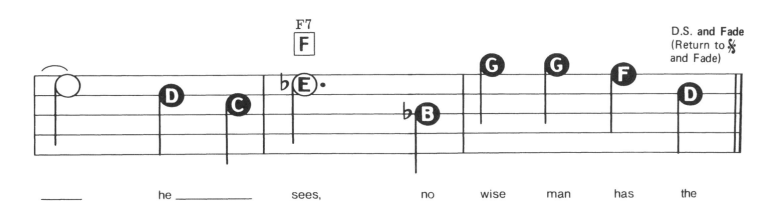

_____ he _____ sees,   no wise man has the

What's Love Got to Do with It

Registration 7
Rhythm: Slow Rock

Words and Music by Terry Britten
and Graham Lyle

213

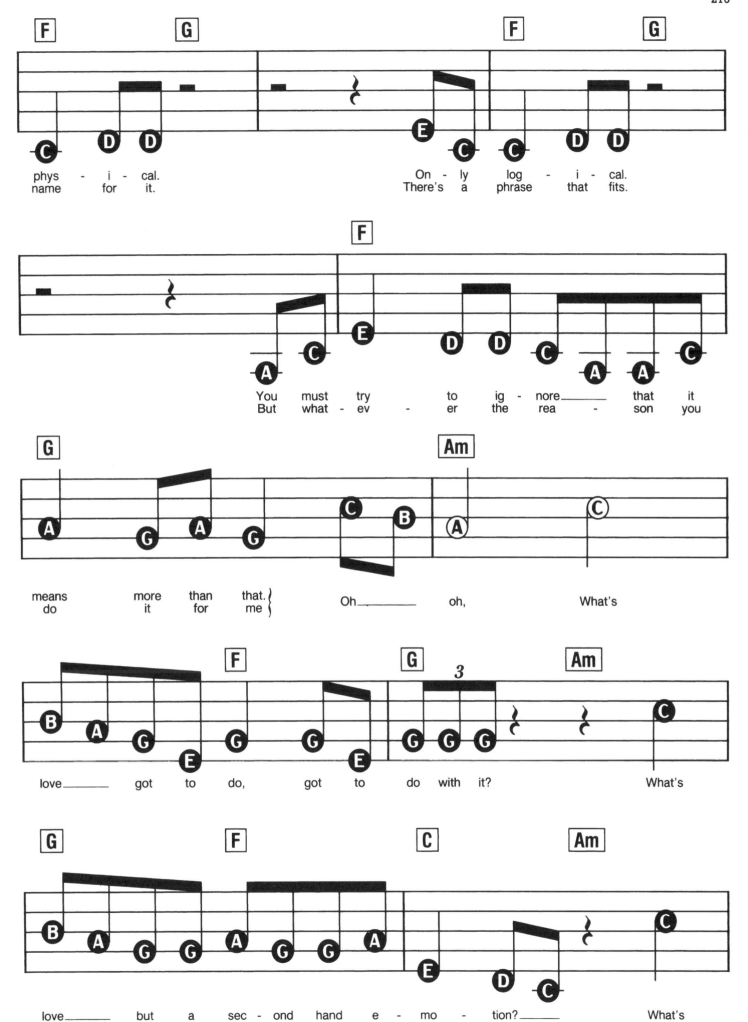

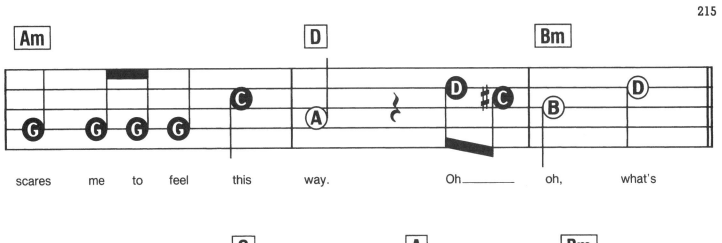

scares me to feel this way. Oh___ oh, what's

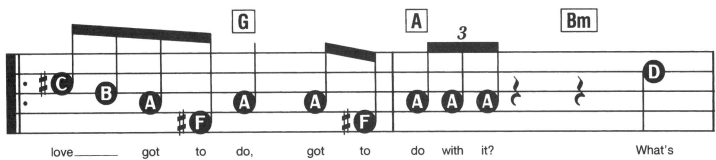

love___ got to do, got to do with it? What's

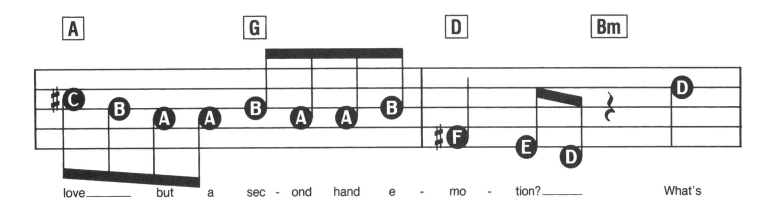

love___ but a sec - ond hand e - mo - tion?___ What's

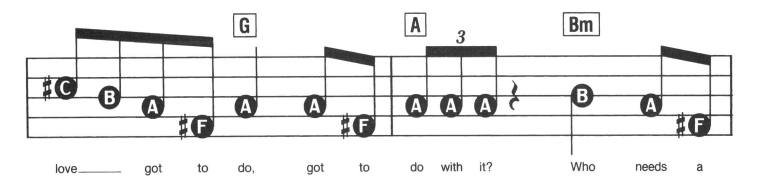

love___ got to do, got to do with it? Who needs a

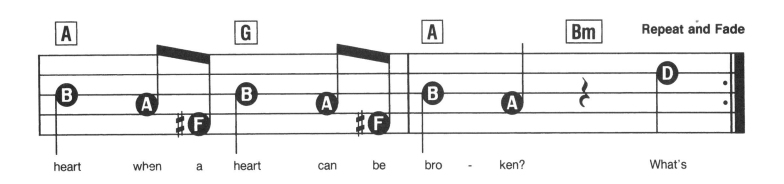

heart when a heart can be bro - ken? What's

The Wind Beneath My Wings

Registration 3
Rhythm: Rock

Words and Music by Larry Henley
and Jeff Silbar

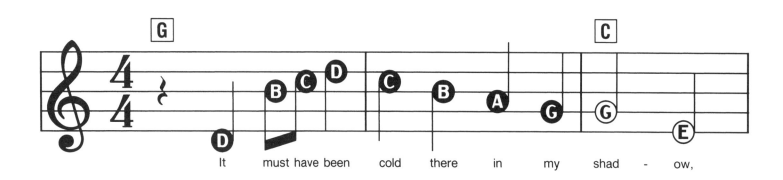

It must have been cold there in my shad - ow,

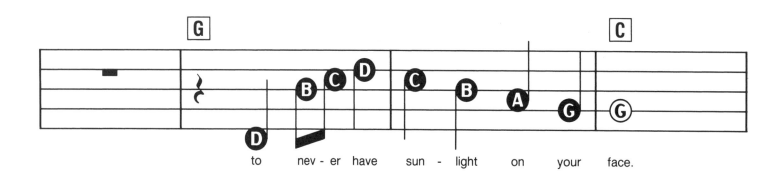

to nev - er have sun - light on your face.

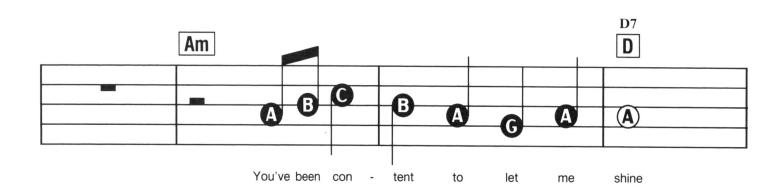

You've been con - tent to let me shine

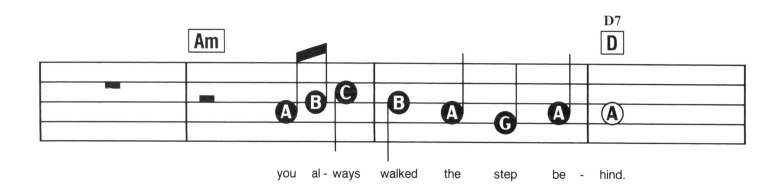

you al - ways walked the step be - hind.

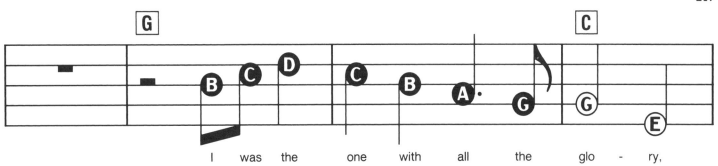

I was the one with all the glo - ry,

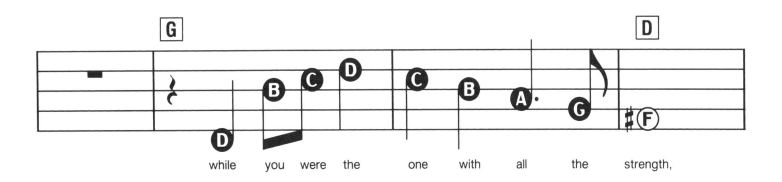

while you were the one with all the strength,

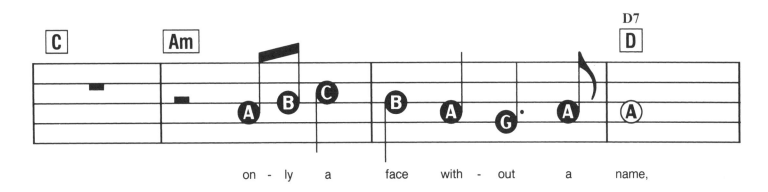

on - ly a face with - out a name,

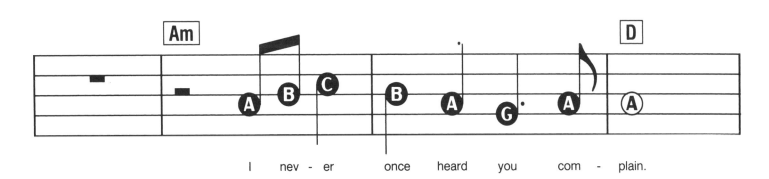

I nev - er once heard you com - plain.

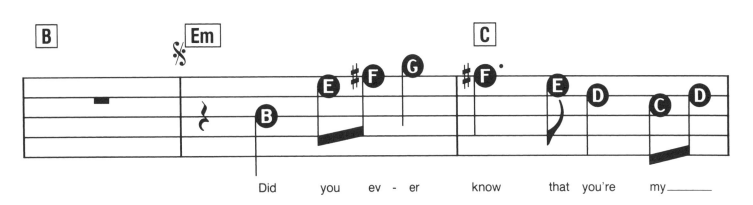

Did you ev - er know that you're my____

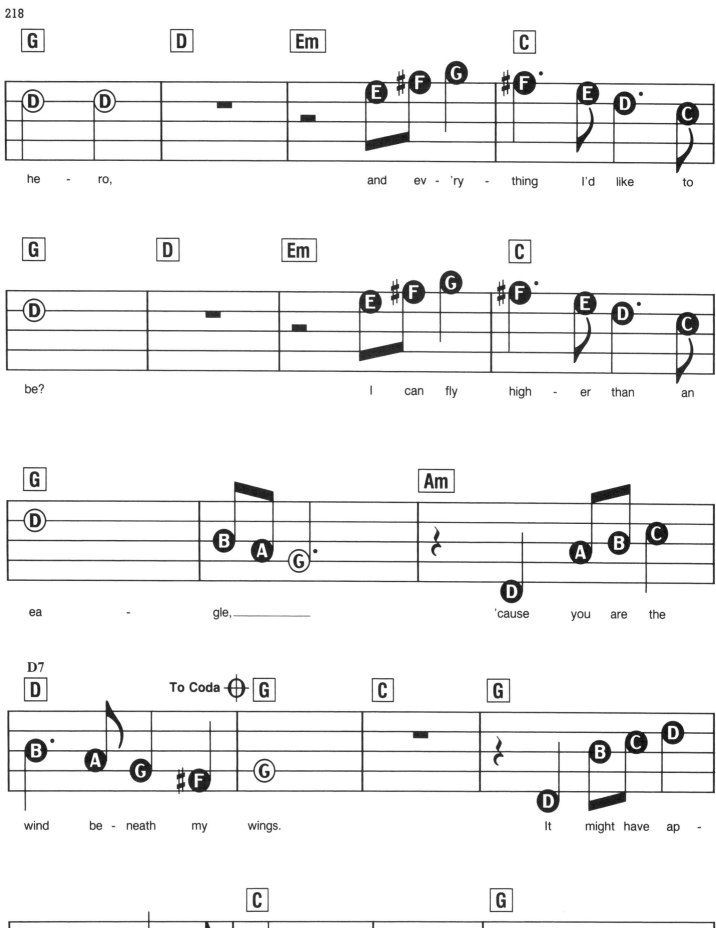

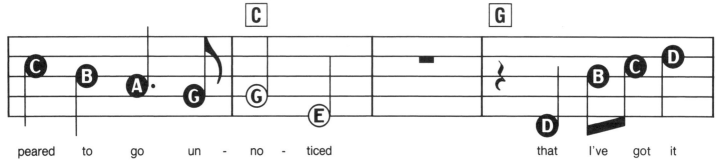

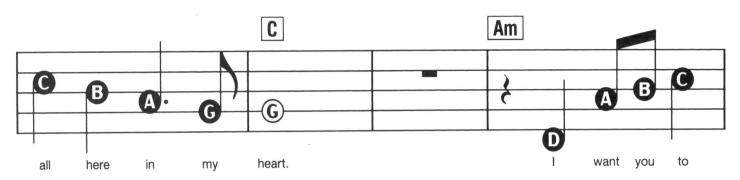

all here in my heart. I want you to

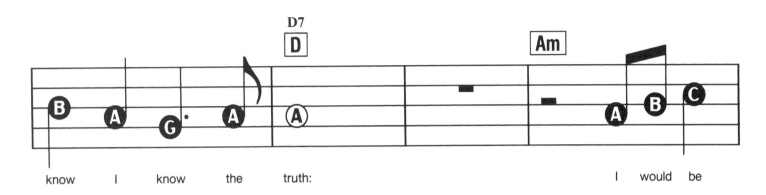

know I know the truth: I would be

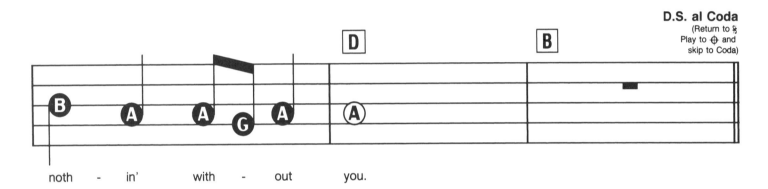

noth - in' with - out you.

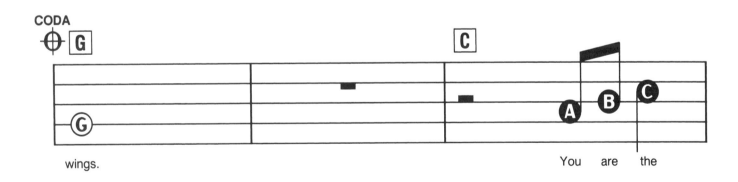

wings. You are the

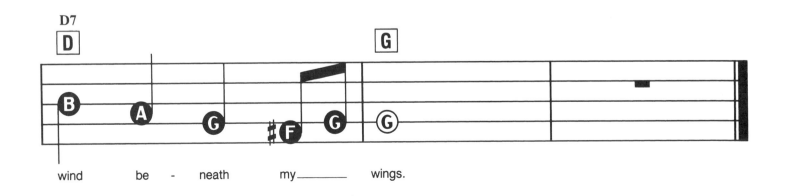

wind be - neath my wings.

Volare
(Nel blu, dipinto di blu)

Music by Domenico Modugno
Original Italian Text by D. Modugno and F. Migliacci
English lyric by Mitchell Parish

Registration 1
Rhythm: Swing

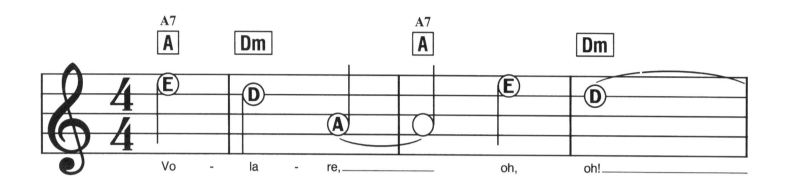

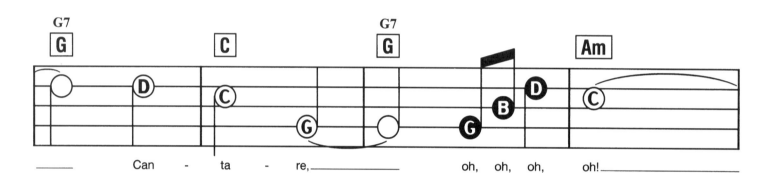

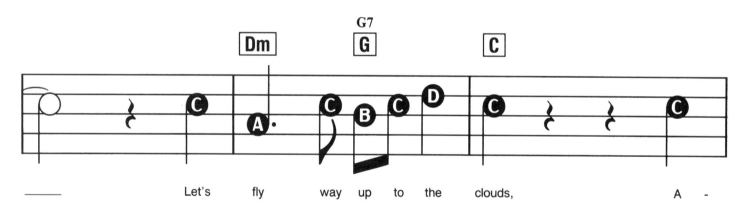

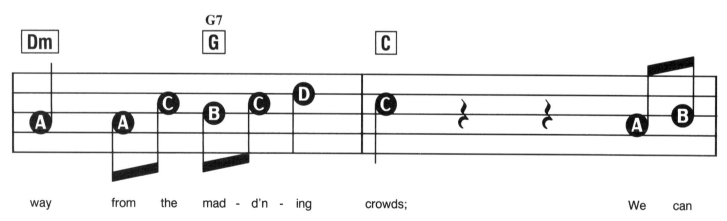

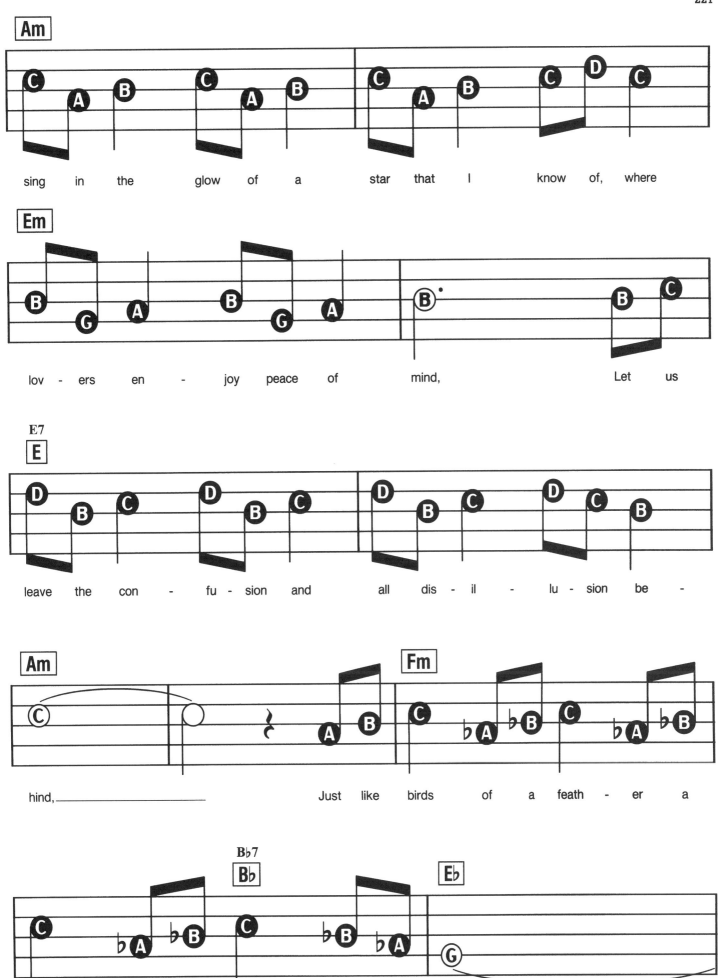

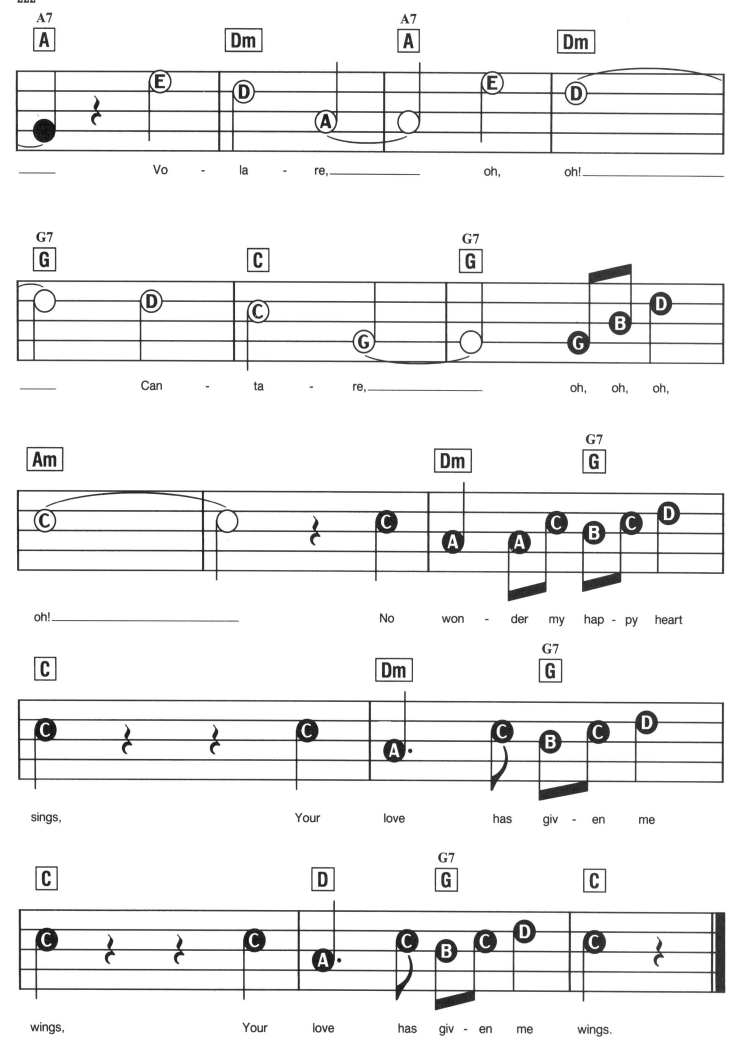

Registration Guide

- Match the Registration number on the song to the corresponding numbered category below. Select and activate an instrumental sound available on your instrument.

- Choose an automatic rhythm appropriate to the mood and style of the song. (Consult your Owner's Guide for proper operation of automatic rhythm features.)

- Adjust the tempo and volume controls to comfortable settings.

Registration

1	Mellow	Flutes, Clarinet, Oboe, Flugel Horn, Trombone, French Horn, Organ Flutes
2	Ensemble	Brass Section, Sax Section, Wind Ensemble, Full Organ, Theater Organ
3	Strings	Violin, Viola, Cello, Fiddle, String Ensemble, Pizzicato, Organ Strings
4	Guitars	Acoustic/Electric Guitars, Banjo, Mandolin, Dulcimer, Ukulele, Hawaiian Guitar
5	Mallets	Vibraphone, Marimba, Xylophone, Steel Drums, Bells, Celesta, Chimes
6	Liturgical	Pipe Organ, Hand Bells, Vocal Ensemble, Choir, Organ Flutes
7	Bright	Saxophones, Trumpet, Mute Trumpet, Synth Leads, Jazz/Gospel Organs
8	Piano	Piano, Electric Piano, Honky Tonk Piano, Harpsichord, Clavi
9	Novelty	Melodic Percussion, Wah Trumpet, Synth, Whistle, Kazoo, Perc. Organ
10	Bellows	Accordion, French Accordion, Mussette, Harmonica, Pump Organ, Bagpipes

THE GRAMMY AWARDS
SONGBOOKS FROM HAL LEONARD

These elite collections of the nominees and winners of
Grammy Awards since the honor's inception in 1958
provide a snapshot of the changing times in popular music.

PIANO/VOCAL/GUITAR

GRAMMY AWARDS RECORD OF THE YEAR 1958-2011

Beat It • Beautiful Day • Bridge over Troubled Water • Don't Know Why • Don't Worry, Be Happy • The Girl from Ipanema (Garôta De Ipanema) • Hotel California • I Will Always Love You • Just the Way You Are • Mack the Knife • Moon River • My Heart Will Go on (Love Theme from 'Titanic') • Rehab • Sailing • Unforgettable • Up, Up and Away • The Wind Beneath My Wings • and more.
00313603 P/V/G.....................................$16.99

THE GRAMMY AWARDS SONG OF THE YEAR 1958-1969

Battle of New Orleans • Born Free • Fever • The Good Life • A Hard Day's Night • Harper Valley P.T.A. • Hello, Dolly! • Hey Jude • King of the Road • Little Green Apples • Mrs. Robinson • Ode to Billy Joe • People • Somewhere, My Love • Strangers in the Night • A Time for Us (Love Theme) • Volare • Witchcraft • Yesterday • and more.
00313598 P/V/G.....................................$16.99

THE GRAMMY AWARDS SONG OF THE YEAR 1970-1979

Alone Again (Naturally) • American Pie • At Seventeen • Don't It Make My Brown Eyes Blue • Honesty • (I Never Promised You A) Rose Garden • I Write the Songs • Killing Me Softly with His Song • Let It Be • Me and Bobby McGee • Send in the Clowns • Song Sung Blue • Stayin' Alive • Three Times a Lady • The Way We Were • You're So Vain • You've Got a Friend • and more.
00313599 P/V/G.....................................$16.99

THE GRAMMY AWARDS SONG OF THE YEAR 1980-1989

Against All Odds (Take a Look at Me Now) • Always on My Mind • Beat It • Bette Davis Eyes • Don't Worry, Be Happy • Ebony and Ivory • Endless Love • Every Breath You Take • Eye of the Tiger • Fame • Fast Car • Hello • I Just Called to Say I Love You • La Bamba • Nine to Five • The Rose • Somewhere Out There • Time After Time • We Are the World • and more.
00313600 P/V/G.....................................$16.99

THE GRAMMY AWARDS SONG OF THE YEAR 1990-1999

Can You Feel the Love Tonight • (Everything I Do) I Do It for You • From a Distance • Give Me One Reason • I Swear • Kiss from a Rose • Losing My Religion • My Heart Will Go on (Love Theme from 'Titanic') • Nothing Compares 2 U • Smooth • Streets of Philadelphia • Tears in Heaven • Unforgettable • Walking in Memphis • A Whole New World • You Oughta Know • and more.
00313601 P/V/G.....................................$16.99

THE GRAMMY AWARDS SONG OF THE YEAR 2000-2009

Beautiful • Beautiful Day • Breathe • Chasing Pavements • Complicated • Dance with My Father • Daughters • Don't Know Why • Fallin' • I Hope You Dance • I'm Yours • Live like You Were Dying • Poker Face • Rehab • Single Ladies (Put a Ring on It) • A Thousand Miles • Umbrella • Use Somebody • Viva La Vida • and more.
00313602 P/V/G.....................................$16.99

THE GRAMMY AWARDS BEST COUNTRY SONG 1964-2011

Always on My Mind • Before He Cheats • Behind Closed Doors • Bless the Broken Road • Butterfly Kisses • Dang Me • Forever and Ever, Amen • The Gambler • I Still Believe in You • I Swear • King of the Road • Live like You Were Dying • Love Can Build a Bridge • Need You Now • On the Road Again • White Horse • You Decorated My Life • and more.
00313604 P/V/G.....................................$16.99

THE GRAMMY AWARDS BEST R&B SONG 1958-2011

After the Love Has Gone • Ain't No Sunshine • Be Without You • Billie Jean • End of the Road • Good Golly Miss Molly • Hit the Road Jack • If You Don't Know Me by Now • Papa's Got a Brand New Bag • Respect • Shine • Single Ladies (Put a Ring on It) • (Sittin' On) the Dock of the Bay • Superstition • U Can't Touch This • We Belong Together • and more.
00313605 P/V/G.....................................$16.99

THE GRAMMY AWARDS BEST POP & ROCK GOSPEL ALBUMS (1990-2012)

Call My Name • Come on Back to Me • Deeper Walk • Forever • Forever We Will Sing • Gone • I Need You • I Smile • I Will Follow • King • Leaving 99 • Lifesong • Looking Back at You • Much of You • My Love Remains • Say So • Somebody's Watching • Step by Step • Tunnel • Unforgetful You • You Hold My World • Your Love Is a Song • and more.
00313680 P/V/G.....................................$16.99

ELECTRONIC KEYBOARD

THE GRAMMY AWARDS RECORD OF THE YEAR 1958-2011 – VOL. 160

All I Wanna Do • Bridge over Troubled Water • Don't Know Why • The Girl from Ipanema (Garôta De Ipanema) • Hotel California • I Will Always Love You • Just the Way You Are • Killing Me Softly with His Song • Love Will Keep Us Together • Rehab • Unforgettable • What's Love Got to Do with It • The Wind Beneath My Wings • and more.
00100315 E-Z Play Today #160 ....$16.99

PRO VOCAL
WOMEN'S EDITIONS

THE GRAMMY AWARDS BEST FEMALE POP VOCAL PERFORMANCE 1990-1999 — VOL. 57

Book/CD Pack

All I Wanna Do • Building a Mystery • Constant Craving • I Will Always Love You • I Will Remember You • My Heart Will Go on (Love Theme from 'Titanic') • No More "I Love You's" • Something to Talk About (Let's Give Them Something to Talk About) • Unbreak My Heart • Vision of Love.
00740446 Melody/Lyrics/Chords.................$14.99

THE GRAMMY AWARDS BEST FEMALE POP VOCAL PERFORMANCE 2000-2009 – VOL. 58

Book/CD Pack

Ain't No Other Man • Beautiful • Chasing Pavements • Don't Know Why • Halo • I Try • I'm like a Bird • Rehab • Since U Been Gone • Sunrise.
00740447 Melody/Lyrics/Chords.................$14.99

MEN'S EDITIONS

THE GRAMMY AWARDS BEST MALE POP VOCAL PERFORMANCE 1990-1999 – VOL. 59

Book/CD Pack

Brand New Day • Can You Feel the Love Tonight • Candle in the Wind 1997 • Change the World • If I Ever Lose My Faith in You • Kiss from a Rose • My Father's Eyes • Oh, Pretty Woman • Tears in Heaven • When a Man Loves a Woman.
00740448 Melody/Lyrics/Chords.................$14.99

THE GRAMMY AWARDS BEST MALE POP VOCAL PERFORMANCE 2000-2009 – VOL. 60

Book/CD Pack

Cry Me a River • Daughters • Don't Let Me Be Lonely Tonight • Make It Mine • Say • Waiting on the World to Change • What Goes Around...Comes Around Interlude • Your Body Is a Wonderland.
00740449 Melody/Lyrics/Chords.................$14.99

Prices, contents, and availabilbility subject to change without notice.

HAL•LEONARD® CORPORATION

7777 W. BLUEMOUND RD. P.O. BOX 13819 MILWAUKEE, WI 53213

www.halleonard.com

1212